The World of Small States

Volume 10

Series Editors

Petra Butler, Faculty of Law, Victoria University of Wellington, Wellington, New Zealand

Caroline Morris, School of Law, Queen Mary University of London, London, UK

Small states differ considerably in their geography, history, political structures, legal systems and wealth. Nevertheless, because of their size, small states face a set of common challenges including vulnerability to external economic impacts such as changing trade regimes and limited ability to diversify economic activity; limited public and private sector capacity, including the legal and judicial infrastructure. A number of small states have experienced colonization and must accommodate the legacy of one or more forms of colonial law alongside the customary law of the indigenous people. Many small states are islands. These are particularly susceptible to environmental impacts such as natural disasters and climate change. Small states can also be flexible, adaptable, sites of social development and innovation, and have an influence in the world disproportionate to their size.

The importance of research into small states is increasingly recognised by the global legal community. Small states are microcosms which allow us to study and gain insight into the challenges of big states. Their small size makes research easier and the testing of solutions more easily. Small states, however, also have unique problems for which unique solutions must be designed. For example, in a small state with a correspondingly-sized legal profession, ethical guidelines in regard to the appointment of judges have to take into account to the small size of the profession.

The aim of this exciting and unique series is to be the essential compendium for every legal researcher interested in small states but also for practitioners and policy makers working in small state.

Alice Cunha • Baldur Thorhallsson
Editors

Small States and Big Powers

Portugal and Iceland's Foreign Relations

Springer

Editors
Alice Cunha
Universidade Nova de Lisboa
Lisboa, Portugal

Baldur Thorhallsson
Faculty of Political Science
Centre for Small State Studies
University of Iceland
Reykjavík, Iceland

ISSN 2627-5996 ISSN 2627-6003 (electronic)
The World of Small States
ISBN 978-3-031-42344-4 ISBN 978-3-031-42345-1 (eBook)
https://doi.org/10.1007/978-3-031-42345-1

This work was supported by EEA Grants

This Springer imprint is published by the registered company Springer Nature Switzerland AG
The registered company address is: Gewerbestrasse 11, 6330 Cham, Switzerland

Paper in this product is recyclable.

Acknowledgments

This book is the result of the "EURO-ATLANTIC: The European and Atlantic dimensions of Portugal and Iceland's foreign policies" bilateral initiative, funded by EEA Grants Portugal (2021–2022).

This project was a partnership between the Portuguese Institute of International Relations (IPRI-NOVA) and the Centre for Small State Studies and the Institute of International Affairs at the University of Iceland.

The project's PI, Alice Cunha, and co-PI, Baldur Thorhallsson, would like to thank EEA Grants for the funding to develop this research; their institutions for all the administrative support; the researchers, António Raimundo, Auður Birna Stefánsdóttir, Nuno Severiano Teixeira, Pia Hansson, Skafti Ingimarsson, and Snaefridur Grimsdottir, who accepted to be part of this project and to deliver their scientific contributions; participants at the projects' seminars "Small states and big powers" held in Lisbon in October 2021 and in Reykjavík in August 2022; the editors of "The World of Small States" series, Caroline Morris and Petra Butler; and Springer for publishing and disseminating the results of this project.

This work was sponsored by:

EEA Grants Portugal (Grant FBR_OC1_61, bilateral initiative "EURO-ATLANTIC: The European and Atlantic dimensions of Portugal and Iceland's foreign policies")

Instituto Português de Relações Internacionais—Universidade NOVA de Lisboa, funded by Portuguese funds through FCT—Fundação para a Ciência e a Tecnologia under the project UIDB/04627/2020.

Centre for Small State Studies and Institute of International Affairs—University of Iceland

Contents

Editors and Contributors

About the Editors

Alice Cunha is Assistant Professor with Habilitation in International Relations at the NOVA University of Lisbon—School of Social Sciences and Humanities (NOVA FCSH), and Researcher at the Portuguese Institute of International Relations (IPRI), where she has worked on European Integration, an area in which she has published extensively. Her main research interests are related to enlargement studies, Europeanization, European funds and Portuguese foreign policy. She is a member of the European Union Liaison Committee of Historians.

Baldur Thorhallsson is a Professor of Political Science, and founder and Research Director for the Centre for Small State Studies, at the University of Iceland. His research focus has primarily been on small European states, small state theory and Iceland's foreign policy. His recent articles are included in *The Hague Journal of Diplomacy*, *Scandinavian Journal of History* and *Global Affairs*. His latest edited books are titled *Iceland's Shelter-Seeking Behavior: From Settlement to Republic* (Cornell University Press 2021), *Small States and the New Security Environment* (co-editor) (Springer 2021) and *Small States and Shelter Theory: Iceland's External Affairs* (Routledge 2019). He holds a PhD (1999) and MA (1994) in Political Science from the University of Essex in the United Kingdom.

Contributors

Alice Cunha Universidade NOVA de Lisboa, Lisbon, Portugal

Snaefridur Grimsdottir University of Iceland, Iceland

Pia Hansson University of Iceland, Iceland

Skafti Ingimarsson University of Iceland, Iceland

António Raimundo University of Minho, Braga, Portugal

Auður Birna Stefánsdóttir University of Iceland, Iceland

Nuno Severiano Teixeira Universidade NOVA de Lisboa, Lisbon, Portugal

Baldur Thorhallsson Faculty of Political Science, Centre for Small State Studies, University of Iceland, Iceland

Chapter 1
Portugal and Iceland: Foreign Policy Constructed by Smallness?

Baldur Thorhallsson and Alice Cunha

1.1 Introduction

The core aim of this book is to test the common assumptions of the small states literature that all small states are similar units and behave in the same manner in the international system. It will examine the cases of Iceland and Portugal and their relations with larger states and membership in regional organisations from the mid-twentieth century until today.

Portugal and Iceland are regarded as small states not only among most scholars of small state studies but also by the countries' allies in NATO and the European project when compared to the larger participating states, such as Spain, France, Germany, Italy, the United Kingdom. However, there are considerable differences in Portugal and Iceland when it comes to the variables generally used to define the size of states, that is the number of inhabitants, military capacity, the size of their economy (GDP) and the size of their foreign service (public administration). Indeed, as can be seen in Table 1.1, with the exception of territorial area, the size and capabilities of the two countries vary considerably.

We will compare the foreign policies of Iceland and Portugal considering their commonly identified status as small states and place them within the shelter theory framework.[1] We will also test whether their different size and capabilities matter in their relations with larger states and in regional organisations. Accordingly, the book

[1] Thorhallsson (2010, 2011, 2019).

B. Thorhallsson
Faculty of Political Science, Centre for Small State Studies, University of Iceland, Reykjavik, Iceland
e-mail: baldurt@hi.is

A. Cunha (✉)
Universidade NOVA de Lisboa, Lisbon, Portugal
e-mail: alice.cunha@fcsh.unl.pt

A. Cunha, B. Thorhallsson (eds.), *Small States and Big Powers*, The World of Small States 10, https://doi.org/10.1007/978-3-031-42345-1_1

Table 1.1 Iceland and Portugal: Comparison of key 'size' variables

	Population (Thousands)	Territory (sq. km)	Real GDP (PPP) ($ Billion)	GDP (per capita) ($ Thousands)	Military spending ($ Million)
Iceland	357	103,000	19.16	52,300	21 (0.083% share of GDP)
Portugal	10,242	92,090	331.64	32,000	3753 (1.44% share of GDP)

Sources: Central Intelligence Agency World Factbook: Population (est. 2022), territory, real GDP (est. 2020), and GDP per capita (est. 2020); NATO, Defence Expenditure of NATO Countries (2014–2022): Portugal (est. 2022); The Proposed State Budget 2023, Iceland, Cooperation on Security and Defence (figures for 2022)

aims to shed light on whether the perceived smallness of Portugal and Iceland as well as their different size and capabilities have played a role in the trajectories they have chosen in international cooperation.

The book will also take account of the countries' location on the periphery of Europe and on the Atlantic Ocean and their different history (Portugal a former Empire and Iceland a former dependency in the Danish Kingdom). Despite having followed distinct paths, Portugal and Iceland have some important similarities in their foreign policy, namely in relation to the European and the Atlantic dimensions and their participation in regional organisations. We examine their decisions to join regional organisations, that is the European Free Trade Area (EFTA) and NATO, and why Portugal chose to join the European Union (EU) while Iceland opted for membership of the European Economic Area (EEA) but not of the Union. The book will also cover the countries' bilateral relations with other important parts of the world, namely Africa (in the case of Portugal), and the Nordic states and China (in the case of Iceland). Thus, the objective of the book is to examine whether Iceland and Portugal's relationships with larger powers and their membership in regional organisations follow a similar pattern commonly identified in small state studies.

1.2 Does Smallness Construct States in the Same Way?

Portugal (with about 10.2 million inhabitants) and Iceland (with about 360,000 inhabitants) are both small states according to the traditional small state literature in the field of International Relations (IR). Population size is the most common single variable in defining the size of states and most studies in political science and economics categorise small states as having resident populations of below 10 or

15 million.[2] This is also the common practice in European studies.[3] However, other studies place the threshold as low as one million[4] or one and a half million.[5]

Moreover, the IR small state literature generally claims that small states need to form alliances to compensate for their vulnerability. They rely on larger states and regional and international organisations in order to survive and prosper.[6] Recently, the theory of shelter was created to bring together core assumptions of the small state literature and explain small state behaviour in the international system.[7] The aim of this book is to test whether these assumptions hold true for two small states which differ considerably in size, i.e. Iceland (a state which is a small state by every traditional criterion) and Portugal (which is not regarded as a small state by scholars who place the threshold of small states as low as one or one and a half million).

It is not a coincidence that the number of inhabitants is the most common variable in defining the size of states. Population size creates special static advantages, disadvantages, and needs. If a state/entity has a small population, whether it is a tiny enclave (such as Luxembourg) or controls a vast expansive territory (such as Greenland), and whether it is extraordinarily rich or deeply impoverished, the small population creates certain needs and challenges that have to be compensated for. A state with a small population will find it hard to field a large military force with diverse capabilities. Small states may not be able to defend themselves from hostile attacks and rely on other states and international organisations for defence.[8] For instance, Iceland does not have an army, as reflected in its limited defence expenditure (see Table 1.1). Moreover, the economies of small states are bound to be small, which leads them to depend on foreign trade and be vulnerable to international economic fluctuation.[9] Small population size also creates constraints on the size and skill set of a state's diplomatic forces.[10] Small states are in need of the diplomatic support provided by larger states and international organisations.[11]

---

[2] Armstrong and Read (2000), Jalan (1982), Katzenstein (1984, 1985), Kuznets (1960), Ross (1983), Vital (1967).

[3] For example, see Grön et al. (2015), Steinmetz and Wivel (2013), Thorhallsson and Wivel (2006), Thorhallsson (2000).

[4] Easterly and Kraay (2000).

[5] Butler and Morris (2017).

[6] E.g. see Rothstein (1968), Keohane (1969), Leeds et al. (2002), Huth and Russett (1988), Ikenberry (2001), Morrow (1991), Jackson and Nei (2015).

[7] Thorhallsson (2010, 2011, 2019), Bailes et al. (2016).

[8] Handel (1981), Bailes and Thorhallsson (2013).

[9] Katzenstein (1984, 1985).

[10] Corbett and Connell (2015).

[11] Vayrynen (1971).

1.3 Are the Foreign Policies of Portugal and Iceland Constructed by History, Geography, and Size?

The history of Portugal and Iceland is very different and this shapes their political discourses. However, they have followed a similar pattern in terms of security and defence since the beginning of the Cold War and became founding members of NATO in 1949. Their geographical location as well as important strategic location have led to close cooperation with both the superpower on the other side of the Atlantic, the United States (US) and the old Atlantic powerhouse, the United Kingdom (UK). Neither country took part in the European project originally but since the 1970s they have sought a deeper engagement in the project. Since 1994, Iceland has had the status of associated member of the European Union through its membership of the European Economic Area, while Portugal has been a member of the EU since 1986. The two countries are Member States of the Schengen Area. They share the same values of democracy and rule of law and are committed to human rights. In the international arena, they are also strong supporters of multilateralism, and are members of numerous and all the most important international organisations.

Nevertheless, there are marked differences in our two cases. While both countries are peripheral and have around the same territorial size (see Table 1.1), Iceland is the most sparsely populated country in Europe. Portugal has a single land border with Spain, whereas Iceland is an island country. Iceland is close to the Arctic while Portugal is close to Africa.

Throughout Portugal's eight-century history and until the mid-1970s—when it fully embraced the democratic regime—, Portugal had to deal with continental pressure and the search for a maritime alternative; this led to the Portuguese Discoveries after 1415 and the building of the Empire, which lasted until 1999. Ever since 1976, Portugal has been a fully-fledged European country with an Atlantic calling, and this has been essential to the definition of the country's foreign policy axis, namely Europe, the Atlantic, the Portuguese-speaking world, the Portuguese communities (*diaspora*), the internationalisation of the Portuguese economy and the reinforcement of multilateralism.

While Europe is the prevailing axis, the Atlantic stands mostly for security. On the other hand, the Portuguese communities are a result of the successive migratory waves from the late nineteenth century onwards, while the internationalisation of the economy is an endeavour for further economic development, and the multilateralism axis results from the value and support of multilateral institutions at the service of the common good.

The Portuguese-speaking world emerged and was consolidated with the Portuguese Empire—with its creation but also after its end—following the country's special relationship with Portuguese speaking African countries, as well as with Brazil and East Timor. All of these countries constitute the Community of

Portuguese-speaking Countries (CPLP),[12] created in 1996, aimed at not only promoting and disseminating the Portuguese language, but also cooperating in several domains, such as education, environment, justice and migrations.

Soon after the tempestuous process of decolonisation in 1974–1975, Portugal reassumed bilateral relations with Angola; although on an equal basis (formally, at least) for the first time, this was not without some post-colonial tensions. Nevertheless, the relationship between the former colony and its one-time master was restored, is mutually beneficial, and Angola is mostly an important market for Portugal in terms of capital projects and jobs. Alongside African countries, Brazil also enjoys strong bilateral cooperation with Portugal on the economic front and in multilateral fora on political matters.

Iceland straddles the Mid-Atlantic rift and its location between Greenland and Norway has had a profound influence on its affairs. Iceland was a major hub in the Allies' defences of the North Atlantic during the Second World War. The country's central location in the middle of the GUIK-gap, which forms a naval warfare choke point between Greenland, the United Kingdom and Iceland, made it strategically important for world powers throughout the Cold War. The US military base in Keflavík/Iceland was essential in the US and NATO defence plans against a possible attack by the Soviet Union. Their aim was to prevent the Soviet navy from breaking into the open Atlantic on either side of Iceland and reaching the east coast of North America, the UK and the European continent.

Decision-makers in Washington are currently worried about the increased Russian naval activity in the Arctic and the North Atlantic, and the possibility of further economic and military activity of China in these areas. Iceland is back on the geopolitical map after having been side-lined by its allies following the end of the Cold War.

Iceland is one of the five prosperous Nordic states and has adopted many of its closest neighbours' domestic characteristics. Recently, Iceland defined itself as one of the Arctic states, in an attempt to benefits from increased economic and political opportunities in connection with the opening of the Arctic Ocean. Previously, Icelanders had tried to distinguish themselves from the Arctic regions, such as Greenland and other indigenous communities, and emphasised their old Norse and European heritage.

In the Second World War, Iceland came under American influence after centuries as part of the Danish Kingdom. In the mid-thirteenth century, Iceland formally became part of the Norwegian kingdom after settlers in Iceland in the ninth and tenth centuries had maintained close ties with Norwegian rulers. The kingdom united with the Danish kingdom and Sweden under the Kalmar Union around 1400.

Iceland achieved Home Rule in 1904 and become a sovereign state in 1918 in a union with Denmark. In 1944, the union was dissolved, and Iceland became a

---

[12]The nine Member-States are Angola, Brazil, Cape Verde, Guinea Bissau, Mozambique, Portugal, and Sao Tome and Principe (the original Member-States), East Timor became a member in 2002, and Equatorial Guinea joined in 2016.

republic after a century-long peaceful struggle for independence. The population at the time was about 127,000. Many Icelanders believe the independence struggle was won by national unity built on Icelandic culture and uniqueness led by distinguished national heroes.[13] This historical narrative ignores the development that led to the sovereignty of many small European nations/states in the early twentieth century.

In the post war period, Iceland joined all the main international and regional organisations, such as the Nordic Council and NATO, and made a bilateral defence agreement with the United States in 1951. However, Icelanders have always been hesitant to take part in the European project and reluctantly joined the European Free Trade Area in 1970, the European Economic Area in 1994 and Schengen in 2001. Iceland applied for membership of the European Union after the collapse of its economy in 2009 but the accession process has been on hold since 2013. Icelandic politicians continue to play the 'nationalistic uniqueness' card with considerable success even though the country has been swept by globalisation. Rapid modernisation, which reached new heights in the Second World War with British and American occupations, together with closer engagement with the outside world in the 1970s and 1980s, are still slowly but steadily making their mark on the country's domestic and external affairs.

1.4 Do All Small States Need Shelter?

The book will place the cases of Portugal and Iceland within the shelter theory framework. Shelter theory claims that all small states, regardless of their size, depend on the economic, political, and societal shelter provided by larger states, as well as regional/international organisations. Thus, what distinguishes Iceland and Portugal from large states is their lack of capabilities, despite their difference in the size. In the late 1960s, scholars of small states already defined the size of states according to their vulnerability, that is their ability to cope with weaknesses associated with their size. In 1967, Vital argued that 'It is the capacity of the state to withstand stress, on the one hand, and its ability to pursue a policy of its own devising, on the other, that are the key criteria.'[14] He continued 'A small state is more vulnerable to pressure, more likely to give way under stress, more limited in respect of the political options open to it, and subject to a tighter connection between domestic and external affairs. In other words, the smaller the human and material resources of a state, the greater are the difficulties it must surmount if it is to maintain any valid political options at all and, in consequence, the smaller the state, the less viable it is as a genuinely independent member of the international community.[15]

[13] Hálfdanarson (2001).

[14] Vital (1967, p. 78).

[15] Vital (1967, p. 77).

In the 1980s, Katzenstein set out in detail how small states are particularly vulnerable during times of economic and political crises—a common finding in security and defence studies (as discussed above).[16] Shelter theory takes the assumption further and argues that the importance of shelter is related to three interrelated features: the reduction of risk in the face of a possible crisis event, help in absorbing shocks during a crisis situation, and assistance in dealing with the aftermath of the crisis.

According to shelter theory, these vulnerabilities can be categorised in three ways: political, economic, and societal vulnerability. Political shelter takes the shape of direct and visible diplomatic or military backing, as well as other strategic coverage at any given time of need by another state or a regional/international organisation, and/or organisational rules and norms.

Economic shelter can include direct economic assistance, a currency union, help from an external financial authority, beneficial loans, favourable market access and a common market, all of which are provided by a more powerful country or by an international organisation.

Societal shelter can contain the diffusion of foreign people and ideas to avoid social stagnation and to make up for a lack of indigenous knowledge. The theory argues that cultural transactions with the outside world, in terms of a transfer of messages, norms, values and lifestyles, are essential for the prosperity of a small community and form a crucial part of their societal shelter. The social and cultural relationships of small states with the outside world are elements that have been neglected by the traditional literature. These are especially important for small peripheral communities, such as Iceland and Portugal. If they do not have close cultural relations with Europe's core, at any time in history, they are in danger of becoming isolated and being deprived of access to the latest know-how. This will affect their ability and their well-being. For example, since 1948, the Benelux states have had wide-ranging and privileged access to each other's higher educational institutions and labour markets. Moreover, since the 1950s, they have had access to the French and German societies through the European project. This access has been and continues to be an essential source of their prosperity. Germany and France have also served as a role model for their legislation and state institutions more generally. Hence, according to shelter theory small states not only need political and economic shelter to thrive, but also societal shelter.[17]

Shelter theory diverges from other theories in further important ways. It rejects the basic assumption of neorealism, that all states are "functionally undifferentiated" units and face the same challenges and opportunities in the international system. Bandwagoning behaviour, according to this view, is an alliance between two formally equal entities that only differ in their capabilities. Shelter theory dismisses this premise and insists that small states not only have different capabilities, but they

[16] Katzenstein (1984, 1985).

[17] Thorhallsson (2010, 2011, 2019).

are fundamentally different social units that operate according to a different logic from their larger counterparts.

In addition, shelter theory claims that small states seek shelter provided by larger states and regional/international organisations for domestic reasons as much as for international purposes. Importantly, small states do not exclusively seek shelter based on outside threats—central as they may be—but also to counter the challenges inherent in being a small society. Accordingly, external shelter not only protects small states in the international sphere, but also helps them overcome some of their domestic limitations, such as lack of indigenous knowledge, underdeveloped infrastructure, and their limited public administration capacity. Traditional theories fail to consider the ability of small states to maintain minimum state structures, which are required to form and conduct domestic policies, and the extent to which they seek the necessary resources through international collaboration.

Moreover, shelter theory argues that small states often benefit disproportionately from international cooperation, including institutional membership, as compared with large states. For instance, the traditional literature underestimates the role of regional and international organisations such as the World Health Organisation (WHO), International Monetary Fund (IMF), the Nordic Council, and the European Union in providing political, economic, and societal shelter to small states.

Finally, a small state needs to find an international actor which is willing to provide it with shelter. This often comes at a certain cost and may involve a deep penetration of the small state by the larger state or the regional/international organisation, often with transformative effects on the small state and its society. Hence, relationships between small states and large states are not limited to the international system, which is covered by most of the international relations literature. The shelter relationship may have considerable domestic consequences for political, economic, and social developments in the small state. Where the quest for protection and insurance is successful, a price must often be paid in terms of sacrifice of autonomy at home and abroad.

To summarise, shelter theory seeks to combine external and domestic dimensions into an integrated framework capable of explaining small state behaviour in world politics. Do these assumptions hold true for both Iceland and Portugal? Will scholars of small states have to take greater account of the difference in size of small states in case studies which consist of states with a population of less than one million inhabitants (such as Iceland) and around ten million inhabitants (such as Portugal)? These are fundamental questions for the small state' literature. Small state studies may be in danger of overlooking key explanatory variables in small states' foreign policy if they do not take account of their different size and capabilities.

1.5 The Layout

The book examines Portugal and Iceland's relations with seven significant actors (states and regional organisations) to determine whether these have provided the two countries with political, economic and societal shelter, as already outlined in this first chapter. The next two chapters examine their engagement with the European project. Special attention will be given to their membership of EFTA and their different European policy. Chapters 4 and 5 analyse their security and defence policy with a particular focus on their NATO membership and close relations with the United States.

The remaining three chapters analyse whether Iceland and Portugal's special relations with different world actors provide them with shelter. Accordingly, the sixth chapter examines whether Iceland's close bond to the other Nordic states provides it with shelter. Chapter 7 looks at whether Portugal's largest and resource-rich ex-African colony, Angola, has provided its former powerhouse with shelter in recent years. Studies in International Relations usually deal with colonies as receivers in their relations with former colonial powers. We want to examine whether the transformation of Portugal from a colonial power to a small peripheral European state has turned this usual assumption of IR on its head. Thus, a particular focus is given to the relations of Portugal and Angola in the recent global financial meltdown and subsequent Eurozone crisis, when Portugal went through great difficulties. Special attention is also given to societal relations between the countries in connection with Angola as a potential provider of societal shelter to Portugal. Chapter 8 examines whether Iceland's relations with China have provided shelter to the much smaller entity. The chapter will focus in particular on the countries' relations during the collapse of the Icelandic economy at the time of the 2008 international financial crisis and why Iceland, at the height of the crisis, requested shelter from China. The concluding section of this volume, Chap. 9, titled "The many shades of shelter: Portugal and Iceland's seek for political, economic and societal shelter", summaries our main findings.

References

Armstrong HW, Read R (2000) Comparing the economic performance of dependent territories and sovereign microstates. Econ Dev Cult Chang 48(2):285–306

Bailes AJK, Thorhallsson B (2013) Instrumentalising the European Union in small state strategy. J Eur Integr 35(2):99–115

Bailes AJK, Thorhallsson B, Thayer BA (2016) Alliance theory and small state alliance 'shelter': the complexities of small state alliance behaviour. Third World Thematics 1(1):9–26

Butler P, Morris C (eds) (2017) Small states in a legal world. Springer, New York, NY

Corbett J, Connell J (2015) All the world is a stage: global governance, human resources, and the 'problem' of smallness. Pac Rev 28(3):435–459

Easterly W, Kraay AC (2000) Small states, small problems? Income, growth, and volatility in small states. World Dev 28(11):2013–2027

Grön CH, Nedergaard P, Wivel A (eds) (2015) The Nordic countries and the European Union: still the other European community? Routledge, New York, pp 32–50
Hálfdanarson G (2001) Íslenska þjóðríkið – uppruni og endimörk. Hið íslenska bókmenntafélag og ReykjavíkurAkademían, Reykjavík
Handel M (1981) Weak states in the international system. Frank Cass, Totowa, NJ
Huth P, Russett B (1988) Deterrence failure and crisis escalation. Int Stud Q 32(1):29–45
Ikenberry GJ (2001) After victory: institutions, strategic restraint and the rebuilding of order after major wars. Princeton University Press, Princeton, NJ
Jackson MO, Nei S (2015) Networks of military alliances, wars, and international trade. PNAS 112(50):15277–15284
Jalan B (ed) (1982) Problems and policies in small economies. Croom Helm, London
Katzenstein P (1984) Corporatism and change: Austria, Switzerland and the politics of industry. Cornell University Press, Ithaca
Katzenstein P (1985) Small states in world markets: industrial policy in Europe. Cornell University Press, Ithaca
Keohane RO (1969) Lilliputians' dilemmas: small states in international politics. Int Organ 23(2): 291–310
Kuznets S (1960) Economic growth of small nations. In: Robinson EAG (ed) Economic consequences of the size of nations. Macmillan, London, pp 14–34
Leeds BA, Ritter JM, Mitchell SML, Long AG (2002) Alliance treaty obligations and provisions, 1815-1944. Int Interact 28:237–260
Morrow JD (1991) Alliances and asymmetry: an alternative to the capability aggregation model of alliances. Am J Polit Sci 35(4):904–933
Ross G (1983) The great powers and the decline of the European states system. Longman, London
Rothstein RL (1968) Alliances and small powers. Columbia University Press, New York
Steinmetz R, Wivel A (eds) (2013) Small states in Europe: challenges and opportunities. Routledge
Thorhallsson B (2000) The role of small states in the European Union. Ashgate, Farnham, Surrey
Thorhallsson B (2010) The Icelandic crash and its consequences: a small state without economic and political shelter. In: Steinmetz R, Wivel A (eds) Small states in Europe: challenges and opportunities. Ashgate, Farnham, Surrey, pp 199–216
Thorhallsson B (2011) Domestic buffer versus external shelter: viability of small states in the new globalised economy. Eur Polit Sci Symp 10(3):324–336
Thorhallsson B (ed) (2019) Small state and shelter theory. Iceland's external affairs. Routledge, London
Thorhallsson B, Wivel A (2006) Small States in the European Union: What do we know and what would we like to know? Camb Rev Int Aff 19(4):651–668
Vayrynen R (1971) On the definition and measurement of small power status. Coop Confl 6(1): 91–102
Vital D (1967) The inequality of states: a study of the small power in international relations. Clarendon Press, Oxford

Baldur Thorhallsson is a Professor of Political Science, and founder and Research Director for the Centre for Small State Studies, at the University of Iceland. His research focus has primarily been on small European states, small state theory and Iceland's foreign policy. His recent articles are included in *The Hague Journal of Diplomacy*, *Scandinavian Journal of History* and *Global Affairs*. His latest edited books are titled *Iceland's Shelter-Seeking Behavior: From Settlement to Republic* (Cornell University Press 2021), *Small States and the New Security Environment* (co-editor) (Springer 2021) and *Small States and Shelter Theory: Iceland's External Affairs* (Routledge 2019). He holds a PhD (1999) and MA (1994) in Political Science from the University of Essex in the United Kingdom.

Dr. Alice Cunha is Assistant Professor with Habilitation in International Relations at the NOVA University of Lisbon—School of Social Sciences and Humanities (NOVA FCSH), and Researcher at the Portuguese Institute of International Relations (IPRI), where she has worked on European Integration, an area in which she has published extensively. Her main research interests are related to enlargement studies, Europeanization, European funds and Portuguese foreign policy. She is a member of the European Union Liaison Committee of Historians.

Chapter 2
Portugal, the European Union and Shelter Theory

Alice Cunha

2.1 Introduction

Portugal's history in the European Union (EU) is just a very small part of its almost nine centuries of history, but it is one of the utmost importance.

In fact, EU accession on 1 January 1986 was a turning point for Portugal and, domestically, this triggered a process of EU-driven change, of Europeanisation. As a result, it is now impossible to understand Portugal's recent history without recognising the structural contribution of European integration to the country's political, economic and social development.

After 35 years of membership, Portugal has acquired a statute of maturity within the EU. However, the country's connection with the European integration process can be traced back to before the start of this official process to when intellectuals were reflecting on the idea of Europe and European unification, cooperation and federation, and took action in pursuit of these goals.

After accession, Portugal established a clear strategic focus and directed efforts and resources toward its EU membership. Since that time, it has achieved its two main objectives: democratic consolidation, on the one hand, and economic development (albeit with limitations), on the other. It has been committed to European values, joined all major deepening projects, such as the Schengen Area, the Economic and Monetary Union (EMU) and the Permanent Structured Cooperation (PESCO), and has benefited from EU funding. Overall, the EU has not only become "a full-time job"[1] for Portugal, but the country has strived to be "European by all

[1] Cunha (2023)

A. Cunha (✉)
Universidade NOVA de Lisboa, Lisbon, Portugal
e-mail: alice.cunha@fcsh.unl.pt

A. Cunha, B. Thorhallsson (eds.), *Small States and Big Powers*, The World of Small States 10, https://doi.org/10.1007/978-3-031-42345-1_2

means"[2] possibly in its attempt to overcome its geographic periphery (continently speaking) and smallness and to be part of EU decisions; it has therefore always supported more integration to avoid the risk of marginalisation.

The main purpose of this chapter is to use shelter theory to explain and understand Portugal's involvement in European integration and, more specifically, its EU membership. This chapter will explain why Portugal joined the EU in 1986 and will thus analyse whether EU membership provides the country with political, economic and societal shelter.

The small states International Relations' literature generally claims that small states (namely countries like Portugal with a population of less than 15 million) need to form alliances to compensate for their vulnerability, and that they rely on regional and/or international organisations to survive and prosper. For Portugal, it was not really a question of survival in the late 1970s/early 1980s, but one of which path would provide political security, economic prosperity and a new societal project (or even new national purpose) following the end of its nearly six-century old Empire. In twenty first century Portugal, engagement with regional organisations, notably the EU, remains a commitment and the country continues to seek further political and economic advantages.

On the one hand, Portugal's size affects and limits its capacity to influence as a EU Member State, but on the other, its size and above all its low level of economic development have also created solidarity among other Member States and, by extension, different kinds of shelter. Many theoretical frameworks can explain European integration and Portugal's membership, including shelter theory. This chapter is divided into three sections analysing the role played by European integration in providing the country with political, economic and societal shelter.

2.2 Political Shelter: Increasing the International Scale of Interests

This first section will analyse whether EU membership has provided Portugal with political shelter. History shows and literature unanimously confirms that political reasons were the over-riding motivation for the request for EU membership: to secure democracy (and not fall into a communist regime), ensure post-decolonisation insertion on the international stage and to become part of the Western Bloc.

After decades under the rule of an authoritarian regime (*Estado Novo*), the foundation of the democratic period on 25 April 1974 entailed a profound redefinition of Portuguese foreign policy, with the end of the Empire and the search for a new calling in the European continent. Nevertheless, European integration and EU membership were not an immediate foreign policy option after the fall of the

[2]Cunha (2021, p. 59).

authoritarian regime. It was only in 1976 that joining the former European Economic Community (EEC, now EU) became a conscious political goal that implied making a choice for democracy and a market economy; indeed, this became Portugal's chief political and economic priority since the EU was regarded as a source of both political security and economic development that, in turn, entailed making many changes domestically to comply with EU rules and regulations.

The history of the Iberian enlargement officially begins with Portugal submitting its membership application to the EEC on 28 March 1977 and ends on 1 January 1986 when both Portugal and Spain joined the EEC. This must be contextualised against the overarching background of the Cold War, during which it was important for the EU to guarantee stability in the Iberian Peninsula and to support the Portuguese transition and democratisation process to ensure that the country would not become a communist regime. Nevertheless, as Fishman points out, while the EU did not make the Southern Europe democracies when they were negotiating their accession, they did shape them.[3] But it was ultimately a win-win situation as both Portugal and the EU were able to consolidate democracy in Southern Europe in the late 1970s. At the time, Portugal did what others small states had been doing since the second half of the twentieth century, namely seeking shelter in multilateral organisations, including the EU. While the EU also gained geopolitically, it was Portugal seeking shelter and not the other way around as the EU does not invite States to apply for membership. Moreover, Portugal somehow acquired a "debt of gratitude" which was paid by agreeing to the Central and Eastern enlargement rounds for countries with similar difficulties to those faced by Portugal twenty years earlier, even though this had negative economic consequences for Portugal.

The long and complex accession process may be considered Portugal's most important political-diplomatic undertaking of the democratic regime and even "the priority of priorities",[4] although there was no referendum on the country's EU accession. After EU membership, Portugal entered into permanent negotiations as a Member State and it has taken part in the decisions that enabled the EU's further deepening and widening.[5]

In the first years of Portuguese membership to the EU, several important changes took place in the organisation itself. These included the change of designation from the EEC to European Union, treaty revisions (Single European Act, Maastricht Treaty), the completion of the internal market and the four freedoms of movement, the creation of the Schengen Area and the Economic and Monetary Union, as well as the first major reform of the Common Agricultural Policy. Moreover, there were major geopolitical changes with the collapse of the Soviet Union and reunification of Germany.

---

[3] Fishman (2003, p. 32).

[4] On the Portuguese EU accession process, see: Cunha (2018), Cunha (2017a), Lã and Cunha (2016).

[5] For wide-ranging overviews on Portugal's EU membership: Lã et al. (2019), Ferreira-Pereira (2014), Mateus (2013), Lopes (1993).

Portugal became a well-integrated Member State, adapting well to EU's institutions, rules and procedures and the decision-making process. It has complied with the obligations of EU membership while also benefitting from it, but it has also earned the trust of its European counterparts and the reputation of a stable, bridge-building country. Nevertheless, small states like Portugal are not small versions of big states and the country has managed to preserve its identity while being a member of the EU and other international organisations.

Overall, the benefits of EU membership continue to outweigh the costs. Membership led to the Europeanisation of the country's foreign policy, which is heavily dependent on the EU. Notwithstanding, Portuguese foreign policy officially has three main axes: European, Atlantic and Lusophone, which have remained constant throughout the country's history and its various types of political regime. But whereas the Atlantic axis has been weakening for some years now, the European axis has become stronger due both to domestic circumstances and also the continentalisation of the EU. Teixeira even argues that "there is no alternative to European membership. All the other [foreign policy options] have not proved to be credible or even constitute alternatives. They can be compensation vectors, but not the central axis of [the Portuguese] foreign policy".[6]

The EU is in constant "survival mode"—internally with its 27 Member States and externally with its geopolitical positioning—, but the Covid-19 pandemic and its immediate and short-term consequences have raised questions about the ability of the EU and its institutions to take prompt and coordinated action in a spirit of solidarity. Nevertheless, the pandemic has accentuated the EU's importance to Portugal, namely with the joint acquisition of vaccines (saving time, money and other resources) and the funding made available for economic and social recovery.

At a different level, as an EU Member State, Portugal is also represented in a number of other international organisations that provide diplomatic backing and allow the negotiation of more favourable agreements. Thus, Portugal is not only a member of a regional organisation (the EU) but also delegates power to the EU to represent it in other regional or international organisations (such as the World Trade Organisation to negotiate more favourable trade agreements), which is quite unique in the multilateral system.

Portugal has delegated sovereignty to the EU on a wide range of policy domains (e.g. agriculture and fisheries, environment, trade, transport); it no longer fully controls its land borders, does not print money, and even had to alter its Constitution three times to comply with EU law, which takes precedent over Portuguese law.

Despite always positioning itself in favour of deeper integration, Portugal's involvement with the EU over the last three decades has been through different phases. Goucha Soares refers to the Euro-sceptical period, the Euro-enthusiastic phase and the Euro-realistic stage.[7] The Euro-sceptical period lasted from 1986 until the end of the transition period and the first Portuguese EU Council rotating

[6]Teixeira (2017, p. 34).

[7]Goucha Soares (2007, pp. 463–473).

presidency in 1992 when the Social-Democrat Government took a cautious approach to European integration, marked by discretion, mostly dedicated to meeting the many challenges caused by accession, and politically aligned with the United Kingdom. The Euro-enthusiastic phase corresponds to the years between the first and second EU Council presidency in 2000. Also due to the success of the 1992 presidency, the official Government discourse changed from moderation to a pro-European attitude, which would be heightened during the Socialist Government from October 1995; this was fostered by the deep transformations made to infrastructures and successfully becoming a founding member of the single currency, which ultimately led to more confidence in European affairs and public recognition of the benefits of accession. The Euro-realistic stage started at the turn of the century and is characterised by a weak enthusiasm in the European project, when the membership advantages are not the only ones evident, and some obligations, such as the ones related to the Euro Area membership, also stand out. Today, the country knows the rules that go hand in hand with being an EU Member State and the associated benefits and constraints, and it manages its political positions accordingly.

Like other small states, the size and skills of Portugal's diplomatic forces as well as its defence and security capacity are limited. This brings it within Baldacchino and Wivel's definition of a small state, namely one characterised by the limited capacity of their political, economic and administrative systems and that typically find themselves as the weaker party in asymmetric relationships.[8]

On the other hand, EU membership allows Portugal to overcome these limitations to some extent. For instance, holding the EU Council's rotating presidency is particularly important for small and medium-sized countries, even though the ability to promote national priorities was reduced by the Lisbon Treaty. The presidency gives the country greater international visibility and allows it to include certain topics on the EU agenda, such as Africa and Brazil. As we will see below, as a Member State, Portugal can also increase the international scale of its interests.

The resolution of the East Timor case is a good example of the political shelter from the EU to Portugal. East Timor was a former Portuguese colony, occupied by Indonesia in December 1975. The Indonesian invasion received tacit support from major Western governments, including the United States, but neither Portugal nor the United Nations (UN) accepted or recognised East Timor's annexation. In spite of several UN resolutions over the years, they were unable to find a solution to the East Timor issue. Given the national interests of the great powers in Indonesia, they were unwilling to use their political and military forces to help East Timor or, for that matter, to back the Portuguese endeavours to do so.

Until Portugal became an EU Member State, the former ten Member States had taken a neutral position on this issue; they had not supported East Timor and abstained in votes within the UN General Assembly, not only due to the demands of Cold War politics, but also because there were no supporters of the East Timor cause in the EU at the time.

---

[8] Baldacchino and Wivel (2020, pp. 2–19).

After joining the EU, Portugal raised the issue of self-determination for East Timor in the European institutions, but it took a long time for the EU as a whole to adopt a common position due to trade issues. For example, France and the United Kingdom supplied arms to the Suharto regime, and other Member States did other business with the regime. The situation would not change until two decades later following the international publicity of the Santa Cruz massacre on 12 November 1991 which raised awareness of the East Timor case in international public opinion, including in the EU Member States. The EU subsequently issued its first statement condemning Indonesia and, ultimately, its support of a political solution in 1999 with the Referendum on Autonomous Status.

The added value of the European Union in the continued pressure from Portuguese diplomacy was crucial to overcoming this situation. UN and EU membership (multilateralism) favoured the Portuguese efforts towards East Timor independence and pressuring the other EU Member States, and enabled Portugal to emphasise its interests internationally more effectively.[9] In the end, the EU's support of East Timor independence was only clear after the collapse of Indonesia's dictatorship in 1998 when the strong trade ties with some Member States would no longer be affected. However, the EU's role in resolving the East Timor conflict resulted from a series of actions (European Parliament resolutions, inclusion in the Council of Ministers agenda) and it demonstrates how the EU's soft power can provide political shelter for small Member States such as Portugal in cases of great interest to them.

According to Thorhallsson,[10] political shelter takes the shape of direct and visible diplomatic or military backing, as well as other strategic coverage at any given time of need by another state or international organisation. The case of East Timor clearly fits the category of diplomatic backing as it was increasingly debated in the EU and progressively made EU Member States adopt a common position, largely for humanitarian reasons.

Shelter theory claims that small states need shelter in order to survive and prosper. Although Spain, Portugal's only land neighbour, has always had the economic and political resources to provide Portugal with comprehensive shelter, Portugal has never sought shelter from Spain; quite the opposite. For more than five centuries and precisely until both countries joined the EU, Portugal strived to diversify its extra peninsular alliances.[11]

The traditional International Relations literature underestimates the role of regional and multilateral organisations, such as the EU, in providing political shelter to small states. However, there is less risk of a multilateral organisation backing out from providing shelter, as the risk is shared and they operate according to agreed rules.[12]

---

[9] See: Gomes (2010, pp. 67–89).

[10] Thorhallsson (2019).

[11] Teixeira (2021).

[12] Thorhallsson (2018, p. 77).

Portugal first became a member of an international organisation in 1865 when it joined the International Telecommunication Union; since that time, it has had an impressive track-record of joining a wide range of regional and international organisations. It is a member of almost 90 organisations, some of a political and economic nature (such as the United Nations, the North Atlantic Treaty Organisation, the Community of Portuguese Speaking Countries, the International Criminal Court, the International Monetary Fund, World Trade Organisation), and others with scientific and technical scope (e.g. European Telecommunications Satellite Organisation, International Council for the Exploration of the Sea, the International Organisation of Vine and Wine or the International Organisation for International Carriage by Rail).[13] This clearly shows that Portugal has always sought international cooperation and, in some cases and to some extent, shelter from these organisations, particularly the bigger ones that may provide security and economic support. This is in keeping with the small states' preferences "for multilateral organisations because they reduce the power asymmetry between states, decrease the transaction costs of diplomacy, and impose constraints on large states",[14] as well as the tendency for small states to seek multilateral shelter in international organisations since the second half of the twentieth century. In addition, small states benefit from the stable organisational norms, rules and procedures, most of which are established by treaty and therefore tend to provide small states with a stronger negotiating position.

Developments in the field of security have been meagre. Little sovereignty has been delegated in this domain despite the growing importance given by the EU to its role in geopolitics and foreign affairs (e.g. creation of the European Security and Defence Policy and the Strategic Compass). Europe as a whole still relies primarily on American and NATO protection for their security, as recently shown with the Russian invasion of Ukraine on 24 February 2022.

As a small state, Portugal recognises that it cannot ensure its security entirely alone and that it must depend on (or seek shelter from) other organisations, such as NATO.[15] In this particular domain, EU and NATO membership are complementary.

2.3 Economic Shelter: Securing Funding

This second section will examine the extent to which EU membership provides Portugal with economic shelter. Besides belonging to the internal market, one of the EU's greatest achievements, the country has benefited from a huge amount of EU funding. On the other hand, belonging to the Euro Area has also brought austerity measures.

[13] Teixeira and Cunha (2021–2023).

[14] Thorhallsson and Steinsson (2016, p. 1).

[15] See: Teixeira (2022).

According to the traditional International Relations small states literature, Portugal is a small state: it has 92,000 sq. km in land area, just over 10 million inhabitants; a Gross Domestic Product (GDP) of around 188 billion euros[16]; only between 23 to 28 thousand members of the armed forces (in 2021, and according to different entities) and spends around 2% of its GDP on defence[17]; it has a diplomatic corps that comprises approximately 500 diplomats; and the percentage of public servants vis-a-vis of total employment is low.[18] It also falls in this category into EU Studies literature and according to EU standards (also in terms of population, land area, GDP), which has its own implications, such as fewer seats in the European Parliament and fewer votes under the qualified majority voting in the Council of Ministers. The country only has some seniority thanks to its accession date, which means its integration began earlier than over half the other members. These traditional variables should not, however, undermine other qualitative factors, such as the country's political willingness or prioritisation, or even new variables such as the "perceptual size" (how domestic and external actors regard the State) and the "preference size" (ambitions and prioritisation of the governing elite and its ideas about the international system), which help explain small states' behaviour in an international organisation like the EU.[19]

Portugal's economic history is not only closely linked with external funding as it has been fundamental to assure the needs of the national economy.[20]

Small population size and a small economy both lead to the country's dependence on foreign trade. The EU's implementation of the internal market was closely linked to the need to promote economic and social cohesion. Southern Europe countries, including Portugal, received significant financial compensations with the aim of reducing the consequences of further liberalisation of the European market,[21] and this was decisive for the structural changes that took place in the country. Ever since, Portugal has benefited from the free movement of goods, capital and labour.

According to Thorhallsson's definition,[22] Portugal's EU membership includes several aspects of economic shelter as it belongs to a common market and a currency union (the Euro Area), and benefits from direct economic assistance by means of EU structural and investment funds (ESI, in their current designation) in the form of grants and loans.

---

[16] Source: Banco de Portugal, Séries para a economia portuguesa—PIB Anual, Lisboa. In 2019, the GDP was around 203 billion euros. The −8.40 difference in 2020 was due to the economic effects of the Covid-19 pandemic, still more than the Euro Area average of −6.80.

[17] Diário de Notícias, "Forças Armadas. Afinal quantos militares há em Portugal? Da falta de rigor à conveniência política", 19 February 2022. https://www.dn.pt/sociedade/forcas-armadas-afinal-quantos-militares-ha-em-portugal-14603184.html. Accessed 4 July 2023.

[18] Source: Eurostat, Brussels. https://ec.europa.eu/eurostat/cache/digpub/european_economy/bloc-4d.html?lang=en. Accessed 4 July 2023.

[19] Thorhallsson (2006, p. 8).

[20] Rodrigues and Cunha (2022).

[21] See: Lains (2007, pp. 14–40).

[22] Thorhallsson (2011, p. 4), Thorhallsson (2019).

While the official narrative in Portugal has not always been that of the "money bazooka", obtaining European funds has always played a relevant or even priority role, especially during the negotiation of the multiannual financial frameworks, the EU long-term budget. It is widely recognised by all stakeholders that ESI funds have contributed to the country's economic and social development, despite the inequalities that persist and the country's inability to move away from the "cohesion country" label.

Nonetheless, there is no consensus on whether the funds have been properly managed and spent, and there are also issues of transparency and accountability. Some argue that "the evolution of Portuguese society and economy in the 25 years of European Portugal illustrates a semi-failure in real convergence at the European level"[23] and thus failure to make the country's economy more competitive and its society more cohesive. Others claim that the Portuguese economic growth and convergence with the most economically developed Member States between 1986 and 2016 was quite modest[24]; since the 2000s, Portugal has been growing less and on an accentuated diverging path which means it is constantly lagging behind the EU economically. Projections also show that the Portuguese economy will end 2023 with the lowest GDP growth in the EU, when compared to pre-pandemic standards.

Nevertheless, ESI funds have undoubtedly been a lever for development since Portugal joined the EU.[25] The aim of bringing Portuguese economic development more in line with that of its European counterparts and the European average was not only one of the main reasons for applying for membership but ESI funds proved central for that purpose.

As a Member State, one of the key axes of Portugal's participation in the EU has been optimising the benefits of membership, namely through the building and modernisation of infrastructure, the reduction of regional asymmetries and access to ESI funds. Since 1986, Portugal has benefited from large, mostly non-refundable, sums from structural and investment funds, which have provided the country with the necessary resources to invest in certain areas previously neglected due to the lack of financial means.

As part of its obligations, Portugal must also contribute to the EU budget. But unlike other small EU members—that may subsidise larger but less developed members, because the EU budget is dependent on the level of earnings—, Portugal has always been a net recipient, has never paid more than it received from the EU and the difference in public transfers with the EU is generally quite disproportionate: the largest was in 2012 at the time of a serious economic crisis and intervention from the European Troika)[26] when it received 5722.9 billion euros and contributed 1830.4 billion euros. In the first years after accession, the difference between the payment

[23] Mateus (2013, pp. 24–25).

[24] Marques (2017, pp. 39–54).

[25] Martins (2016, p. 338).

[26] The European Troika was formed by the European Commission, the European Central Bank and the International Monetary Fund, hereafter "Troika".

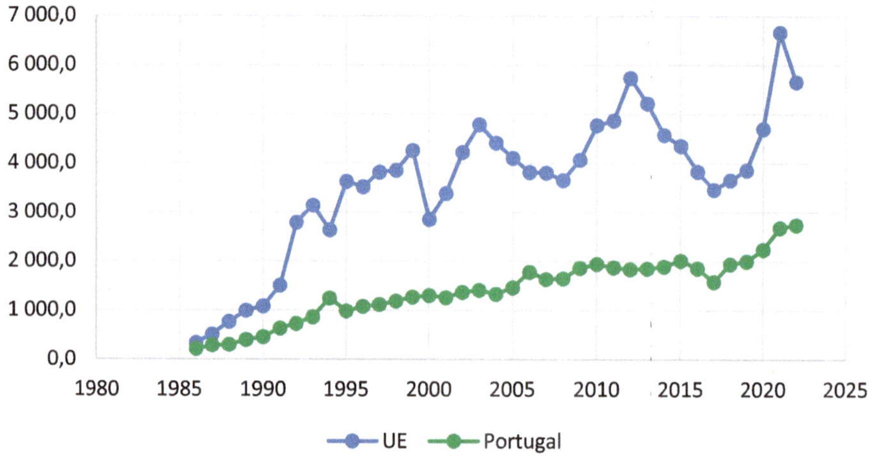

Fig. 2.1 Transfers to and from the EU, 1986–2022 (in Euro). Source: Data available at PORDATA, in million Euro (PORDATA, "Transferências públicas com a União Europeia", Lisboa. https://www.pordata.pt/portugal/transferencias+publicas+com+a+uniao+europeia-2363. Accessed 4 July 2023)

and receipt of transfers was smaller, with the balance growing over the years in favour of Portugal, as illustrated in Fig. 2.1.

In total, between 1986 and 2022 (last year with official data available) Portugal received 133,020.9 billion euros and paid 52,110.7 billion euros, thus with a positive balance of 80,909.9 billion euros. This sum further confirms the strengthening of economic shelter provided by the EU through European solidarity. But in addition to these direct transfers, the indirect economic and financial benefits associated with EU membership such as access to the internal market and the free movement of people, goods, services and capital, must not be overlooked.

In the context of a pandemic that is unprecedented since the creation of the EU, and the subsequent health, economic and social crisis, EU funds remain a top priority on Portugal's agenda. By 2030, Portugal will have received 58 billion euros, 30 billion euros of which under the Multiannual Financial Framework 2021–2027, 15 billion euros from the "Next Generation EU" recovery programme and an additional 12 billion euros from the "Portugal 2020" programme. Prime-Minister António Costa went as far as to call it "a money bazooka", with the country receiving 1 million euros per hour [27] and the state budget continuing to be heavily dependent on EU funding. This unprecedented amount—roughly half of the sum the country received from 1986 to 2019—is not only a clear manifestation of the economic

[27] Expresso, "Um milhão de euros por hora", 26 October 2021. https://expresso.pt/newsletters/expresso-fundos-europeus/2021-10-26-Um-milhao-de-euros-por-hora-c7cc5ad5. Accessed 4 July 2023.

shelter granted by the EU, but another opportunity for the country to reverse its relative economic decline.

European integration permitted a national process of economic modernisation, especially of infrastructure, and the improvement of living conditions for the Portuguese. However, the introduction of the single currency and the associated possibility of sanctions if Euro Area rules, notably the stability pact, were violated, led to economic and fiscal difficulties that impacted the enthusiasm for the benefits of membership. That was further exacerbated by the economic and financial crisis that resulted in financial assistance from the Troika from May 2011 to May 2014 and which was the period of greatest friction and discontent with the EU to date, even though most Portuguese believe the country has benefited from EU membership.

But, even then, the EU provided economic shelter by taking part in the Troika that provided a bailout for Portugal so that it could cope with the crisis and its consequences albeit at the cost of various and severe austerity measures and social reforms. To that extent, the quality rather than the existence of the shelter between the sheltering (the EU) and the sheltered state (Portugal) may also be questioned. In some Member States, the financial crisis became the European sovereign debt crisis, to which the EU had to respond to mitigate its consequences. At first, the EU had neither the instruments to deal with the sovereign debt crisis nor a strategy to face the related problems but it later created the European Financial Stabilisation Mechanism to provide financial assistance to any EU country experiencing or threatened by severe financial difficulties—first used to provide financial assistance conditional on the implementation of reforms to Ireland and Portugal between 2011 and 2014—, and the European Stability Mechanism also to provide financial assistance for the Euro Area countries.

The total financial assistance package for Portugal amounted to 78 billion euros to make up for the sudden halt to inflows of external finance.[28] As each member of the Troika had to finance one third of the total loan to Portugal, the European Central Bank and European Commission combined supported two thirds. Despite this vital aid at that time of crisis, it came at a cost for the Portuguese as it entailed spending cuts, cutbacks in salaries, pensions and social security, and increases in taxes. These measures were widely regarded as tough and caused social unrest, something that is infrequent in Portugal.

EU membership does not, per se, prevent an economic crisis from hitting the country. These can also derive from domestic factors and, in fact, there have been six economic recessions in Portugal since the 1980s. Nonetheless, EU Member States are better equipped to deal with and recover from such problems as they benefit from economic shelter from the EU. The EU did not abandon its compromise of solidarity with EU members, even though it came with a cost.

[28] "Portugal. Memorandum of Understanding on Specific Economic Policy Conditionality", 17 May 2011. https://ec.europa.eu/economy_finance/eu_borrower/mou/2011-05-18-mou-portugal_en.pdf. Accessed 4 July 2023.

During this crisis, Portugal started to search for new extra-European strategic partnerships, notably with China and Angola, for foreign investment and the internationalisation of the Portuguese economy, as well as to debate the strategic potential of post-colonial relations and the Community of Portuguese Speaking Countries (CPLP).[29] However, these discussions were largely limited to the period of the economic crisis and only resulted in immediate share purchases of companies operating in strategic sectors such as banking and energy.

Another current and tangible example of economic shelter provided by the EU is the recovery from the Covid-19 pandemic. The abovementioned ESI funds enabled Portugal to be better equipped to deal with the sanitary, economic and social crisis; moreover, the country also benefited from the activation of the general escape clause of the Stability and Growth Pact, the Temporary Framework for State Aid measures to support the economy in the Covid-19 outbreak, the creation of a new instrument for "Support to mitigate Unemployment Risks in an Emergency" (SURE), designed to protect jobs and employees affected by the coronavirus pandemic, and the European Central Bank's Pandemic Emergency Purchase Programme on asset purchase of private and public sector securities.

In the last two decades, the Portuguese economy has been stagnant; the country is poorer than other comparable Member States and has not reached the EU's average development levels. In addition, some Member States such as the Czech Republic, Estonia, Lithuania and Slovenia, together with Poland and Hungary, that joined the EU in the Central and Eastern enlargement in 2004, with a lower level of economic development than Portugal, have already surpassed Portugal, which is still one of the poorest and least economically developed countries in the EU. For Lains, "slower growth was a consequence of the changes in economic policy that occurred after the Maastricht Treaty. As such, Portugal's longer-term convergence performance was superior under the earlier European policy regimes but suffered from higher levels of economic and financial integration",[30] mainly derived from the creation of the Economic and Monetary Union and ensuing policies. Overall, the country is still far from being on track for steady real convergence with the EU core economies, a central objective for Portugal since membership. In this case, it may not be considered simply as a cost of shelter but more a consequence, in connection with the political, economic and even monetary evolution of the shelter-provider organisation. In any case, "the choice of the EU as strategic protector presents a small state with a dilemma not unrelated to, but sharper than, the choices involved when looking to another state or an alliance like NATO" as it "must open itself to more profound transformations than in any other strategic relationship" in exchange for the benefits.[31]

Although Portugal's participation in the EU is still largely unchartered territory, the evidence of economic shelter is strong.

---

[29] See: Raimundo (2022).

[30] Lains (2019, p. 1095).

[31] Bailes and Thorhallsson (2013, p. 110).

2.4 Societal Shelter: Belonging to a New Societal Project

The third and last section aims to evaluate whether Portugal's engagement in the European project has provided it with societal shelter—which involves the diffusion of ideas, the importance of cultural transactions and the transfer of norms[32]—, namely using some indicators such as the Portuguese feelings towards the EU, turnout for European Parliament elections and student exchanges.

For the Portuguese, the EU has been a source of prosperity and a synonym for democratic stability, geopolitical security and even of a cultural belongingness to the Western world; this was not changed by the crisis in the late 2000s/early 2010s even though the EU was seen as synonymous with austerity politics and economic recession at that time. Portugal was one of the countries hardest hit by the crisis, which led to the request for financial assistance in 2011 and consequently to unpopular austerity measures. EU membership was never questioned by any important sector of Portuguese society even during the difficult period of the Adjustment Programme when Europe-wide indicators of public trust in European institutions fell and in spite of the political, economic and social discontent. Europeanism proved to be resilient in Portugal; no political party, not even new emerging parties, advocated withdrawing from the Euro Area or the EU no matter how controversial the economic policies imposed by the Troika were.

This is explained in part by the fact that the two major parties, the Socialist and the Social Democratic parties, as well as those on the left side of the political spectrum (Communist Party, the Left Bloc) are still key players for linking public opinion to European issues in the country; the EU remains mainly the domain of a political elite, with parties using it to fit their political agenda. Their visions of Portugal's EU participation vary from defending "more Europe", to a "better Europe" or "another path for Europe".[33] And although Euroscepticism has increased among civil society—more so than among political parties—the financial crisis is seen as a consequence of the failure of the domestic political system to implement the structural reforms required at that time by the Economic and Monetary Union, and not something driven exclusively by EU membership.

Nevertheless, the 2010–2014 financial crisis and ensuing Troika bailout was perceived as the low point for EU solidarity in Portugal and the EU was seen as a source of austerity measures and social sacrifices. In 2011, only 39% of the Portuguese considered EU membership to be a good thing versus 79% 20 years earlier.[34] In 2021, 73% of Portuguese have trust in the European Union—the highest levels observed in all Member States—, 62% have a positive image of the EU, and 76% are

[32] Thorhallsson (2019).

[33] Cunha (2017b, p. 109).

[34] Data collected from Standard Eurobarometer No. 31 June 1989 to Standard Eurobarometer No. 75 August 2011, Spring, Brussels. https://europa.eu/eurobarometer/surveys/browse/all/series/4961. Accessed 4 July 2023.

optimistic about the future of the EU. And an impressive 84% feel that they are citizens of the EU.[35]

One way of measuring involvement with the EU is the turnout in European elections. Despite being the only directly elected EU institution and its increased powers, participation by the Portuguese in the European parliamentary elections has been poor and has decreased steadily. After a 72.42% turnout in the 1987 elections (the first for Portugal), in part explained by the fact they were simultaneous with legislative elections, the participation rate fell to 51.10% in 1989; 35.54% in 1994; 39.93% in 1999; 38.60% in 2004; 36.78% in 2009; 33.67% in 2014; and, finally, 30.75% in 2019.[36] Furthermore, Portugal's voter turnout in European elections has generally been below the European average.

The large amount of EU funding and the construction of the first EU funded infrastructures clearly demonstrated the benefits of accession and led to a more positive public perception of EU membership in the first years after accession. However, foreign affairs are not an area of interest for most citizens, and successive governments over the years have been unable to transmit the importance of the EU to the country and its citizens, more specifically what it means in concrete terms to be European and to live in the EU. Moreover, the European accomplishments still tend to be nationalised and its failures Europeanised.

Before accession, the country "sought for a new identity and to meet its European destiny".[37] The destiny was clearly achieved with accession to the EU and a political goal thus fulfilled. EU membership entailed the Europeanisation of Portuguese society[38] not only by means of norms, such as the free movement of people or the institution of European citizenship (something unique in the universe of multilateral organisations to date, and also a product of the evolution of European integration towards developing and broadening its political sphere), but also with the creation of the ERASMUS programme or the European Solidarity Corps, both aimed at promoting better knowledge of other European people and Member States among young people. So far, over 100 thousand Portuguese students have participated in the ERASMUS programme since 1987, which illustrates the EU's societal outreach.

On a different level, Portugal is the EU's Member State with the largest number of emigrants as a proportion of its resident population. Around 1.5 million Portuguese live in another European country, including Switzerland and the United Kingdom. The latest data show that France continues to be the favourite destination (with around 600 thousand Portuguese nationals), almost the same number as nationals from other EU countries residing in Portugal (around 590.3 thousand).[39]

---

[35] European Commission (2021, pp. 10, 13, 15 and 29).

[36] Source: Comissão Nacional de Eleições, Lisboa. https://www.cne.pt/content/eleicoes-referendos. Accessed 4 July 2023.

[37] Arquivo Mário Soares, Lisboa, 00814.022, image 3, 1977.

[38] Magone (2004).

[39] Observatório da Emigração (2021); Gabinete de Estratégia e Estudos (2021), Resident Foreign Population in Portugal, Lisboa.

2.5 Conclusion

Portugal is a good example of how a small state (by EU standards) follows the pattern commonly identified in small state studies in terms of its relationships with regional organisations, namely the EU. This chapter has shown that over the years Portugal has depended to different extents on the political, economic and even societal shelter provided by the EU since it joined the organisation.

Thereafter, that Portugal wanted to capitalise on the political, economic and social advantages provided by EU membership. The country has managed to be at the core of European integration, and this is expected to continue in the near future with Portugal remaining committed to the European integration process and to projects that deepen the EU; in other words, it is ultimately being sheltered by the EU, which is undoubtedly the most important regional organisation for Portuguese national interest. This importance was recently highlighted by the government when it took office in March 2022, as the Prime Minister, António Costa, took direct responsibility for European Affairs, which had formerly come under the Foreign Office.

Notwithstanding, Portugal remains a poor country in an increasingly differentiated and asymmetric EU and has delegated several dimensions of its sovereignty in the process. Given that shelter theory depends on the proportion of benefits to cost, in 35 years of EU membership the advantages have outweighed the costs and no "Portuguese exit" (in line with Brexit) is expected in the near future, namely due to the great disparities between the power and potential of Portugal alone and that of Portugal as an EU member.

From the political shelter point of view, Portugal first received political shelter from the EU when it applied for membership in 1977 with a view to securing the full democratisation of the country; as a full EU member since 1986, it has gained diplomatic backing as well as more favourable agreements negotiated in international fora.

In relation to economic shelter, the EU has enabled Portugal to take part in the internal market, to adopt the single currency and have access to EU funding. Despite being granted direct economic and financial assistance during both economic growth and crisis conjunctures, the latter had costs which caused some social unrest and mistrust in the good nature of the European integration project.

Finally, regarding societal shelter, the Portuguese identify themselves as Europeans not only geographically but also in terms of lifestyle and shared values; they are generally pro-EU, find EU membership positive and take advantage of opportunities it offers, such as living, studying and/or working in other EU Member States.

Nevertheless, and despite the predominance of EU membership, Portugal has a universal foreign policy, which is rare for a small country; in fact, the other vectors of its foreign policy, namely the Atlantic and the Lusophone, also bring political, economic and societal value to the EU.

References

Bailes AJK, Thorhallsson B (2013) Instrumentalizing the European Union in small state strategies. J Eur Integr 35(2):99–115

Baldacchino G, Wivel A (2020) Small states: concepts and theories. In: Baldacchino G, Wivel A (eds) Handbook on the politics of small states. Edward Elgar Publishing, Cheltenham, pp 2–19

Cunha A (Coord) (2017a) Os Capítulos da Adesão. Assembleia da República, Lisboa

Cunha A (2017b) Assuntos Europeus no Parlamento. Os Debates. Assembleia da República, Lisboa

Cunha A (2018) Dossiê Adesão. História do Alargamento da CEE a Portugal. Imprensa de Ciências Sociais, Lisboa

Cunha A (2021) Gone with the pandemic?: Portugal and EU solidarity. In: Kaeding M, Pollak J, Schmidt P (eds) European solidarity and the future of Europe. Views from the capitals. Palgrave Macmillan, London, pp 59–61

Cunha A (2023) União Europeia. In: Teixeira NS, Cunha A (ed) Portugal Multilateral. Dicionário, Volume III. Almedina, Coimbra, pp 221–239

European Commission (2021) Standard Eurobarometer 95 Spring 2021. European Union, Brussels

Ferreira-Pereira L (ed) (2014) Portugal in the European Union. Assessing twenty-five years of integration experience. Taylor and Francis, London

Fishman RM (2003) Shaping, not making, democracy: the European Union and the post-authoritarian political transformations of Spain and Portugal. In: Royo S, Manuel PC (eds) Spain and Portugal in the European Union – the first fifteen years, vol 8. Frank Cass, London, pp 31–46

Gomes JJP (2010) A internacionalização da questão de Timor. Relações Internacionais 25:67–89

Goucha Soares A (2007) Portugal and the European Union: the ups and downs in 20 years of membership. Perspect Eur Polit Soc 8(4):463–473

Lã JR, Cunha A (Org) (2016) Memórias da Adesão. À Mesa das Negociações. Bookbuilders: Santa Cruz

Lã JR, Cunha, A, Nunes PS (Org.) (2019) As Décadas da Europa. Bookbuilders, Santa Cruz

Lains P (2007) Os caminhos da integração: da autarcia à Europa do euro. In: Lobo MC, Lains P (eds) Em Nome da Europa: Portugal em Mudança (1986–2006). Principia, Cascais, pp 14–40

Lains P (2019) Convergence, divergence and policy: Portugal in the European Union. West Eur Polit 42(5):1094–1114

Lopes JS (ed) (1993) Portugal and EC membership evaluated. Pinter Publishers, London

Magone JM (2004) The developing place of Portugal in the European Union. Transaction Publishers, London

Marques A (2017) Três Décadas de fundos comunitários em Portugal. Competitividade: as oportunidades perdidas. Relações Internacionais 53:39–54

Martins V (2016) O Day After: Pesada Herança ou uma Porta Aberta para o Futuro? In: Lã JR, Cunha A (eds) Memórias da Adesão. À Mesa das Negociações. Bookbuilders, Santa Cruz, pp 331–343

Mateus A (Coord.) (2013) 25 Anos de Portugal Europeu. A Economia, A Sociedade e os Fundos Estruturais. Fundação Francisco Manuel dos Santos, Lisboa

Observatório da Emigração (2021) Portuguese emigration Factbook 2020. Observatório da Emigração, Lisboa

Raimundo A (2022) Portugal's contemporary relations with Africa: a limited 'shelter'? In: Cunha A, Thorhallsson B (eds) Small states and big powers: Portugal and Iceland's foreign relations. Springer, Cham

Rodrigues NC, Cunha A (eds) (2022) Portuguese economic development and external funding in the modern era. Sussex Academic Press, Sussex

Teixeira NS (2017) Portugal e a integração europeia, 1974-2015: uma introdução histórica. In: Teixeira NS, Pinto AC (eds) A Europeização da Democracia Portuguesa. Imprensa de Ciências Sociais, Lisboa, pp 19–34

Teixeira NS (2021) As opções estratégicas nacionais na defesa da independência. Paper presented at the seminar "A Diplomacia e a Independência de Portugal", Sociedade Histórica da Independência de Portugal, Lisboa, 3 November 2021
Teixeira NS (2022) Portugal and NATO: enduring alliance or necessary shelter? In: Cunha A, Thorhallsson B (eds) Small states and big powers: Portugal and Iceland's foreign relations. Springer, Cham
Teixeira NS, Cunha A (Coord.) (2021–2023) Portugal Multilateral. Dicionário, Vols. I, II and III. Almedina, Coimbra
Thorhallsson B (2006) The size of states in the European Union: theoretical and conceptual perspectives. Eur Integrat 28(1):7–31
Thorhallsson B (2011) Domestic buffer versus external shelter: viability of small states in the new globalised economy. Eur Polit Sci 10:324–336
Thorhallsson B (2018) A small state in world politics: Iceland's search for shelter. Stjórnmál og Stjórnsýsla - Icelandic Rev Polit Adm 14(special issue on power and democracy in Iceland):61–82
Thorhallsson B (ed) (2019) Small states and shelter theory. Iceland's external affairs. Routledge, New York
Thorhallsson B, Steinsson S (2016) Small state foreign policy. In: Oxford research encyclopedia of politics. Oxford University Press, Oxford, pp 1–25

Dr. Alice Cunha is Assistant Professor with Habilitation in International Relations at the NOVA University of Lisbon—School of Social Sciences and Humanities (NOVA FCSH), and Researcher at the Portuguese Institute of International Relations (IPRI), where she has worked on European Integration, an area in which she has published extensively. Her main research interests are related to enlargement studies, Europeanization, European funds and Portuguese foreign policy. She is a member of the European Union Liaison Committee of Historians.

Chapter 3
A Reluctant European: Iceland and European Integration

Baldur Thorhallsson

3.1 Introduction

The main aim of this chapter is to use shelter theory to explain and understand Iceland's participation in the European project. This chapter will analyse why Iceland joined EFTA, the EEA and Schengen and why the country has not joined the European Union (EU). It will examine whether membership of EFTA, the EEA and Schengen provides Iceland with political, economic and societal shelter.

Iceland was a latecomer in the European project. There was considerable opposition to all moves by Icelandic governments to take part in European integration from the time of its membership in EFTA in 1970, and the following free trade agreement with the European Community in 1972, membership in the EEA in 1994, and Schengen in 2001. In the aftermath of the Icelandic economic collapse in 2008, Iceland applied for membership of the European Union in the summer of 2009. Icelandic governments had refrained from applying for membership at other key moments, such as when its main trading partner, the United Kingdom, and its close neighbouring states Denmark, Norway and Ireland applied for membership in 1961, and the applications of all of its fellow EFTA member states in the early 1990s. Iceland's application for membership in 2009 was extremely controversial and was put on hold as soon as a new government took office in 2013. It has been frozen ever since.

The first section will examine to what extent membership in EFTA and the EEA provides Iceland with economic shelter. It will also discuss why Iceland has not followed most other small European states and joined the EU. Are there economic reasons for Iceland's non-membership of the EU?

B. Thorhallsson (✉)
Faculty of Political Science, Centre for Small State Studies, University of Iceland, Reykjavik, Iceland
e-mail: baldurt@hi.is

A. Cunha, B. Thorhallsson (eds.), *Small States and Big Powers*, The World of Small States 10, https://doi.org/10.1007/978-3-031-42345-1_3

The aim of the second section is to analyse whether Iceland's engagement in the European project has provided it with societal shelter. Most evaluations of the EEA Agreement and EFTA membership fail to consider the importance of societal concerns for the EFTA/EEA member states. This section is dedicated to six subjects (EU norms and values, the EU/EEA grant programmes, the free flow of people, a stimulus towards more modern administrative practices, modernisation of legislation, and involvement in European crisis management) and how they have provided the small Icelandic community on the edge of Europe with important societal shelter.

This third section will analyse whether membership of EFTA, the EEA and Schengen has provided Iceland with political shelter. We will examine Iceland's adherence to the EU's foreign policy (regulated by the EEA), boarder control and police collaboration in Schengen, and the structure of the EEA Agreement and Iceland's limited ability to have a say on EEA rules.[1]

3.2 Economic Shelter: Opportunities and Risks

Most Western European states demonstrated increased interest in free trade during the 1950s, but Iceland did not follow in their footsteps. The Icelandic government justified its abstention from free trade by making an example of Iceland as a small state and the sensitivity of its small market. The United States (US) ensured that Iceland's demands were met in the Organisation for European Economic Co-Operation (OEEC). The US was willing to sacrifice its free trade principals in order to please the Icelandic government due to Iceland's strategic importance in the North Atlantic.[2]

In 1952, Iceland's exports consisted almost entirely of marine products (92.3%). The national fishing limits were therefore of such importance to the Icelandic government that they were extended to 4 miles in 1952, making the creation of the European Economic Community (EEC) of little interest to Icelanders. However, Iceland participated in the negotiations on a free trade area in Western Europe in 1957–59 but nothing came of them. In the late 1950s, Iceland was not invited to participate in the creation of EFTA as the Icelandic government had extended its fishing limits to 12 miles in 1958 and was 'virtually at war with the U.K. over the 12 miles'.[3]

The political climate in Iceland changed in the early 1960s. A new liberal government, the Government of Reconstruction, made up of the centre right Independence Party and Social Democratic Party (SDP), made radical changes to the

---

[1]This chapter draws extensively on the chapter by Thorhallsson B (2019) European Integration: Genuine or False Shelter? In: Thorhallsson B (ed.) Small States and Shelter Theory: Iceland External Affairs. Routledge.

[2]Gunnarsson (1996, p. 89).

[3]Benediktsson (2003, p. 62).

national economy and brought it in line with other countries in Western Europe. It also began to consider joining EFTA and the EEC. By modernising the Icelandic economy, the government wanted to make the country better equipped to undertake the obligations arising from membership of free trade associations and economic alliances.[4] Notwithstanding, it concluded that Iceland's small, underdeveloped economy, characterised by high tariffs and other trade barriers, was not ready for membership. The government was also hampered by the Secretary-General of EFTA's refusal to grant the exemptions that the Icelandic government proposed,[5] as well as the continued tensions with Britain over fishing limits.[6]

In 1961, the Icelandic government carefully examined the advantages and disadvantages of EEC membership. Although the interest groups hired for consultation on the matter were all in favour of applying for membership, the Icelandic government concluded that the various provisions in the Treaty of Rome were unfavourable for small states and chose instead to apply for associated membership despite a lack of clarity on what exactly this meant. The government's decision was based on the following arguments: firstly, the small size of the nation made it impossible to accept the EEC's concept of equal right to employment and the right of establishment[7]; secondly, Iceland had a much higher volume of trade with Eastern Europe than other Western European countries and provisions on the manufacturing industry, agriculture and trade with Eastern Europe were seen as an obstacle to full membership; thirdly, it believed Iceland would need a long period of adaptation before abolishing its protective tariffs; fourthly, and perhaps most importantly, Iceland was not willing to grant other states the same rights to its fisheries as its own nationals.[8]

President de Gaulle eventually declared his opposition to EEC enlargement. As a result, discussions between Icelandic officials and their foreign counterparts came to an end, as did domestic discussions about European cooperation. The "herring boom" brought economic prosperity to the country in the 1960s and the government no longer saw any need for favourable trade deals.

However, the Icelandic government was still interested in joining EFTA and the opportunity presented itself when Britain started exploring ways to strengthen the organisation by, for example, bringing Iceland and Ireland in as members.[9] The main advantage of EFTA membership was that it would facilitate Iceland's exports of fish and other marine products and improve its competitive position within European markets.[10] EFTA membership became even more attractive following a slump in Iceland's fisheries due to a sudden decline in the herring stock and the closure of an important market for fish in Nigeria; moreover, the position of Icelandic exporters

[4] Gíslason (1993, p. 59).

[5] Andersen (1961, p. 30).

[6] Ólafsson (1961).

[7] Benediktsson (1961), Independence Party (1961), Alþýðublaðið (1962).

[8] Alþýðublaðið (1961).

[9] Icelandic GATT committee (1965a).

[10] Icelandic GATT committee (1965b).

within EFTA and the EU was about to worsen due to their planned tariff reduction on marine products. The slump in fisheries and the closure of the Nigerian market eventually led to a deep economic downturn for Iceland. The government had planned to modernise the manufacturing industry and diversify the economy but instead it relied almost entirely on the export of marine products.[11] Furthermore, EFTA and the EU were planning a free trade agreement. Joining EFTA would now make a free trade agreement possible with the EEC, which had been one of the government's main reasons for pressing for membership originally.[12]

In January 1969, Iceland began negotiations on accession to EFTA. The government was successful in securing nearly all of its original objectives. For instance, Iceland signed a very favourable deal for its marine exports to Britain and was also permitted to continue its trade with Eastern Europe. The Nordic countries created an industrial development fund for Iceland and made lamb exports to their markets easier. Despite some serious implications for manufacturing, interest groups in the industry in Iceland were strongly in favour of EFTA membership, which made it much easier for the Icelandic government to go ahead with its application.[13] The government assured the interest groups that it would take all necessary measures to counter any risks to the sector arising from EFTA membership, be they in the areas of taxation, finance, technical matters, customs, or others.[14] In the end, joining EFTA not only resulted in substantial economic growth for the country but also prepared the Icelandic industrial sector for external competition by modernising the sector.[15] While some sectors in Iceland, such as agriculture, were against European integration, the fisheries sector wanted to improve its position in the European market and had advocated EEC membership in 1961.

Iceland joined EFTA in 1970. The European Community (EC) agreed that same year to open negotiations on free trade agreements with EFTA member states, and Iceland was offered a free trade agreement that covered industrial products. This was not the result the government had been looking for since the vast majority of the country's exported goods was fish and other marine products. During these negotiations, Iceland decided in 1972 to extend its fishing limits to 50 miles. This came at a very sensitive time and brought great difficulties in the negotiations.[16] Nevertheless, Iceland managed to negotiate a very favourable free trade agreement in 1972, which proved to be of great advantage to Icelandic fish exporters.[17] Continued disputes between Iceland and the EC over fishing limits meant this protocol did not come into effect until they were resolved in 1976. By that time, Iceland had extended its fishing limits to 200 nautical miles. The extensions of fishing limits were a defining feature

[11] Jónsson (2010, pp. 84–85).

[12] Kristinsson (1987, p. 73).

[13] Benediktsson (2000, p. 86).

[14] Á döfinni (1993, p. 12).

[15] Jónsson (2010).

[16] Ásgeirsson (1972, p. 105).

[17] Hjaltason and Hannibalsson (1997, p. 270), Jónsson (1976, p. 167).

of Iceland's foreign policy in the post war period until 1976[18] and were the foundation of economic sustainability and prosperity in the country,[19] These benefits remained unchanged until the EU completed its internal market expansion in 1992. When Spain and Portugal joined the EC in 1986, quotas and tariffs were also placed on saltfish from Iceland.

In the late 1980s, Iceland put considerable effort into securing free trade of marine products with other EFTA states and succeeded in making this one of the core objectives of the EFTA states in their negotiations on the EEA. The EC argued that fish and marine products should not be categorised in the same way as manufactured goods[20] but should be negotiated under the same conditions as stipulated in its Common Fisheries Policy (CFP), which the Icelandic government strongly opposed.[21] Iceland finally reached an agreement whereby 90% of Icelandic fish products were categorised as tariff free. The Icelandic government deemed this to be a great success[22]; Iceland had to give up its fishing rights to 3000 tons of redfish equivalents in exchange for 30,000 tons of capelin, which was considered a very small price to pay for almost tariff free access to the entire European market.

As part of these negotiations, Iceland became a founding member of the EEA in 1994. The government believed this further secured its long-term interests; under the EEA agreement, Iceland places provisions on foreign parties within the fisheries and power sectors, agricultural imports are limited, and non-nationals are prohibited from buying coastal properties.[23] Furthermore, the government negotiations succeeded in granting Iceland the right to take special security measures regarding employment and residence, such as placing limits on the flow of people, due to its unique circumstances as a small state. Perhaps the greatest influence of EEA membership on the small island state was that it granted Iceland access to the EU internal economic market and required Iceland to adopt EU legislation and implement the 'four freedoms', that is freedom of goods, services, capital and people (except in the areas of agriculture and fisheries). Hence, Iceland has already adopted about two thirds of EU legislation into its national legislature.[24] Moreover, along with the other EFTA/EEA states (Norway and Liechtenstein), Iceland also participates in various EU programmes such as research cooperation and education (discussed in the section on societal shelter). Despite these advantages, Iceland is obliged to adopt EU legislation (EEA rules) and yet it does not have access to the EU's decision-making processes in return (see discussion in the section on political shelter).

[18] Benediktsson (2003, p. 20).

[19] Guðmundsson (2006).

[20] Stephensen (1996, pp. 55–57).

[21] Benediktsson (2003, p. 23).

[22] Stephensen (1996, p. 56), Morgunblaðið (1991).

[23] Stephensen (1996, pp. 55–57).

[24] Institute of International Affairs (2014).

Reports published by the Institute of International Affairs in 2014 and by the Icelandic Prime Minister's Office in 2007 maintain that the EEA agreement has provided the small Icelandic state with important economic shelter. These benefits had already been noted in a Ministry for Foreign Affairs report in 2000 on Iceland's position in European cooperation, which mentions advantages such as improved market access, increased participation in European cooperation projects, particularly within the fields of research and development, greater capital injection into the small Icelandic economy, increased complementarity between economic and commercial legislation, greater liberalisation, and encouragement of modernised administration practices. It also claims that the EEA agreement has put Iceland in an extremely advantageous position in that it can abstain from European cooperation projects that are not beneficial to the state whilst enjoying access to all aspects of the cooperation the Icelandic government regards as beneficial.[25]

The single market is of great importance to Iceland, as can be seen from the fact that the EU and EFTA member states are by far its most important trading partners. Iceland mainly exports fish and marine products to the EU. However, there are certain costs that follow the access to the internal market. For instance, the EFTA/EEA contribute to the so-called EEA and Norway Grants. These payments were originally created on a temporary basis but were expanded in 1999 and have come to be regarded as the EFTA/EEA states' membership fee for access to the internal market. In return, the EU has granted the EFTA/EEA states short term exemptions from certain import duties on marine products, which have been valuable for the Icelandic fishing industry.[26] Norway has shouldered the burden of most of the payments to the grants and, as such, provides Iceland with partial economic shelter, as the injections are based on a country's GDP relative to that of the other EFTA/EEA states. This was particularly important during Iceland's economic difficulties following the economic crash in 2008, when Iceland was exempt from paying the 33% increase in the contribution between periods during the crisis.[27]

Nonetheless, the economic crash in 2008 demonstrated that Iceland merely receives partial economic shelter from its relations with the EU within the EEA framework, and that the country's participation in the free movement of capital in the EEA exposed the small economy to considerable external risk. This can be seen in the collapse of nearly the entire financial sector in Iceland in the first week of October 2008 which resulted in the largest drop in the country's GDP ever recorded. Subsequently, Iceland had to face many challenges, notably a marked rise in unemployment, high inflation, and a significant reduction in wages.[28] The Icelandic bank loans amounted to more than ten times the country's GDP and, thus, it was impossible to rescue the banks or guarantee foreign liabilities to creditors.[29]

---

[25] Icelandic Ministry for Foreign Affairs (2000, pp. 7–12).

[26] Sveinsson (2016).

[27] Institute of International Affairs (2014).

[28] Thorhallsson and Kirby (2012).

[29] Central Bank of Iceland (2010).

The Icelandic government failed to take account of and adopt necessary measures to cope with the free flow of capital within the EEA.[30] First, a small economy poses limitations on the domestic market, the small state budget and the national currency, and, at the time of the 2008 international financial crisis, Iceland could not sustain the outflow of capital. In essence, the small domestic financial sector outgrew the state's capacity to defend it. The Icelandic government had no insurance for these risks within the EEA agreement. Left without an ally or shelter and unable to prevent the fall of its financial sector, Iceland's economy collapsed when the international financial crisis swept across the globe.

Second, according to shelter theory, the public administration in small states faces structural problems related to their smallness. Iceland's administration was unable to cope with policymaking and legislation in the financial sector. This was visible in particular due to the lack of staff and expertise within the administration, which contributed to inadequate supervision of the financial sector and a disregard of the risks associated with the expansion of the economy and the repercussions for the small Icelandic society.[31] Iceland failed to take account of weaknesses associated with its small economy within the EEA, and the EEA and the EU did not provide shelter in the economic crisis.

3.2.1 *The 2009 Membership Application: A Missed Economic Shelter Opportunity?*

Only 9 months after the economic crash in the summer of 2009, the Icelandic government submitted a membership application to the EU. There was a pro-EU momentum in Iceland after the 2008 economic crisis and many saw EU membership and the adoption of the euro as a fundamental source of economic shelter for the crippled Icelandic economy. In the immediate aftermath of the crisis, many in the business community and the main labour unions came out in favour of membership, while all of the political parties softened their positions, especially in regard to the possible adoption of the euro.[32] The crash gave the Social Democrats the opportunity to make EU membership their main election issue and a precondition for the creation of a coalition government with the Left Green Movement in 2009.

However, the application was soon sidelined by the Ice-save dispute, which dominated Icelandic politics until the end of the parliamentary term in 2013 and triggered a nationalist backlash and greater Euroscepticism. The Ice-save debate was particularly difficult for the Europhiles in Iceland because the EU stood firmly by its member states, United Kingdom and the Netherlands, in their effort to get Iceland to compensate their citizens for lost investments in savings schemes operated by the

[30] Office of the Prime Minister (2010).

[31] Thorhallsson (2012).

[32] Thorhallsson and Rebhan (2011).

Icelandic banks. The EU was no longer seen as a possible saviour after the immediate shock of the crash. Indeed, the crash and the associated Ice-save dispute came to be seen by many as "proof" that Icelanders should stand on their own due to the uniqueness of the nation, its small size and the country's geographical location. Moreover, the euro crisis and the European economic crisis, and their consequences for the hard-hit small states of the EU, made it very difficult for the Europhiles to sell the narrative that EU membership was a boon for small states. Moreover, the coalition partner of the Social Democrats in government, the Left Green Movement (LGM), opposed EU membership but reluctantly accepted the EU application in order to secure a seat in government and create the first left-wing government in Icelandic history. The Left Greens were badly split on whether or not to continue the EU accession process, which caused deep friction within the government and weakened the accession process.

The economic crisis only led to a temporary change in Iceland's European policy. The economic preferences of Iceland's political parties remained remarkably stable despite the application for EU membership. The Independence Party and the LGM continued to oppose membership and the centre agrarian Progressive Party's position (which came out in favour of EU membership shortly after the economic crash) quickly returned to its policy of firm opposition to membership.[33] All the parties oppose membership of the Common Fisheries Policy (CFP) and the workings of the Common Agricultural Policy (CAP), while supporting protectionism in domestic agricultural production in Iceland. They have come out in full support of retaining Iceland's currency, the Icelandic króna, and are opposed to the transfer of power over the country's monetary affairs. The EU project is seen as putting constraints on businesses and restricting Iceland's ability to trade with other parts of the world. Furthermore, the parties also appeal to nationalist rhetoric, arguing that EU membership is an unacceptable loss of Iceland's sovereignty and independence (undermining the uniqueness of the nation and its identity), as well as a loss of control over its natural resources. Moreover, EU opponents commonly argue that as a small state within the EU, Iceland would not have any influence within the Union and would be unable to defend its interests. They also note that Iceland would be a net contributor to the Union in terms of the direct transfer of money. Opponents of EU membership also point to the economic success of Iceland since the mid-1990s and argue that Iceland's living standards have risen enormously, in part because it was not a member of the EU. They point out that the government and the Central Bank have been able to form their own economic and monetary policy without EU interference, that Iceland recovered relatively quickly from the 2008 economic crash, and it presently has one of the highest economic growth rates in Europe.

There are two main reasons for Iceland's status as a non-EU member state. First, the European project clashes with the largest political party's vision of Icelandic identity and its emphasis on the self-determination of the nation—its freedom and independence (this is also manifested in its protectionist policies in the agricultural

[33]Thorhallsson and Rebhan (2011).

and fishing sectors). The Independence Party has been in most governments since the creation of the Republic and has constructed Iceland's foreign policy. Material and ideational factors and domestic politics are nicely knitted together and strongly shape Iceland's engagement with the European project, making it only a partial participant. The fisheries and agrarian sectors have formed a powerful force within the party due to the over-representation of MPs from the rural and coastal areas in the Althing, to the determent of representatives from the more populated areas, especially in the Greater Reykjavík area. The fisheries sector has held a special status in the party due to its economic importance and the direct connections between many of its MPs and the sector.[34] The party has always emphasised Iceland's independence struggle and used nationalist rhetoric to appeal to voters. The Conservatives have both shaped and been influenced by the nationalist discourse in Iceland. The party's ideology has roots in the concepts of freedom and independence. Its political discourse is founded on these concepts, which are extensively referenced in all contexts concerning domestic and foreign affairs. Membership of the EU is seen as contrary to these core values of the party.

Second, the political and economic shelter provided by the United States partly explains Iceland's partial engagement in the European project in the twentieth century. The close association between pro-American politicians in Icelandic politics, who were usually to the right and centre of Icelandic politics, may have had a lasting effect on the political positions of the centre and right where bilateral relations, in particular with the US, were seen as key. For instance, a number of Icelandic elites were convinced that the United States would retain a military presence in Iceland, and that the US would rescue Iceland during the financial crisis. Without these misperceptions and miscalculations in the 1990s and 2000s, Icelandic governments might have been more open to exploring EU membership and the adoption of the euro.

After a troubled accession process, the first act of a newly formed coalition government (comprised of the Independence Party and the Progressive Party) in the spring of 2013 was to put the EU accession negotiations on hold. The centre-right government later made it clear that Iceland should not be considered as a candidate country for EU membership, but they did not formally withdraw the application. The cross right-left coalition government formed in January 2018, comprised of the Left Green Movement, the Independence Party and the Progressive Party, has opted to maintain this status quo although it has no intention of reopening the access negotiations nor of formally withdrawing the membership application.

Membership of the European Union is still a debated issue in Icelandic politics. At present, the question of EU membership is not the most important political issue, but it is always at the forefront of all discussion about Iceland's external affairs. It is a highly divisive topic and the opposite camps fundamentally disagree on whether or not membership would provide Iceland with shelter or be highly costly for the society at large. On the other hand, the pro-European parties in the Althingi, the

[34] Thorhallsson and Vignisson (2004).

SDA, the Reform Party and the Pirate Party are committed to holding a referendum on whether or not to resume the negotiations. Accordingly, the EU accession process will not resume without the approval of the majority of the electorate in a referendum. However, the vast majority of Icelandic politicians still consider that the costs associated with full participation in the European project outweigh the benefits.

3.3 Societal Shelter: For the Icelandic Youth?

The EEA Agreement has provided Iceland with important societal shelter. As such, the EEA's wide-reaching effects on the society must be recognised and appreciated instead of dismissing the body as merely economic. Our research has identified six different subjects which bear evidence to the societal shelter provided by the EEA.

First, the EEA Agreement was approved in Althingi in 1992 with a very narrow margin. Subsequently, there were such loud calls for a national referendum on the Agreement that they even drove the President, Vigdís Finnbogadóttir, to contemplate whether she should refuse to sign the Agreement and, thus, call a referendum—a move that the Icelandic president had never previously taken. The President finally signed the Agreement on the grounds that Icelandic youth would otherwise lose access to educational programmes within the Agreement and that it would allow Iceland to move closer to Europe, limit American influence within the country, and uphold the traditional neutrality of the presidential office. These actions signal some of the most important characteristics of societal shelter, i.e. the transfer of norms, values, and more general messages to small communities.[35] In that regard, the small Icelandic society has gone through a phase of Europeanisation since signing the EEA Agreement to an extent that nobody had anticipated.[36]

Second, the EEA Agreement has provided the small Icelandic society with important access to EU institutions of higher education, with educational opportunities, research and funding that support domestic innovation. This access is of the utmost importance to Iceland and highlights our findings that Iceland enjoys societal shelter via membership of the EEA when it comes to research, education, and innovation. From 1995 to 2016, Iceland received approximately 200% return on the country's contribution to the EU programmes, i.e. it receives 2 euros for every 1 euro the government puts in. The disproportionate allocation of funds to small EU/EEA member states compared to their larger counterparts is vividly illustrated in the EU educational funds. For instance, Iceland was by far the highest recipient per person via the Erasmus+ programme within the period 2014–2016,[37] and the European Commission estimated that 28,710 Icelanders received direct benefits

[35] Thorhallsson (2008, p. 94).

[36] Lægreid et al. (2004).

[37] Icelandic Centre for Research (2017, p. 4 and pp. 13–14).

from the Erasmus+ programme between 1992 and 2017.[38] Moreover, our research shows that Icelanders most often collaborate and establish networks with researchers from Scandinavia and large EU member states, which increases innovation and creative contributions. Although it is hard to quantify the marked effects this has had on Icelanders, these interactions have been a contributing factor to the growth in the country's scientific research and artistic development in recent decades, and have increased the output of its firms and research institutions, thus strengthening the international competitiveness of the small Icelandic state.

Third, the free movement of people as stipulated under the EEA has not only provided the Icelandic nation with various opportunities abroad, but has also been an important element in the country's economic management. The concept of movement of people, both to and from small states, is a key aspect of shelter theory. In fact, the EEA Agreement has made Iceland's labour market quite flexible as people have taken advantage of its provisions to seek employment abroad and thus escape risk of unemployment in Iceland; this was particularly relevant following the economic crisis in 2008 when emigration from Iceland exceeded immigration, a pattern that lasted until 2011.

Fourth, several policy fields within Iceland have been transformed by EEA legislation, which has modernised the otherwise small and peripherical society. For instance, the EEA has had a radical effect on environmental and competition law. As smaller communities have small policy-making networks and often limited competition, shelter implications may be greater than in larger communities with bigger markets and more varied competition. Also, Europeanisation has taken place within the judicial sector as well as in policing, immigration and border control,[39] and regarding human rights legislation.[40]

Fifth, the public administration has had to make significant changes in order to comply with EEA rules. The Europeanisation of the Icelandic public administration and the resulting decline in nepotism and ministerial interference have brought about an increase in good governance in policy areas that fall within the parameters of the EEA Agreement. Political favouritism still thrives within the three policy areas that are not negotiated under the EEA Agreement, namely fisheries, agriculture, and rural development.[41] Furthermore, the EEA bodies rarely involve politicians, and decision-making is mostly in the hands of civil servants. Hence, Icelandic civil servants have more influence than politicians in EEA matters.[42]

Sixth, the cooperation between the Icelandic government and the EU on crisis management is increasing, as was seen during the Covid-19 pandemic and regarding border control. The Icelandic government started participating in the EU Civil Protection Mechanism in 2001, which was incorporated into the EEA Agreement

[38] European Commission (2017a, b).

[39] National Commissioner of the Icelandic Police (2016).

[40] Thorhallsson and Thorarensen (2014).

[41] Icelandic National Audit Office (2011).

[42] Lægreid et al. (2004).

in 2014. Moreover, the Commission's Emergency Response Coordination Centre (ERCC) coordinates all the actions of the Civil Protection Mechanism with the European External Action Service (EEAS) and other member states. For example, at the start of the Covid-19 pandemic the ERCC assisted Iceland and other member states with the repatriation of nationals stranded abroad.[43] The Icelandic government also contributes to the EU's Integrated Political Crisis Response mechanism (IPCR) in the Council, a supportive unit for rapid and coordinated decision-making at EU-level during major crisis situations. As such, the IPCR was activated for informal sharing in the early stages of the Covid-19 pandemic. Furthermore, the IPCR provides a framework for the coordination of cross-sectoral crises at the highest political level of the EU and brings affected member states, EU institutions and other key actors together. Iceland is also an associated member of several European agencies that deal with crisis management, such as the European Centre for Disease Prevention and Control (ECDC) and the European Food Safety Authority (EFSA). Iceland secured an agreement for vaccines against Covid-19 via Sweden, which can export vaccines to EEA countries based on agreements between pharmaceutical companies and the EU.[44]

3.4 Political Shelter: Benefits and Costs

As regards border control, membership of Schengen and associated agreements have provided Iceland with important political shelter through soft security, namely through agreements such as the EU Judicial Cooperation Unit (Eurojust), the EU law enforcement agency (the European Police Office/Europol), and the European Union Agency for Law Enforcement Training (CEPOL). Iceland is also a participating member in the European Border and Coast Guard Agency (Frontex), the European Arrest Warrant, and a member of the External Borders Fund, the Dublin System (which deals with asylum applications), and the EURODAC Regulation (which oversees a European database for fingerprints). Iceland also signed the Prüm Decision in 2009, which defines rules for operational police cooperation, including joint patrols and procedures for efficient data exchange in areas such as DNA profiling, fingerprints and vehicle registration data. However, alterations have not been made to the national legislature to implement the EU rules for this cooperation to take place, and the Icelandic police force is also in need of further funding from the state to use the database.

Schengen membership has provided the small island state with several benefits. In 2016, the National Commissioner of the Icelandic Police published an evaluation report on Iceland's Schengen membership. The report came when large numbers of

[43] Information received from a high-ranking official in the Icelandic public administration (B), 26 February, 2011.

[44] Gunnarsson (2020), Icelandic Ministry of Health (2020).

asylum seekers and an increase in foreign nationals traveling to Europe had led to some Schengen members strengthening their border control due to the heightened risk of terrorist activities. Four years earlier, the Ministry of Interior had also commissioned a similar report and found that it was in Iceland's interests to remain in the Schengen agreement. Moreover, Iceland participates in a number of sharing mechanisms with Schengen states, the most important of which are the Visa Information System (VIS), the Schengen Information System (SIS), and the EU asylum fingerprint database EURODAC. Participation in these mechanisms also gives Iceland the opportunity to receive education and training, e.g. for the national police force,[45] and the Icelandic Coast Guard (ICG) who have participated in Frontex operations since 2010, which has "made (the ICG) more qualified to fulfil our duties in Iceland". Information sharing is of particular importance when there is an increased risk of terrorism as Icelandic border control officers do not need to check travel documents within the Schengen zone and can instead focus on other travellers. The police enforcement agency at Keflavík airport maintains that Schengen membership has increased border security in Iceland.

Nevertheless, Schengen membership comes with certain disadvantages. According to the report from the National Police Commissioner many people within the Schengen area are unregistered; the identification of some people residing in Iceland was not checked on entry; domestic inspection mechanisms lack resources; the Icelandic police force has limited use of the SIS database and they sometimes conduct random checks on EU citizens at the border; there is inadequate follow-up on foreign visas domestically; and automatic boarder clearing devices at Keflavík airport are limited. Also gaps in border security give rise to risks for member states, such as an increase in human trafficking and terrorism.

European integration has been a driver for increased capacity building in cyber security domestically. The Post and Telecommunications Authority (PTA) in Iceland cooperates with the European Union Agency for Network and Information Security (ENISA) via the PTA Computer Security Incident Response Team (CERT-IS) and learns from the agency on how to counter cyber security risks.[46] Furthermore, the implementation of the EU directive on Network and Information Security (NIS) will not only entail a significant increase in cyber security in sectors such as health, finance, energy, transport and digital infrastructure, but also require CERT-IS experts to be on duty 24 h a day.[47]

As for the structure of the EEA Agreement, the EEA Council (which is officially composed of the foreign ministers of the EEA/EFTA and EU countries, using the 'troika' format of the EU Council presidency) has very limited scope. Icelandic minister's attempts to use it to foster the development of the EEA agreement and solve disputes in the Joint Committee have been unsuccessful due to the EU's lack of interest in the EEA Council's work. Also, the EEA Joint Parliamentary Committee,

---

[45] Office of the Prime Minister (2007).

[46] CERT-IS (2016).

[47] Vísir (2017).

which is composed of members of parliament (MPs) from both sides, is only a talking club and has no powers. Moreover, few people in Iceland know about these EEA bodies other than the public officials who work with them, and politicians who show an interest in their operations (Thorhallsson 2015). However, as a Schengen member state, Iceland's Minister of Interior is entitled to attend the Council's ministerial meetings, thus giving the country a voice within the Council; however, they have seldom taken the opportunity to do so and some are even unaware of this possibility to voice their concerns.

The Icelandic public is largely unaware that the concept of free movement of people is an obligation under the EEA Agreement, not Schengen, and there have been no public discussions on the role of Icelandic ministers to use the Council to shave a say on Schengen affairs. Similarly, EEA legislation rarely comes up in public debates. In the early days of EEA membership, local council officials criticised the cost of implementation and argued that EEA rules were too costly for small Icelandic municipalities, claiming that they should be exempt from applying them in full.[48]

Iceland has to implement EEA rules without having any real say on them. Even though Iceland can refuse to adopt EU laws relating to the EEA and Schengen areas, Icelandic politicians consider it in the country's interest to adopt them, to avoid challenging Iceland's EEA and Schengen membership.[49] The binding effects of political, economic and societal shelter that are associated with EEA membership require sovereignty and assets to be pooled. In general, small states are often under pressure to adopt transnational regulations. They are in danger of having limited influence on the regulations they are required to implement and feeling pressured to follow the policies of the shelter provider. The EFTA/EEA states are a prime example of this.

The Icelandic government has also sought shelter from the EU by consistently aligning its foreign policy with that of the EU even though it is seldom invited to participate in prior political dialogue.[50] It strives to show a united front with its western allies in the hope of getting support in return. For instance, in 2012, Iceland aligned itself with 64 out of 70 EU foreign policy declarations, and in 2014, Iceland participated in 35 out of 36 EU foreign policy declarations. Non-alignment is usually due to the fact that the Icelandic government has not been given sufficient time to align its policies with EU decisions.[51] Interestingly, when Iceland had a euro-sceptic minister of foreign affairs (2013–2016/2017), EU foreign policy declarations were still accepted even though they troubled the minister.

Nevertheless, on some occasions Iceland has been reluctant to follow US-EU decisions. For example, following the sanctions on Russia in March 2014 over

[48]Thorhallsson (2015).

[49]Thorhallsson (2015).

[50]Interview with high-ranking official in the Icelandic Ministry for Foreign Affairs, December, 2016.

[51]Interview with high-ranking official in the Icelandic Ministry for Foreign Affairs, January 2017.

Ukraine and counter-sanctions on Iceland imposed by Russia in August 2015, the Prime Minister stated that Iceland could not blindly impose the EU sanctions on Russia[52] as they were costly for the marine sector and thus the Icelandic economy. Subsequently, Iceland refrained from participating in EU declarations on the sanctions from 2015 to 2022 despite implementing the sanctions.

In theory, Iceland is free to lift the sanctions on Russia without prior consultation with its allies, but our study finds that it feels obliged to comply with the foreign policy preferences of its close allies in order to continue receiving shelter. Thus, EEA's partial shelter is problematic for Iceland. For instance, if we look at the case of the Faroe Islands, which are not members of EFTA or the EEA but are a home-rule entity and part of the Danish Kingdom, they chose not to impose sanctions and enjoyed a significant increase in trade with Russia.[53] In the case of Iceland, shelter does not come without costs but the government has decided to sacrifice domestic economic interests and instead, follow their foreign allies in policy making.

Apart from aligning itself with the EU foreign policy declarations, Iceland does not participate in EU external politics. Most Icelandic political parties are of the opinion that participation in the EU Common Foreign and Security Policy and in decision-making on the European Security and Defence Policy would not bolster the country's defences, as the political shelter provided by the US and NATO is generally considered sufficient in that regard.

3.5 Conclusion

Iceland's membership in EFTA, the EEA and Schengen have provided important economic, societal, and political shelter in term of soft security cooperation. Most evaluations conducted on the EEA Agreement do not consider the importance of societal effects for the EFTA/EEA member states and, thus, do not conceptualise the EEA as a societal shelter provider. Our findings indicate that EEA membership has provided Iceland with valuable societal shelter, namely in terms of modernising/Europeanising norms and values of the small peripherical society, the free flow of people, stimulating more modern administrative practices, modernising legislation, and its involvement in European crisis management.

Schengen membership has secured easy access for Icelanders to other Nordic states (and Europe at large) and facilitated collaboration between the Icelandic police force and its European counterparts. Moreover, EEA membership has enhanced the notion of Iceland as a fully committed part of the western alliance and aligned Iceland's foreign policy to that of the EU. Such alignments enable small states to maintain their shelter. These findings indicate that the partial political shelter in soft

[52] Eyjan (2016).

[53] Wall Street Journal (2015).

security that Iceland received following membership in Schengen and the EEA was more important than anyone anticipated at the time of entry.

EFTA and EEA membership has modernised the Icelandic economy and granted exporters beneficial access to their most valuable market. Accordingly, EFTA membership and participation in the EU's internal market have provided the small Icelandic market with essential economic shelter.

However, there are risks associated with membership of EEA and Schengen. They do not provide political and economic shelter at times of economic crises. The structure of EEA gives Icelandic politicians limited opportunities to have a say on EEA rules and the Icelandic government applies EU policies reactively without considering domestic implications, such as the country's smallness. Moreover, debates on EFTA and EEA membership were highly controversial in the small Icelandic society and caused a costly division. This is currently the case with the EU membership.

To conclude, Iceland's experience with European engagement has been mixed when it comes to shelter theory. While membership of EFTA, EEA and Schengen provide essential economic and societal shelter, and partial political shelter, it also has its limitations: Iceland cannot count on the EU as a political and economic shelter provider during times of need.

References

Á döfinni (1993) Iðnaðurinn og upphaf EFTA aðildar. Á döfinni 2

Alþýðublaðið (1961) Íslendingar og markadsbandalög Evrópu – síðari hluti. Alþýðublaðið 14 July

Alþýðublaðið (1962) Aukaaðild hentar Íslandi bezt. Alþýðublaðið, 6 February

Andersen H G (1961) Unpublished memo from the Icelandic ambassador in Brussels, Ministry of Commerce, 30 August

Ásgeirsson Þ (1972) Samningur Íslands vid Efnahagsbandalag Evrópu. FjÁrmÁlatÍdindi 2:104–108

Benediktsson B (1961) Unpublished speech at the 1961 national convention of the Independence Party

Benediktsson E (2000) Ísland og Evrópuþróunin 1950–2000. Fjölsýn forlag, ReykjavÍk

Benediktsson E (2003) Iceland and the European development. Almenna bókafélagid, ReykjavÍk

Central Bank of Iceland (2010) Peningastefnan eftir höft: Skýrsla Seðlabanka Íslands til efnahags- og viðskiptarÁðherra. http://www.sedlabanki.is/lisalib/getfile.aspx?itemid=8358. Accessed 4 July 2023

CERT-ÍS (2016) Ársskýrsla CERT-ÍS 2016. Póst- og Fjarskiptastofnun. https://www.cert.is/files/CERT-IS_arsskyrsla_fyrir_arid_2016.pdf

European Commission (2017a) Countries and regions: Iceland, last updated 15 December 2017

European Commission (2017b) Erasmus+ Factsheet for Iceland. https://www.erasmusplus.is/media/30-ara-afmaeli/erasmusplus-factsheet-is-hd.pdf. Accessed 4 July 2023

Eyjan (2016) Sigmundur Davíð: Getum ekki bara elt ESB og tekið þátt í viðskiptaþvingunum blindandi. Eyjanpressanis, 6 January

Gíslason GÞ (1993) ViðreisnarÁrin. Almenna bókafélagid, ReykjavÍk

Guðmundsson GJ (2006) The cod and the cold war. Scand J Hist 31(2):97–118

Gunnarsson GÁ (1996) Ísland og Marshallaðstodin: Atvinnustefna og stjórnmÁlahagsmunir. Saga 34:85–130

Gunnarsson OÆ (2020) Svíar munu sjá Íslendingum fyrir bóluefni. Fréttablaðið

Hjaltason J, Hannibalsson Ó (1997) Med spriklið Í sporðinum: Saga SH 1942–1996. Hið Íslenska bókmenntafélag, ReykjavÍk

Icelandic Centre for Research (Rannís) (2017) Þátttaka Íslands í áætlunum ESB á sviði rannsókna, menntunar og menningar. https://www.rannis.is/media/esb-skyrsla/Skyrslan%2D%2D-tolfraedi-ESB-aaetlana.pdf. Accessed 4 July 2023

Icelandic GATT committee (1965a) Aðild Íslands ad EFTA. Unpublished memo, Ministry of Commerce, 20 April

Icelandic GATT committee (1965b) Rökin með og móti aðild að EFTA. Unpublished memo, Ministry of Commerce, 1 July

Icelandic Ministry for Foreign Affairs (2000) Staða Íslands Í Evrópusamstarfi: Skýrsla Halldórs ÁsgrÍmssonar utanrÍkisrÁðherra til Alþingis. Ministry for Foreign Affairs, ReykjavÍk

Icelandic Ministry of Health (2020) COVID-19: Aðgengi Íslands að bóluefni Pfizer tryggt. www.stjornarradid.is/efst-a-baugi/frettir/stok-frett/2020/11/11/COVID-19-Adgengi-Islands-ad-boluefni-Pfizer-tryggt/. Accessed 4 July 2023

Icelandic National Audit Office (2011) Skýrsla um eftirfylgni. Rikisendurskodun, Reykjavik

Independence Party (1961) StjórnmÁlaÁlyktun landsfundar SjÁlfstædisflokksins 1961. The Independence Party, ReykjavÍk

Institute of International Affairs (2014) Aðildarviðræður Íslands við ESB

Jónsson ÓH (1976) Ísland og efnahagsbandalögin. FjÁrmÁlatÍðindi 2:124–174

Jónsson G (2010) Coming to terms with Europe, Iceland's Entry into EFTA and its Implications. In: Bryn K, Einarsson G (eds) EFTA 1960-2010. Elements of 50 years of European history. University of Iceland Press, Reykjavík, pp 77–97

Kristinsson GH (1987) Ísland og Evrópubandalagið. Icelandic commission on security and international affairs, ReykjavÍk

Lægreid P, Steinthorsson RS, Thorhallsson B (2004) Europeanization of central government administration in the Nordic states. J Common Mark Stud 42(2):347–369

Morgunblaðið (1991) Íslenskt atvinnulÍf og evrópskt efnahagssvæði. Morgunblaðið, 12 July

National Commissioner of the Icelandic Police (2016) Mat ríkislögreglustjóra á Schengen-samstarfinu. https://www.innanrikisraduneyti.is/media/frettir-2016/Schengen-mat.pdf. Accessed 4 July 2023

Office of the Icelandic Prime Minister (2007) Tengsl Íslands og Evrópusambandsins: Skýrsla Evrópunefndar um samstarfið á vettvangi EES og Schengen og um álitaefni varðandi hugsanlega aðild Íslands að Evrópusambandinu. https://www.forsaetisraduneyti.is/media/frettir/SkyrslaEvropunefndar-.pdf. Accessed 4 July 2023

Office of the Icelandic Prime Minister (2010) Viðbrögð stjórnsýslunnar við skýrslu rannsóknarnefndar Alþingis Skýrsla starfshóps forsætisráðuneytisins. https://www.forsaetisraduneyti.is/media/Skyrslur/Skyrsla-starfshops-6-mai2010.pdf. Accessed 4 July 2023

Ólafsson D (1961) Afstaða Íslands gagnvart markadsbandalögunum, unpublished memo, Ministry of Commerce, 22 July

Stephensen ÓÞ (1996) Áfangi Á Evrópuför. The University of Iceland Press, ReykjavÍk

Sveinsson GB (2016) Frumvarp til laga um breytingu á lögum um Evrópska efnahagssvæðið, nr. 2/1993, með síðari breytingum (Uppbyggingarsjóður EES 2014–2021). (Lagt fyrir Alþingi á 145. löggjafarþingi 2015–2016). http://www.althingi.is/altext/145/s/1116.html. Accessed 4 July 2023

Thorhallsson B (2008) Evrópustefna íslenskra stjórnvalda: Stefnumótun, átök og afleiðingar. In: Ingimundarson V (ed) Uppbrot hugmyndakerfis: Endurmótun íslenskrar utanríkisstefnu 1991–2007. Hið íslenska bókmenntafélag, Reykjavik, pp 67–136

Thorhallsson B (2012) The Icelandic economic collapse: how to overcome constraints associated with smallness? Eur Polit Sci 12(3):320–332

Thorhallsson B (2015) Iceland – a reluctant European? In: Eriksen EO, Fossum JE (eds) The European Union's non-members: Independence under hegemony? Routledge, New York, pp 118–136

Thorhallsson B (2019) European integration: genuine or false shelter? In: Thorhallsson B (ed) Small states and shelter theory: Iceland external affairs. Routledge

Thorhallsson B, Kirby P (2012) Financial crisis in Iceland and Ireland: does EU and euro membership matter? J Common Mark Stud 50(5):801–818

Thorhallsson B, Rebhan C (2011) Iceland's economic crash and integration takeoff: an end to European Union scepticism? Scand Polit Stud 31(1):53–73

Thorhallsson B, Thorarensen B (2014) Iceland's democratic challenges and human rights' implications. In: Carey HF (ed) European institutions, democratization, and human rights protection in the European periphery. Lexington Books, Lanham, pp 223–244

Vísir (2017) Ólíklegt að Ísland sleppi við netárásirnar. Visiris, 14 May. http://www.visir.is/g/2017170519344/oliklegt-ad-island-sleppi-vid-netarasirnar. Accessed 4 July 2023

Wall Street Journal (2015) Faeroe Islands boom by selling Salmon to Russia. wsjcom, 20 February

Baldur Thorhallsson is a Professor of Political Science, and founder and Research Director for the Centre for Small State Studies, at the University of Iceland. His research focus has primarily been on small European states, small state theory and Iceland's foreign policy. His recent articles are included in *The Hague Journal of Diplomacy*, *Scandinavian Journal of History* and *Global Affairs*. His latest edited books are titled *Iceland's Shelter-Seeking Behavior: From Settlement to Republic* (Cornell University Press 2021), *Small States and the New Security Environment* (co-editor) (Springer 2021) and *Small States and Shelter Theory: Iceland's External Affairs* (Routledge 2019). He holds a PhD (1999) and MA (1994) in Political Science from the University of Essex in the United Kingdom.

Chapter 4
Portugal and NATO: Enduring Alliance or Necessary Shelter?

Nuno Severiano Teixeira

According to the traditional "small states" literature in the field of International Relations, Portugal, with around 10 million inhabitants, falls into this category.[1]

On the other hand, the small states International Relations literature also usually argues that "small states" need to form alliances in order to enhance their strengths and compensate for their vulnerabilities. They establish long term and privileged relations with larger states and join regional or international organizations in order to survive and thrive in the international scene.[2] This is also the case with Portugal.

A European country, Portugal is also an Atlantic country. A small semi-peripheral power with a single land border, Portugal has always experienced an unstable balance between continental pressure of Spain and the search for a maritime alternative in the Atlantic. From these geopolitical constraints and this continuous attempt at balance stem long-term movements that have shaped structural continuities or historical invariants in the strategic options and features of Portuguese foreign policy, which we can define as models of international insertion. From the modern ages to the present day, Portugal has known two different models of international insertion.

The first one is the classical model, characterised by four main invariants. First, a contradictory perception between the continent and the sea, between Europe and the Atlantic. Second, the strategic distancing from Europe (perceived as the Spanish threat) and the affirmation of Portugal's maritime vector and Atlantic option. Third,

[1] See Armstrong and Read (2000, pp. 285–306), Jalan (1999, pp. 39–48), Katzenstein (1984, 1985), Kuznet (1960, pp. 14–34), Ross (1983), Vital (1967).

[2] See Rothstein (1968), Keohane (1971, pp. 161–182), Leeds et al. (2022, pp. 237–260), Fang et al. (2014, pp. 775–80), Huth and Russett (1988, pp. 29–45), Ikenberry (2002), Morrow (1991, pp. 904–933), Jackson and Nei (2015, pp. 15277–15284).

N. S. Teixeira (✉)
Universidade NOVA de Lisboa, Lisbon, Portugal
e-mail: nst@unl.pt

A. Cunha, B. Thorhallsson (eds.), *Small States and Big Powers*, The World of Small States 10, https://doi.org/10.1007/978-3-031-42345-1_4

in the framework of the Atlantic option, two long-duration historical movements in the external orientation of the State: on the one hand, at geostrategic level, the favoured alliance with the maritime power- the British Alliance, the United States of America and finally NATO—on the other, at geoeconomic level, the imperial project in its various cycles: India, Brazil and finally Africa. Fourth, the diversification of extra-peninsular alliances in regard to Spain, and an essentially bilateral diplomacy based on the Lisbon-Madrid-London triangle and, after 1945, Lisbon-Madrid-Washington. This is the model that governs Portugal's international relations for five centuries and these are the strategic guidelines shaping Portuguese foreign policy until the end of authoritarian regime in 1974.

Democratisation in Portugal brought with it the adjustment of this whole framework of foreign policy. Moreover, the transition to democracy and the democratic consolidation in Portugal and Spain, as well as the evolution of the international system itself led, in only 12 years (1974–1986), to the disappearance of this classical five-century old model.

The changes introduced by the democratic regime are not, however, short-term, nor are they limited to foreign policy priorities. They appear to be long-term, and, in all likelihood, they are leading Portugal to a new model of international insertion—the democratic model of international insertion. But what characterises, then, this new democratic model? What changes and what remains the same?

First, that which has remained the same. It stems from structural and geopolitical factors that lingered and has to do, essentially, with the persisting areas of Portugal's strategic interest: Europe, the Atlantic and postcolonial relations.

Second, that which has changed. It stems from historical factors and alters the four main characteristics of the previous model.

First, it changes the perception and contradictory logic between the continent and the sea. Today, Europe and the Atlantic are not only contradictory but also complementary. For Portuguese foreign policy, being Atlantic may represent an added value in terms of Europe, just like being European may represent an added value in terms of the Atlantic and, in particular, the South Atlantic, where postcolonial relations unfold.

Secondly, in the Europe-Atlantic binomial, the geopolitical equation remains but strategic priorities have been reversed: traditionally, Portugal saw itself as an Atlantic and colonial country and, when the weight of the maritime vector was excessive, it sought continental compensations. Today, on the contrary, it sees itself as a European country and it is as a member of the EU that it seeks to value and enhance the Atlantic position and post-colonial relations. Thirdly, and as a result of democratisation in Portugal and Spain, the two peninsular states brought their international positions closer together. This means, at the very least, two things: firstly, that the Portuguese geo-economic instrument has been continentalised with the entry into the European Community and, for Portugal, the single market begins in the Iberian market; secondly, that the diplomatic and strategic instruments of Portugal and Spain have gradually come closer and, for the first time in their history, Portugal and Spain today share the same extra-peninsular alliances: the EU and NATO.

Fourthly, as a result of globalisation, the interdependence of international relations and the enhancement of multilateral diplomatic frameworks, the old bilateral triangle Lisbon, Madrid and maritime power is now joined by a new multilateral triangle, corresponding to Portugal's presence in international organisations in its areas of strategic interest: the EU in Europe, NATO in the Atlantic and the CPLP for postcolonial relations.

In this transition from the classical to the democratic model of international insertion, Portugal changed priorities from Africa to Europe, but the Atlantic remains constant and, in that framework, NATO played an important role as an enduring alliance.

Recently and in parallel with the theory of alliances, the theory of shelter was created and developed in an attempt to bring together the "small states" literature core assumptions and try to explain small state behaviour in the international system.[3]

Founding member of the Atlantic Alliance since its inception, the Portuguese presence in NATO has been analysed in the context of the theory of alliances. The purpose of this essay is to bring the shelter theory to the analysis and to attempt an understanding of which theoretical framework is the most useful to make sense of the Portuguese case: one exclusively or the combination of both?

4.1 Why a Founding Member?

Which were Portugal's position and role in the foundation of the Alliance? To answer this satisfactorily, three preliminary questions must be addressed.

The first question is: why did the negotiating powers decide to invite Portugal to join the Alliance? A neutral country during the Second World War, and home to an unrelenting authoritarian regime, Portugal had been excluded from the post-war reordering of the international scene—not to say marginalized—between 1945 and 1949. Why, then, the invitation to sign the Washington Treaty and become a founding member of the Atlantic Alliance?

The second question, conversely, is: why did Portugal accept the invitation? Why sign the treaty and join the pact when it meant such a radical change in Portuguese foreign policy as relinquishing neutrality, so hard to conquer during the Second World War and so often invoked by the propaganda of the *Estado Novo* as Salazar's and the regime's crown of glory?

Finally, the question of consequences: what were the immediate and medium to long-run consequences of Portugal's admission to NATO for the country's evolution—in foreign policy, domestic policy and, obviously, defence policy and the reforms of the military instrument?

[3]Thorhallsson (2019), Thorhallsson (2011, pp. 324–336), Bailes et al. (2016, pp. 9–26).

Why was Portugal invited? The answer is straightforward and relates to the geopolitical and geostrategic nature of the very grounds underlying the new Atlantic security system. Conceived against the Soviet threat, this system was based on two pillars: the first was the strategic potential of the United States, bringing up the rear and self-guarantee of the whole system; the second, forming the front line and immediate defence, was the ensemble of countries that signed the Brussels Pact in 1948. However, for the system to work properly, it was necessary to ensure not only the protection of the northern and southern flanks but, above all, the articulation between the front and the rear, that is, between the two pillars of the Alliance. This was the main reason why Portugal was invited to join. The territory of the Azores archipelago represented, furthermore, an added strategic value. Already an important military base during the First War, it proved decisive during the Second World War and vital in the course of the Cold War. Included in Pentagon's post-war military defence system, the Azores base had previously been the object of a bilateral agreement between Portugal and the United States in 1948.[4] With NATO, within a multilateral framework, its value was further increased and its role confirmed by the strategic concept of the Atlantic Alliance: in case of an attack coming from the East, the so-called "rapid reinforcement of Europe" relied inevitably on the Azores, this huge natural aircraft carrier in the middle of the Atlantic Ocean. The strategic value of the Azores archipelago prevailed over the authoritarian nature of Salazar's regime. The geopolitical and geostrategic factors were thus the true reasons for inviting Portugal.

But why did Portugal accept the invitation, when doing so entailed such a pronounced change in its international standing, which would lead it from neutrality to alignment?

Ever since the 50s and up to the present day, many have been the attempts by Portuguese historiography to answer this question.[5]

Despite the differences in their theoretical assumptions and political positions, the theses mentioned above rely on a common tenet: they favour the "Statesman" to the detriment of the "deep forces", to use Renouvin and Duroselle's classical terminology. That is, they focus almost exclusively on Salazar's ideological, political and diplomatic positioning and attach less importance to the external environment and internal constraints.

Now, an understanding of the decision-making process must rely both on the attitude of the decision-maker and on the internal and external factors that influence the decision. And, despite the ideological, political and diplomatic motivations at play, Portugal's accession to the Alliance is ultimately linked to those constraints and, in particular, to the reduced leeway of Portuguese foreign policy.[6]

---

[4]Vintras (1975), Marquina (1986, pp. 943–960), Telo (1993).

[5]Carvalho (1953), Nogueira (1980), Nogueira (1981, pp. 226–228), Ferreira (1987, pp. 395–401), Ferreira (1989), Ferreira (1990, pp. 155–157).

[6]Teixeira (1993, pp. 55–80).

Salazar was aware, from an early stage, of the changes in the correlation of forces in the international scene and of the emergence of a new framework of world security, and had highlighted the advance of communism in Europe. It was in 1947, when giving a speech on current international events.[7]

For that reason, when, in 1948, at the UN's general Assembly, Mr. Spaak drew the world's attention to the "Russian threat", Salazar presumably felt his concerns confirmed and his traditional anti-communism justified. However, he had no sympathy for the post-war multilateral diplomacy, let alone the democratic regimes that conducted it, especially the United States of America. It is thus unenthusiastically and even with demur that he receives the formal invitation to sign the North Atlantic Treaty. In the negotiations that preceded admission, between Portugal and the negotiating powers—England and the United States—Salazar insistently raised four objections to the text of the pact: in the first place, the allusion to the UN Charter, from which Portugal had been excluded, and the parliamentary democratic model, which the *Estado Novo* rejected; secondly, the refusal of any solution involving integration or supranationality, for fear that the true aim of the pact might be to obtain, in peacetime, the use of the Azores base—he feared the loss of sovereignty and did not want to lose control of it; thirdly, the case of Spain, which had been excluded from the pact and which Salazar, still under the influence of the concept of Iberian Bloc, deemed essential for western defence; and, finally, the obligatory twenty-year commitment to the Treaty, a length of time he considered to be excessively long, fearing that Portugal might be involved in a new conflict after the neutrality conquered in the Second War.[8]

Except for the guarantees concerning the strategic bases, and although their rejection was diplomatically justified, no other Portuguese request was granted. In fact, none of them seriously affected the great powers.[9]

As the scheduled date for the signing of the treaty approached, Lisbon began to be subject to diplomatic pressure from different countries. On one hand, Spain was pressuring Portugal not to join by invoking the Iberian Pact.[10] On the other, the United States and England urged Portugal to go ahead with the adhesion. Dean Acheson and Ernest Bevin themselves sent personal messages to Salazar on the eve of the council of the ministers which would decide the Portuguese position.[11] The

---

[7] See the speeches "Miséria e medo características do momento actual", of 25 November 1947, and "O Ocidente em face da Rússia", of 28 April 1948, in Salazar (1950) "Miséria e medo características do momento actual - discurso de 25 de Novembro de 1947", in *Discursos e notas políticas*, pp. 287–311 and Salazar (1950), "O Ocidente em face da Rússia, de 28 de Abril de 1948", in *Discursos e notas políticas*, pp. 325–337.

[8] See the exchange of diplomatic notes between London, Washington and Lisbon, particularly the Portuguese pro-memoria of 31 December 1948, the English and North-American *aide-mémoire* of 10 January of 1949, and the Portuguese memorandum of 8 March 1949.

[9] See the English pro-memoria of 17 March 1949.

[10] See the letter by Nicolás Franco, Spanish Ambassador in Lisbon, dated the 20 March 1949.

[11] See telegrams 78, 79 and 80 of the Portuguese Embassy in London dated the de 19 March 1949, Dean Achson's letter dated the 22 March 1949.

pressure over Lisbon was mounting and there was little leeway. Internationally, Portugal's refusal might have a negative impact on countries in the process of pondering their own adhesion. It might open a breach in the West that would only benefit the Soviet Union. In a scenario of worldwide polarisation and exacerbation of the Cold War, a refusal by Portugal, with all its consequences, was too great a risk for Salazar to take before the political leaders and the public opinion of the western world. Moreover, in the context of the peninsula, Portugal's refusal could be further interpreted as a sign of weakness and yielding before Franquist Spain.

In short, refusal meant running a significant risk, the leeway of Portuguese foreign policy was small and alternative options almost none. After three councils of the ministers,[12] the government divided and unenthusiastic, Salazar decided to join the pact. Less through conviction than necessity. On the 4th of April of 1949, Portugal signed the Washington Treaty and became a founding member of the Atlantic Alliance.

Finally, what would be the short and long-term consequences of Portugal's adhesion to the Atlantic Alliance at the various levels: that of domestic policy and that of *Estado Novo*'s foreign and defence policy?

Notwithstanding all the reservations that had delayed Portugal's final decision, its admission in NATO represented paradoxically a victory for Salazar. A victory *malgré lui*, but still a victory.

To begin with, a victory of foreign policy. In the framework of the peninsula, despite Salazar's insistence for Spain to be admitted in the Alliance, the refusal by the western powers proved beneficial for Portuguese foreign policy. The coincidence of Portugal's admission and Spain's exclusion unmistakably reinforced Portugal's position in the peninsula and establish Lisbon as chief interlocutor in the extra-peninsular relations, especially with the United States.[13] Globally, Portugal's adhesion to the Alliance came to confirm the permanence of the historical vectors of Portuguese foreign policy, that is, the Atlantic option and the alliance with maritime power. However, there was a fundamental change in its pole of reference which was the prevalent naval power in the Atlantic: the decline of the Anglo-Portuguese Alliance and the emergence of a new axis on the other side of the Atlantic—the United States of America. That change would constitute the Portuguese answer to the international scene of the second post-war period.

Secondly, insofar as this was a military pact, the consequences of Portugal's admission in the Alliance were naturally felt in the military institution itself and in defence policy. Despite a few clashes, within the military hierarchy, over Portugal's military defence concept, the military institution on the whole supported the adhesion to NATO. They hoped that the ensuing military aid from the United States might make a vital contribution to the professional modernisation and the military re-equipment of the Portuguese Armed Forces, which indeed occurred throughout

[12] Nogueira (1980, pp. 143–144).

[13] Ferreira (1987, pp. 395–401), Jiménez Redondo (1996, pp. 163–191), Jiménez Redondo (1999, pp. 97–111).

the 50s under a "mutual aid plan". On the other hand, this period of professionalisation and modernisation of the Armed Forces was accompanied by a withdrawal of the institution into itself and an absence of military intervention in political life, which further worked in Salazar's favour.

Thirdly, at the level of domestic policy. If it is a fact that Portugal's admission in NATO divided the regime, it is no less true that it caused even deeper and more enduring dissension within the opposition: the communists, siding with the Soviet positions, opposed radically and regarded the Alliance as the military instrument of North-American imperialism[14]; the democratic opposition, on the other hand, seeing in the pact an embodiment of the principles of the United Nations Charter and of democracy, supported enthusiastically the Portuguese accession, hoping that it might entail an implicit condemnation of authoritarianism and a chance, even if remote, of the democratisation of the regime.[15]

The outcome would be the exact opposite: the acceptance of the Portuguese dictatorship in the midst of the Alliance, side by side with western democracies, not only conferred to the regime a measure of international legitimacy, but also favoured the political stability of the regime, aggravating the domestic divisions among the opposition—communists on one side and Democratic Republicans on the other—and cast it into one of its more enduring crises, extending throughout the whole decade of the 50s, until General Humberto Delgado's presidential candidacy.[16]

Hence Portugal's adhesion to NATO, in 1949, launched one of the most stable periods of the history of *Estado Novo*, in terms of both foreign and domestic policy. Only Portugal's admission in the UN, in 1955, and the start of international contestation against Salazar's colonial policy eventually changed the panorama and closed this period.

The Atlantic option and Portugal's presence in the Alliance will remain, however, basic references in the foreign orientation of the Portuguese State until the end of the authoritarian regime and will even be confirmed with the transition to democracy.

In this context, Portugal's NATO accession can hardly be explained through shelter theory and is better accounted for by the classical theory of alliances. To seek shelter was not a deliberate choice, but rather a begrudging decision in which the Portuguese territory was of great strategic value for the alliance and the room for manoeuvre was little for Portuguese foreign policy. Portugal did not seek shelter; it was the shelter provider who sought Portugal instead. But while it is true that the decision favouring accession cannot be explained by shelter theory, it is no less true that its consequences can be understood as having worked for Portugal as a shelter at the military and political level. It was a modernisation factor for the Armed Forces, a factor of diplomatic preponderance vis-a-vis Spain, and also a factor of longevity and internal political stability for the authoritarian regime.

---

[14] Avante!, March 1949, p. 1; Avante!, April 1949, p. 1–2; and Avante!, May 1949, p. 2.

[15] A República, 19 and 25 March 1949, pp. 4 and 1, respectively.

[16] Raby (1988, pp. 163–204).

4.2 Portugal and NATO in the Cold War

From the moment when the Alliance was ratified and Portugal signed his adhesion to it, except for the brief period that followed the revolution of April of 1974, NATO completely vanished as an issue of domestic policy in Portugal. Its consequences were felt, however, throughout the whole period, at the level of foreign policy and defence policy.

For Portuguese foreign policy, Portugal's entry into NATO meant not only the emergence of a new preferential ally—the United States—as a qualitative change in the bilateral relation between the two countries, especially in the field of defence. From 1949, although the military cooperation and the so-called facilities granted by Portugal to the United States ensued from bilateral agreements, their relationship would of necessity acquire a multilateral dimension and be seen as Portugal's contribution to the Alliance's defensive system. As such, to grant or to restrain military facilities was no longer a strictly bilateral problem, but a matter for NATO.

From this moment onwards, and inasmuch as the United States represent the true military mainstay of the Alliance, diplomatic relations between Portugal and the United States, especially involving cooperation in terms of defence, become the fulcrum of Portugal's relationship with NATO. In other words, for Portugal, the transatlantic relationship acquired two dimensions: a bilateral one, involving the United States, and a multilateral one, involving NATO.

In that sense, the 50s are marked by a good bilateral relationship and, within that context, by the signing of agreements on military cooperation. Following the agreement on the Azores base, in 1948, and the Mutual Defense Assistance Act, in 1949, always within the framework of the Atlantic Alliance, Portugal and the United States sign an agreement on mutual assistance in January of 1951, and, in September of the same year, a defence agreement that extended North American rights to facilities in the Azores military base until 1956. In November of 1957, the signing of a supplementary defence agreement renewed the agreement, extending it until December of 1962.[17]

As to defence policy, Portugal's integration in the military system of the Alliance would be rife with consequences. To begin with, consequences at the level of Portugal's strategic concept.

In accordance with the new global and integrated defence concept, the first change soon took place in the institutional organic structure of what would thenceforth be called "National Defence". In 1950, the office of Minister of National Defence is created, which, however, did not correspond to an autonomous ministry. The Minister of Defence is integrated in the Presidency of the Council of Ministers, and is essentially responsible for the strategic orientation of defence policy and the coordination of the three branches of the Armed Forces. The War Ministry, a traditional title that no longer reflected the new strategic concept, was replaced by

---

[17] Vintras (1975), Marquina (1986, pp. 943–960), Magalhães (1987b/1988, pp. 31–32), Telo (1996, pp. 113–131).

the Army Ministry. The Navy Ministry is preserved and, given the growing strategic importance of the Air Force, since the Second World War, a Sub-secretariat of State for Aeronautics is created. It was the beginning of the Air Force as autonomous branch of the Armed Forces, which came into force in 1952. In the scope of the same reform, the General Secretariat for National Defense was also created. It was designed as a consultation and advisory body of the defence minister, at the head of which appeared for the first time the office of Chief of the General Staff of the Armed Forces. This decree was reinforced, in 1952, by the Basic Law of National Defence and, in 1956, by the Law of the General Organization of the Nation during Wartime, enhancing the autonomy of the military institution regarding the political power and creating new bodies, such as the Chief of Staff of the Armed Forces and the Supreme Military Council.[18]

These reforms had a primary objective: to close the gap between the institutional structures of National Defence and the Portuguese Armed Forces and those of the other countries within the Atlantic Alliance.

They all aimed at adapting the Portuguese military instrument to the higher standards of the Alliance and, ultimately, at complying with the military commitments made within the framework of NATO. These commitments basically involved two types of missions: with regard to the Army, the creation of an autonomous division allocated to NATO's missions in mainland Europe; with regard to the Navy and the Air Force, their engagement in missions of anti-submarine warfare and patrolling in the North Atlantic within NATO's commands.[19]

In short, the 1950s were marked, in terms of foreign policy, by a smooth bilateral relationship with the United States, sealed by the signing of defence treaties and the mutual assistance plan, and in terms of defence policy, in the multilateral framework of NATO, by the engagement in the military commitments taken with the Alliance.

The 1960s, on the contrary, were marked by the decolonization conflicts and the difficult relations between Portugal and the United States, by the failed bilateral negotiations over defence agreements, and, multilaterally, by the non-fulfilment of the military commitments with NATO.

Portugal's admission in the UN, in 1955, opened a new period for Portuguese foreign policy, marked by international contestation directed at the colonial policy of the *Estado Novo*.[20] From 1961, Portugal abandoned its engagement with the Atlantic and suspended, almost completely, the military commitments with NATO. The colonial question had become the Portuguese foreign policy's almost exclusive concern.

---

[18] Carrilho (1985, pp. 377–399), Ferreira (1992, pp. 255–262), Afonso and Martelo (1999, pp. 698–699).

[19] About Portugal's commitments with NATO, see, with respect to the Army and the independent division, Macedo (1988), Rocha (1989, pp. 71–73). Sobre as Forças Armadas no seu conjunto e a política de defesa de Portugal, Telo (1996, pp. 225–288).

[20] Martins (1995), Silva (1995, pp. 5–50), Magalhães (1995), Castaño (2015, pp. 9–38).

On the other hand, from a North American point of view, the year of 1961 also coincided with the rise to power of the Kennedy administration and the beginning of its interventionist policy at the international level. The influence of Africanists in the Department of State was heavy and pressure for Salazar to reverse his colonial policy did not take long to arrive. It was substantiated by the so-called Sakwa Plan.[21]

Now, the collision of these two positions—Salazar's intransigence with respect to his colonial policy and Kennedy's liberal interventionism—had immediate effects on the bilateral relations between Portugal and the United States, especially on what concerned bilateral defence cooperation.

The 1957 supplementary defence agreement had a 5-year duration, thus expiring in December of 1962. When, near the middle of the year, the American ambassador to Lisbon requested the Portuguese government the reopening of negotiations with a view to renewing the agreement, Salazar had the firm intention of not negotiating. Not even the US's favourable vote at the UN, nor the signs of a greater tolerance towards the colonial question, nor the visit of the North-American Under Secretary of State George Ball to Lisbon, in a last attempt to secure a deal, managed to change Salazar's mind.[22] Since early 1962, in the scope of a NATO meeting, the Secretary of State Dean Rusk had conveyed to the Portuguese Minister of Foreign Affairs his apprehension regarding the operational problems that might be brought forth by such a situation. In the face of this, the Portuguese government showed itself available to find a solution for the problem, but not without making its position very clear. It issued a note wherein it authorized the stationing and the use of the Azores base, but, it must be stressed, "only *de facto* and during the negotiations".[23] To all practical purposes, the agreement was extended until 1964. Unable to drive away the North Americans, Salazar made it clear that it was nonetheless a *de facto*, and not a *de jure* arrangement, thus apposing on the whole thing the unequivocal seal of precariousness. Precariousness indeed marked the times ahead, since an aggravation of the colonial question, as well as the deteriorating relations between Portugal and the United States in the last years of Salazar's government precluded any possibility of successful negotiation.

Militarily, and from the point of view of defence policy, the 1960s were largely marked by a neglect of the commitments with NATO.

In 1961, the defence minister General Botelho Moniz, whose dealings with the Kennedy administration are known today[24] led a military coup intended precisely to reverse Salazar's colonial policy and to seek a non-military solution, that is, a negotiated political solution for the decolonization conflicts. As the coup failed, all

---

[21] Antunes (1991), Rodrigues (2002), Pinto (2001).

[22] Amaral (1994), Rodrigues (2002, pp. 292–301).

[23] Magalhães (1987b/1988, pp. 32–33).

[24] Mahoney (1983, p. 187 and ff.), Antunes (1991, pp. 175–176 and 207–227), Rodrigues (2002, pp. 54–59).

the political priority was directed towards the empire and all the Portuguese military effort to the colonial theatre.[25]

Completely immersed in the ongoing war in Africa, the Portuguese government was forced to substantially reduce its commitments with NATO.

In the first place, at the Army level, in which the greatest change was felt. The Army's independent division—to which the US administration had ceased to provide military support since 1962, with the explicit purpose of preventing war material granted to the Portuguese Army from being used in the African war theatres—was dismantled.[26]

As to the Navy and the Air Force, despite the reduced engagement in the commitments with NATO, changes were not so radical. Patrolling missions continued and, since the creation of STANAVFORLAND, in 1967, the Atlantic naval force relied on the constant (4–5 months a year) participation of a Portuguese frigate.

At the strategic-military level, during the 1950s, the Atlantic Alliance underwent another development that had an important impact in Portugal: the redefinition of the SACLAND operational theatre and of its command structure. To the two operation zones already defined—WESTLAND and EASTLAND—a third was added: IBERLAND. And although the decision to create the IBERLAND was taken in 1958, divergences between France and England over the command of the operational area made its establishment drag on for years. Only in 1966, coinciding with the French withdrawal from NATO's integrated military structure with all its commands,[27] was a compromise solution reached: the command of IBERLAND would be based on Portuguese territory and its command would be assigned to a North American officer. In February of 1967, the IBERLAND's headquarters were provisionally set up in Sintra, wherefrom it moved, in October of 1971, to the new premises that to this day it occupies in Oeiras.[28]

During the first half of the 1970s, and until the transition to democracy, there were no noteworthy changes in defence policy and Portugal continued to be little engaged in its commitments with NATO, since the conflicts in the three African theatres persisted until 1974.

In foreign policy, on the contrary, there were notable changes. Advances in the bilateral relations between Portugal and the United States allowed for a solution to the pending problem of the Azores base.

With Salazar's exit from the political scene in 1968, and Marcelo Caetano's rise to power, a revision of foreign policy was initiated, particularly in what concerned relations with the United States. Unlike Salazar, Caetano avoided political tension and ideological confrontation, and sought to cooperate as much as possible with the United States government. Portugal's new positioning was favoured by the rise to

[25] Estado-Maior do Exército, *Resenha histórico-militar das campanhas de África (1961–1974)*, vol. 1.

[26] Antunes (1991, pp. 239–243).

[27] NATO/OTAN (1981, p. 52), Delmas (1981, pp. 60–65).

[28] Rocha (1989, pp. 72–74).

power, at roughly the same time, of the Nixon administration, which was itself more benevolent to Lisbon's colonial policy. In light of this, as early as 1969, the Portuguese government informed Washington of its interest in solving the question of the Azores, and proposed to start negotiations to that purpose.

The principles guiding these negotiations were altogether different from those prevalent in Salazar's time. In the first place, Portugal was not asking the US government for any political assurances—which the latter, in any case, was not in a position to give—which prevented political frictions. Secondly, and due to the fact that Portugal was under an embargo on arms supply, Lisbon was forced to negotiate, not for military compensations, but rather for economic-financial ones. This more realistic and pragmatic approach allowed the impasse to be overcome and a new phase for Portuguese-US bilateral relations to begin.

The negotiations were successful, and the agreement was signed in Brussels, after a NATO meeting, in December of 1971. The agreement was essentially based on the following conditions: Portugal extended the facilities in the Azores until February of 1974; and, in return, the United States offered Portugal a vast programme of economic assistance.

This economic assistance programme consisted basically of the following four points: first, a 15-million-dollar loan for 1973 and 1974, redeemable in 15 years at an interest rate of 4.5%; second, the provision of a 400-million-dollar credit line for projects in the scope of economic development; third, the donation of 1 million dollars for development projects in the education sector; fourth and finally, the offer of a hydrographic ship.[29]

It represented a shift in paradigm. If, between 1948 and 1971, the bilateral defence agreements had been based on military compensation, from 1971, a new phase began in which the renewal of facilities was tied to economic-financial compensation. This trend extended beyond the authoritarian regime, into the democratic transition and consolidation, and lasted until the 1989 agreement. From the 90s, the end of the Cold War, Portugal's accession to the European Community, the emergence of other countries requesting the same assistance, the US budget restrictions, and, above all, the question of burden-sharing within NATO, altered significantly the tenets of Portugal's traditional basis for negotiation, that is, the facilities/compensation binomial.[30]

In the last years of the *Estado Novo*, two new events brought about an improvement in relations between the two countries and a strengthening of Portugal's negotiating position.

First, in October of 1971, when, in the General Assembly of the UN, the question was raised of Chinese representation at the Security Council, that is, of which of the Chinese republics was to have a seat at the Council, Portugal voted in favour of North American interests.

[29]Magalhães (1987b/1988, p. 36), Antunes (1986, pp. 152–154).

[30]Pereira (1990, pp. 5–19).

Second, and this would be the crucial element, Portugal's authorization for the use of the Lajes Base, in the Azores, during the Yom Kippur War, in 1973.[31] Portugal's position had such a positive effect on bilateral relations that, despite the embargo on arms supply still in force, Henry Kissinger's Secretary of State endeavoured to secure the supply of missiles required by the Armed Forces for the conduction of war in Africa, especially in Guinea. Missiles that naturally were supposed to arrive in Portugal "through devious ways".[32] Such was then the atmosphere of bilateral relations with the US and multilateral relations with NATO when, in Portugal, the 25th of April of 1974 takes place.

During the Cold War and until the end of the authoritarian regime, Portugal's presence in NATO went through different periods. If, in the 1950s, Portugal maintains its commitments to NATO and benefits from its membership in the alliance, in the 1960s, at the political, diplomatic and military levels, which may be interpreted in terms of shelter theory, the picture is almost totally reversed. The war's military effort in the colonies leads Portugal to suspend many of the military commitments to the alliance and, as a consequence, objections to Portuguese colonial policy rise stemming from the US and other members of NATO. Portugal becomes under an arms embargo not from NATO, but from some of the allies. And not de facto, but de jure, the Lages' agreement is called into question. Not only is NATO failing to work as a shelter, as there are tensions and conflict between allies. The 1970s, however, mark a measure of return to normality. Negotiations on the American presence at the Azores base are reopened but Portugal continues under an arms embargo. The agreed trade-offs are not military in nature but rather of an economic and financial nature, which may be interpreted as economic shelter.

4.3 Portuguese Transition to Democracy and NATO

The end of the authoritarian regime and the process of transition to democracy that begins on the 25th of April of 1974 entailed a profound redefinition of Portuguese foreign policy in line with the programme of the Armed Forces Movement (MFA), which translated, summarily, into the formula "democratization, decolonization, development". Although the MFA programme announced and vouched for the fulfilment of all international commitments binding Portugal, it became clear that those two simple principles—to democratize and to decolonize—would require a reinterpretation of those same commitments and a substantive change in the foreign orientation of the Portuguese State.

However, in what concerns the Atlantic axis, if there were indeed any changes, these had to do with the reaffirmation and the reinforcement of that vector in Portuguese foreign policy. As early as in June of 1974, at NATO's ministerial

[31] Antunes (2000, pp. 41–101).

[32] Themido (1995, pp. 111–147, especially p. 131).

meetings in Ottawa, the minister of Foreign Affairs of the new regime, Mário Soares, reiterates the loyalty to NATO as one of the fundamental principles of the orientation of Portuguese foreign policy, a principle he reasserts once again before the 30th session of UN's General Assembly, in September of the same year.

Between April of 1974 and January of 1986, Portuguese foreign policy oscillated between two basic orientations which also mark two distinct phases: the transition to democracy, corresponding to the pre-constitutional period and ruled by the revolutionary process; and the democratic consolidation, corresponding to the constitutional period and marked by the institutionalization and stabilization of the democratic regime.

The pre-constitutional period was punctuated by struggle over the country's external options, by the exercise of parallel diplomacy and, consequently, by an overall uncertainty regarding foreign policy. Despite the struggle, the indecisiveness and the pervading uncertainty that permeated the provisional governments, especially those in which the military had a more preponderant role, the general orientation of Portuguese foreign policy tended towards a third-worldist option and the pursuance of privileged relations with the new counties arising from the Portuguese decolonization. In a sense, this was the last avatar—albeit now a socializing one—of Salazar's cherished thesis of Portugal's "African vocation". Regardless of that vague and diffuse orientation towards neutralism and the temptation of non-alignment during the process of transition to democracy, neither did the 25th of April, nor the 28th of September, alter the orientation of the Atlantic axis and the military relations with NATO. Only the 11th of March of 1975 ultimately disrupted those relations at the political and military level. And the reason for this was simple enough. In the midst of the Cold War, a NATO member with communist ministers in the government was not in the least reassuring for the Alliance's partners. And Portugal found itself temporarily excluded from the Eurogroup and all classified military information. On the other hand, in Portugal, notwithstanding the criticism directed at NATO and the North American "imperialism" by the forces further to the left, not even the Portuguese Communist Party (PCP) demanded Portugal's exit from the Atlantic Alliance.[33]

The constitutional period which began precisely with the first constitutional government was marked by the clarification of Portuguese foreign policy and a univocal and rigorous definition of Portugal's external positioning. A Portugal which thenceforth committed to its status as a Western country, at once European and Atlantic. If, to these orientations, we add the reinstatement and normalization of post-colonial relations with the new countries emanating from the Portuguese decolonization, we have before us the three main axis of the foreign policy of Portuguese democracy.

[33]See PCP's positions regarding NATO in *Dossier NATO (1979)*, Ed. «Avante!»; and Carvalho (1990).

Between 1976 and 1986, the Atlantic vector and Atlanticism prevailed still, having played an important role, at the level not only of the country's international positioning, but also of internal stabilization and democratic consolidation.[34]

Thus, the Atlantic vector meant, for Portugal, reconciliation with tradition and the endurance of the historical features of its foreign policy. Bilaterally, that Atlanticism substantiated in the strengthening of diplomatic relations with the United States and the renewal of the Lajes Agreements in 1979 and 1983.[35]

In 1977, a joint declaration by Portugal and the US states the willingness of both governments to conclude negotiations over the "facilities" in the Azores base, which eventually happened in June of 1979, and whose outcome was the extension of the lease on the base until 1983. The 1979 agreement also pledged the provision of economic compensation, which materialized in an annual financial aid of 20 million dollars granted to the Autonomous Region of the Azores. With the end of the military embargo on Portugal, the economic aid was eventually accompanied by a military grant: around 60 million dollars for defence.

The aggravation of the situation in the Middle East, the overthrow of the shah of Iran and the Soviet invasion of Afghanistan, in the early 1980s, pressed the need to reinforce Western presence. It was within this framework of strategic reappraisal of the Azores base that the 1983 agreement was signed.

The use of "facilities" in the Lajes base was extended until 1991 and, as compensation, Portugal was once again the recipient of economic and military aid. At the military level, Portugal was awarded a 517.5-million-dollar grant and a 412.5-million-dollar loan for 8 years. As economic compensation, it was given a 75-million-dollar loan and a 320-million-dollar donation. In this scope and imbued with the same spirit, the Luso-American Development Foundation (FLAD) was created.[36]

At the multilateral level, the Atlantic vector translated into the maintenance and reinforcement of Portugal's position in the Atlantic Alliance, as well as the redefinition and renewal of Portuguese commitment to the military engagements with NATO, which the war effort in Africa had forced to put on hold since the 1960s. With respect to the Army, this reassertion of the NATO commitments was substantiated by the creation of the Independent Mixed Brigade (BAI), since then converted into the Air Transport Brigade (BAT), which replaced and, to some extent, reactivated, the former Independent Division of the Army, which essentially furthered the goals of its predecessor in the military missions of NATO's southern flank. With regard to the Navy and the Air Force, patrol missions carried out in the scope of IBERLAND were reinforced. IBERLAND's command was upgraded to command-in-chief—CINCIBERLAND—and the position was entrusted to a Portuguese officer.[37]

[34]Vasconcelos (1989, pp. 129–141), Sá (2009), Sá (2016, pp. 507–520).

[35]Themido (1995, p. 167 and ff).

[36]Magalhães (1987a, pp. 43–51), Stenhouse (1991, pp. 38–41).

[37]Teixeira (1999a, b, pp. 32–33), Telo (2001, pp. 119–122).

The "European option" is, however, the great novelty of post-25th of April foreign policy and, from 1986, a topmost priority in democratic Portugal's external orientation.[38]

Having overcome anti-European resistance which stemmed, first from the Africanist option of the authoritarian regime, and afterwards from the third-worldist temptation of the revolutionary period, Portugal committed entirely, from 1976, to the "European option". The latter was no longer spurred by merely economic and pragmatic motivations as had been the case by the end of the authoritarian regime. Now, it represented a political project and the future of the country. Europeanisation, Atlanticism and post-colonial relations constituted thenceforth the essential orientations and the strategic priorities of Portugal's foreign policy.

If, towards the end of the authoritarian regime, tensions with NATO allies had to do with the colonial war, during the transition to democracy the tensions concern the presence of communists in the Portuguese government. Tensions now involve directly the Alliance, and Portugal is temporarily excluded from some NATO committees. Once again, NATO is not working as a shelter. However, with the consolidation of democracy, the panorama changes. Portugal reaffirms its position as a Western country, both European and Atlantic, and fully resumes its commitments to the Atlantic Alliance. In the transition from Africa to Europe, the Atlantic and NATO played an important role of continuity and stabilisation at the international level, as well as a role in the stability and consolidation of democracy at the internal level. As such, this can be interpreted as political and diplomatic shelter. Just like the renegotiation of the Lages Agreement with economic and financial trade-offs as well as the creation of the Luso-American Development Foundation can be interpreted as economic and social shelter.

4.4 The Post-Cold War Period: Between Atlanticism and Europeanisation

The end of the Cold War, the fall of the Berlin Wall and of the Soviet Union, the dissolution of the Eastern Bloc and the Warsaw Pact, the German reunification and post-Soviet drift in Central and Eastern Europe, as well as the persistence of the United States as the sole global power led to the emergence, since 1989, of a new and unipolar international order and of a new framework of world security.

The new international strategic environment, on the one hand, and the country's new external standing, on the other, shaped the evolution of a new framework for Portugal's international position. The traditional Atlanticism is joined by Europeanisation, and the bilateral and multilateral dimensions of the diplomatic relations with the US and NATO, respectively, are joined by Portugal's new status as a member of the European Union.

[38]Macdonald (1993, pp. 65–87), Teixeira and Pinto (2012, pp. 7–26).

Now, if the European vector represented the great novelty of Democracy's foreign and defence policy, the Atlantic vector, on the contrary, constituted its element of permanence and reunion with the historical tradition, both at the bilateral and the multilateral levels.

At the bilateral level, Portugal's relations with the United States were marked both by a readjustment in US security and defence policies for the post-Cold War era and by Portugal's new European dimension, and finally led, in 1995, to the signing of a new Agreement on Cooperation and Defence, which marked the beginning of a new model of relationship between Washington and Lisbon.

The end of the Cold War brought about a huge change in US security policy, which in the early 90s entered a period of lower investment in the defence sector, at least in its traditional premises. Not only were military bases deactivated all across the North American territory, as US presence in the European theatre was diminished. And, following George Bush's so-called Regional Defense Strategy and Bill Clinton's Bottom-Up Review, the concept of "advanced defence" based on which, since the second post-war period, a worldwide network of North American military bases had been built. US military presence abroad had turned to other priorities: smaller yet more flexible, mobile and effective forces. From that point onwards, the US deactivated, totally or partly, many of their military bases abroad. At the same time, the traditional philosophy that governed the foreign assistance programmes began to change, reducing military aid in favor of economic and humanitarian assistance programmes.

This new atmosphere had an immediate impact on US relations with Portugal, namely concerning the Azores base. This, together with economic development, social stability and the consolidation of democracy, which are confirmed with Portugal's accession to the EU, weighed decisively in the negotiations that were opened for the new agreement in 1991.

The US attempt to strategically play down the Lajes Base and the Portuguese insistence on the model of financial compensation and the extension of the military aid hampered bilateral negotiations and led to a deadlock in 1992. From 1993, positions became more flexible and, in the face of European integration and the country's level of development, Portuguese foreign policy not only was forced to relinquish the traditional "facilities vs. compensation", but, above all, adopted a new way of looking at transatlantic relations. In Portugal's view, the relationship with the single global power transcended the specific question of the Lajes Base, which paved the way for an agreement of a general nature. On the 1st of June of 1995, the ministers of Foreign Affairs of both countries signed, in Lisbon, the Agreement on Cooperation and Defence, but also a technical and labour agreement aimed at the Lajes Base employees.

The new Agreement on Cooperation and Defense did not define specific programmes, but identified the various areas of cooperation: military and defence, scientific and technological and in the domain of economic and commercial relations.[39]

At the multilateral level, Portugal's presence in NATO was still marked by the maintenance and reinforcement of its political-military commitments, but also by the changes and adjustments of the Alliance in the post-Cold War period. And, in parallel, by Portugal's accession to the Community, by its accession to the WEU in 1990 and by its later engagement with the ESDI.

Created for the Cold War and designed against the Soviet threat, NATO not only survived the death of its enemy—the reason for its existence—but also persisted in a world for which it had not been created. In the early 1990s, the US Secretary of State James Baker insightfully pinpointed NATO's quandary: "either extinction or transformation, maintenance of the status quo was impossible". NATO chose transformation and initiated a complex reform process in order to adapt to new functions and new missions. Reforms both at the external and internal levels, with a political and military dimension.[40]

At the external level, NATO's agenda included two major problems: the question of the enlargement to the east and the preservation of the transatlantic link.

The Alliance's first political challenge was the eastern enlargement, a symbolic token of the victory in the Cold War and, at the same time, a way to fill the strategic void left by the dissolution of the Warsaw Pact and a security factor for post-communist Europe.

Confrontation gave way to cooperation. The old enemies became partners and allies. In that process, NATO developed a three-phase initiative: the establishment of a cooperation structure, launched at the Rome Summit of 1991, the North Atlantic Cooperation Council; the offer of a strategic partnership proposed at the Brussels Summit of 1994, the Partnership for Peace; and, finally, the enlargement, decided in Madrid in 1997, and granted to three countries—Poland, Hungary and the Czech Republic. Russia was neither forgotten nor excluded from the new architecture of European security. It was even the object of a special rapprochement substantiated in the Paris Founding Act of 1997, which associated Russia to the Alliance through the Euro-Atlantic Partnership Council.

Throughout the external reform and the enlargement process, Portugal consistently showed a spirit of convergence and openness to the evolution of the Atlantic Alliance. It participated in the establishment of every new institution, it developed cooperation relations in the scope of defence with the Central and Eastern European countries, in the framework of the Partnership for Peace, and actively supported NATO's enlargement. At the Madrid Summit, three new members were invited to join NATO, and Portugal supported, along with other European Countries, the 3 + 2 formula, which meant a wider enlargement not only to Poland, Czech Republic and Hungary, but also to Slovenia and Romania.[41]

[39] Brito (1995, pp. 135–357), Sá (2016, p. 569).

[40] Teixeira (1999a, b, pp. 63–69).

[41] Gama (1997, pp. 51–52).

Since then, the process of enlargement has not ceased and there have been no break-ups. At the Washington Summit, in 1999, the Alliance decided that it should not hamper the entry of new members and defined the principles of the method to adopt: it would welcome candidates who fulfilled the required political and military requirements, that is, who were willing to further the founding political principles of the Alliance—democracy, individual liberty and the rule of law—and whose military capabilities were in a position to contribute to collective security and international stability. In 2009, the enlargement extended to Albania and Croatia. The Alliance now included 28 members. In the spirit of these principles, Portugal was favourable and consistently supported the enlargement process.[42]

The other item in NATO's external agenda concerned the relationship between the two pillars of the Alliance—the American and the European—that is, with the transatlantic relation.

Throughout the length of the Cold War, the transatlantic link had ensured European security and even international peace and stability. In the post-war period, their maintenance continued to be perceived as an essential condition for European security. The evolution towards a unipolar international system with the US as the sole global power, and the EU's institutionalization of the CFSP, reactivation of the WEU and setting in motion of the ESDI, however, pressed for a reassessment of the transatlantic relation.[43]

The Atlantic Alliance immediately reinterpreted the ESDI, not as "an armed wing of the European Union", but rather as "NATO's European pillar". And not only, in the following summits and declarations, from 1992 onwards, did it support this notion of European Security and Defence Identity, the Berlin Summit of 1996 also declared the creation of the ESDI within NATO itself. Portugal supported at all times the development of the ESDI and evolved, in this matter, from a strictly Atlanticist to a Euro-Atlantic position.

Although the establishment of the European Security and Defence Identity by the Treaty of Nice and, at long last, the Common Security and Defence Policy by the Treaty of Lisbon constituted first steps in the direction of an autonomous EU defence capacity, afterwards the core problem was not substantially altered. US intervention in Iraq, in 2003, led to the gravest transatlantic crisis after France's withdrawal from NATO's integrated military structure in 1966, and had profound consequences. The crisis was eventually overcome and the transatlantic link re-established. The direction of the Obama administration's policies, in the US, and France's return to NATO's military structure, in Europe, closed that cycle once and for all. But relations between NATO and the European Union, NATO-CSDP in particular, are still far from resolved. Both at the political and the institutional and operational levels. Proof of that is the ambiguousness of the terms of the NATO-EU strategic partnership in the new strategic concept of the Alliance, approved in Lisbon in 2010.

[42] Teixeira (2011, pp. 257–266).

[43] Teixeira (1998, pp. 68–73).

In the course of this period, the Portuguese position never changed. Following a progressively more Europeanist trend, Portugal supported and integrated from the outset the ESDP and the CSDP, and joined in every international mission carried out in that scope. It advocated, however, at all times, a notion of strategic complementarity between NATO and the EU.

In terms of internal reform, NATO's agenda included two fundamental issues: the restructuring of military commands and the definition of a new doctrine and new missions.

The restructuring of commands aimed at responding and adjusting NATO to the new strategic scenario. Although it preserved in its structure the two strategic commands, the Allied Command Atlantic and the Allied Command Europe, it undertook reforms in lower-level commands: three regional commands in the SACLAND, two regional commands in the SACEUR and, in within both, other sub-regional commands.

For Portugal, the main goal in this reorganization of commands was the preservation of *CINCIBERLAND* in Portuguese territory and its permanence at the level of regional command. The question was raised by Spain's entry into NATO's integrated military structure and the decision concerning the establishment of a command in Spanish territory. This was not a bilateral, but a multilateral question in the NATO framework—the definition of responsibilities between the two strategic commands, *SACLAND* and *SACEUR*. In the end, however, it received a diplomatic solution negotiated between Portugal and Spain, a solution presented to the Alliance and later ratified by its military and political bodies.

The new philosophy of the allied commands merely defined the limits of its strategic commands, and not those of the lower-level commands. These limits and their military responsibilities were, in case of need, defined by the strategic commands, with the establishment, in the areas of mutual interest, a *supporting command* and a *supported command*.

In the spirit of this philosophy, Portugal succeeded in reaching a deal that satisfied its objectives entirely. In the first place, it preserved in its territory not only the Iberian-Atlantic command, but also the level of the same command. In the second place, and for the first time in the history of its presence in the Alliance, the Portuguese territory, mainland and Atlantic, was wholly integrated under the same command: the SACLAND. Ever since the first definition of NATO's military commands, the defence of the Atlantic component of the Portuguese territory had been entrusted to the Atlantic Command, but the defence of the mainland territory was a national responsibility.

In the third place, it managed to prevent the fulfilment of the Spanish claim to a strategic corridor between Gibraltar and the Canaries under the command of the *SACEUR* and, in particular, of Madrid's sub-regional command. Except for a "bubble" over the Canary Islands, resulting from the compromise that had been reached, and which fell under the command of Madrid, the responsibility for all the Atlantic space to the west of the Guadiana River meridian and to the north of the Tropic of Cancer was assigned to *SACLAND*.

Spain, in its turn, upon entering NATO's integrated military structure, managed right away to obtain a sub-regional command in its territory. It managed, moreover, to keep the whole of its territory, including the Canaries, under the same command—the SACEUR—and to shift westward—from Gibraltar to the Guadiana River—the demarcation line between the Alliance's two strategic commands.[44]

After September 11th, changes in the international strategic environment and new threats and risks continued to compel the Alliance to pursue the development of its transformation process, namely the adjustment of its military structures to the new missions.

After the Washington Summit, in 1999, not only did the NATO command remain in Portugal, it was furthermore transformed and enhanced in one of the Alliance's three regional commands: *CINCIBERLANT* was upgraded to *CINCSOUTHLANT*. In 2003, it is transferred from *SACLANT* to *SACEUR*. And, in 2004, it becomes Joint Force Command Lisbon, an operational and deployable command, able to command Alliance missions in any of NATO's areas of responsibility and certified as a NATO Response Force (NRF). In 2006, it took action and demonstrated its effective capacity at the command of relief operations in at least two occasions: the earthquake in Pakistan and Hurricane Katrina.

In June of 2011, in the scope of the transformation process, and in the wake of the reform of military structures which led to a reduction in staff from 13,000 to 9000 posts and in the number of Agencies from 14 to 4, and also the closing of several bases, *Joint Command Lisbon* was deactivated. NATO's flag, however, remained in Portuguese territory, where to *STRIKFORNATO*'s headquarters were relocated from Naples, and which includes US 6th Fleet.

Finally, the last question concerns the new doctrine, that is, the strategic concept of the Alliance. Ever since the end of the Cold War, NATO drafted three strategic concepts, and each new one sought to respond to the evolution of the international scene, namely the change in the strategic environment, that is, the type of threats and risks faced by international security.

In 1991, in Rome, it was a matter of tackling the end of the Cold War, Germany's reunification and the transition to democracy of East-Central European post-communist drifts. Not long after, the dissolution of the Soviet Union came to change once again the international environment. Rome's "strategic concept" pointed towards a new—not strictly military, but progressively more global and integrated—notion of security. From that moment, besides the traditional "collective defence" missions defined by article 5 of the Washington Treaty, a new type of mission began to find its own space which the Alliance came to approve in the Atlantic Council in Oslo, in 1992: missions of humanitarian assistance and peacekeeping operations.

In 1999, at the 50th anniversary summit in Washington, it was essentially a twofold reply: first, to the enlargement of the Atlantic Alliance to the old enemies of the Warsaw Pact, which, in the absence of a peace treaty, recorded in Europe's political geography the victory of the West in the Cold War; second, to the Balkan

[44] Vitorino (1998, pp. 52, 69–70), Gama (1997, pp. 51–52).

secession conflicts. Washington's strategic concept added to the already accomplished logic of geographic enlargement one other enlargement logic: an expansion, to begin with, of the Alliance's area of intervention; and, secondly, of the Alliance's types of missions. The disappearance of the traditional threat, the emergence of new threats and the proliferation of new risks and of a new type of international conflict had a twofold effect on NATO. On the one hand, it was becoming more and more unlikely the need for the traditional collective defence mission and increasingly more likely the pertinence of the new type of mission, which included, besides crisis management and peace-support operations, fight against the proliferation of weapons of mass destruction, terrorism, drug trafficking and organized crime. On the other, these missions appear to be ever less likely within the traditional area defined by the North Atlantic Treaty and gradually more likely outside this area. An issue which instilled in the Alliance the syndrome of the "out of area or out of business" and which led NATO to approve the revision of the strategic concept that provided for these new missions outside the area and, more than that, without the need for a UN mandate, political consensus within NATO being the sole requirement. In the midst of the crisis in Kosovo, and not without international contestation, the revision of the strategic concept was approved, changing NATO, in the early twenty-first century, from a regional defence alliance into a tendentially global security organization. Attending, in Washington, the 50th anniversary summit, in April of 1999, Portugal participated and approved the reform of the Alliance.[45]

In Lisbon, in 2010, it was a matter of tackling the radical changes of the first decade of the twenty-first century. A change primarily in the international system, marked by the transition from a unipolar world under the Western hegemony of the US to a post-Western and tendentially multipolar world. Secondly, a change in the strategic environment, with the emergence of a new picture of threats and risks. Quite beyond the proliferation of weapons of mass destruction, the failed states or the domestic conflicts of ethnic and religious origin, this new post-September 11th scenario was dominated by the threat of transnational terrorism. Changes in the international system and in the strategic environment, together with the experience of a decade within an Alliance engaged in new missions outside its area, especially in Afghanistan, account for the new strategic concept adopted in Lisbon.

Portugal hosted and organized the Lisbon Summit in November of 2010. It took part in every phase of the drafting of the concept and supported the agreed strategic options, which it deemed convergent with the national interest.

In the first place, the emphasis on collective defence and the focus on the Euro-Atlantic area. These were of utmost interest to Portugal, not only because, within the framework of unity and indivisibility of the Alliance's territory, the reaffirmation of article 5 reinforced collective defence, but also because by refocusing on the Euro-Atlantic space, Portugal's centrality came out reinforced and the strategic value of the Portuguese territory was re-established.

[45]Teixeira (1999a, b, pp. 63–69).

In the second place, the reassessment of the Alliance's international responsibilities might very well represent, for Portugal, an opportunity to clarify and reaffirm the doctrine of the intervention of the Portuguese armed forces in international missions. A doctrine no longer dictated by exclusively historical or geographic factors but, just as in the Alliance, by international security criteria.

Finally, the Alliance's partnerships were also of strategic interest to Portugal, inasmuch as it constituted an opportunity for the latter to stress its position within the Alliance. First, if the NATO-EU strategic partnership was given leverage, Portugal would see the value of its strategic centrality renewed, and could more easily profit from its Atlantic belonging in the European framework and, at the same time, its European belonging in the Atlantic framework. Secondly, in the establishment, by the Alliance, of future partnerships in areas wherein Portugal relies on historical experience and privileged insight, such as the Magreb, sub-Saharan Africa and the South Atlantic, where it could work as a facilitator, building bridges with regional partners and reinforcing its position within the Alliance.[46]

Since joining the European Union, Portugal has added to the national dimension a European dimension, with its NATO membership. And throughout the entire post-Cold War period, it proves to be a reliable ally, actively participating in and supporting all the reforms of the Atlantic Alliance: enlargement to the East at the political level; the restructuring of commands at the military level; and the revision of the strategic concept at the doctrinal level. More than that, Portugal participates with its Armed Forces in all of NATO's international missions in Bosnia and Herzegovina, Kosovo and Afghanistan.

The war in Ukraine has radically altered the perception of the threat to Europe's security, and will certainly mark the beginning of a new cycle not only for the European security architecture but also for transatlantic relations. NATO will see its role strengthened and re-legitimised, and collective defence will return to the centre of the Alliance's new strategic concept. But none of this will alter Portugal's relationship with NATO in its core.

4.5 Conclusions

In conclusion, it may be said that, given the strategic value of the Portuguese territory in the Atlantic, Portugal's constant presence in the Alliance and the commitment of the Portuguese Armed Forces to NATO military missions, the theory of alliances remains the most appropriate theoretical framework for an overall understanding of relations between Portugal and NATO. This does not mean, however, that shelter theory fails to provide an adequate and useful theoretical framework for understanding certain historical moments and specific areas of Portugal's relationship with NATO. Despite the fact that it was not Portugal who

[46]Teixeira (2011, pp. 265–266).

sought shelter but instead the shelter provider seeking the Portuguese accession, at that time, it nevertheless worked as a shelter at the military and political level: it represented a modernisation factor for the Armed Forces, a factor of diplomatic preponderance vis-a-vis Spain, and also a factor of longevity and internal political stability for the authoritarian regime. After the Portuguese transition to democracy, it continued to work as a stabilizing factor in the transition to democracy, and in the post-Cold War the Portuguese participation in NATO's peace-keeping operations remains a factor of modernization and internationalization of the Portuguese Armed Forces.

References

Afonso A, Martelo D (1999) Organização do Exército. In: Barreto A, Mónica M F (coord) Dicionário de História de Portugal, vol VII, supl. A/E. Figueirinhas, Porto
Amaral DF (1994) A tentativa falhada de um acordo Portugal-EUA sobre o futuro do ultramar português (1963). Coimbra Ed, Coimbra
Antunes JF (1986) Os americanos e Portugal. Os anos de Richard Nixon (1969–1974). D. Quixote, Lisboa
Antunes JF (1991) Kennedy e Salazar. O Leão e a Raposa, Difusão Cultural, Lisboa
Antunes JF (2000) Portugal na guerra do petróleo. Os Açores e as vitórias de Israel, Edeline, Carnaxide
Armstrong HW, Read (2000) Comparing the economic performance of dependent territories and sovereign microstates. Econ Dev Cult Chang 48(2):285–306
Bailes AJK, Bradley AT, Thorhallsson B (2016) Alliance theory and small state alliance, shelter: the complexities of small state alliance behavior. Third World Thematics 1(1):9–26
Brito N (1995) Para a Acta: O Acordo de Cooperação e Defesa entre Portugal e os Estados Unidos da América. In: Política Internacional, n.° 11
Carrilho M (1985) Forças Armadas e mudança política em Portugal no séc. XX – Para uma explicação sociológica do papel dos militares, IN-CM, Lisboa
Carvalho HM (1953) Portugal e o Pacto do Atlântico. Ed. Gráfica Portuguesa, Lisboa
Carvalho R (1990) Portugal e a NATO. Ed. «Avante!», Lisboa
Castaño D (2015) Portugal e a ONU, a primeira aproximação. R:I n° 47, Lisboa
Delmas C (1981) L'OTAN. PUF, Paris
Estado-Maior do Exército (1988/1989) Resenha histórico-militar das campanhas de África (1961–1974), vol 1. EME, Lisboa
Fang S, Johnson JC, Leeds BA (2014) To concede or to resist? The restraining effect of military alliances. Int Organ 68(4):775–809
Ferreira JM (1987) As ditaduras ibéricas e a fundação da Aliança Atlântica. In: AAVV, O Estado Novo das origens ao fim da autarcia (1926–1959), vol I. Fragmentos, Lisboa
Ferreira JM (1989) Um século de problemas. As relações luso-espanholas da União Ibérica à Comunidade Europeia. Livros Horizonte, Lisboa
Ferreira JM (1990) A ratificação portuguesa do Tratado do Atlântico Norte – Nota introdutória. In: Política Internacional. vol 1, n.° 1, Jan
Ferreira JM (1992) O comportamento político dos militares – forças armadas e regimes políticos em Portugal no século XX. Estampa, Lisboa
Gama J (1997) A política externa. Nação e Defesa 89:52
Huth P, Russett B (1988) Deterrence failure and crisis escalation. Int Stud Q 32:29
Ikenberry GJ (2002) After victory: institutions, strategic restraint and the rebuilding of order after major wars. Princeton University Press, Princeton NJ

Jackson MO, Nei S (2015) Networks of military alliances, wars, and international trade. PNAS 112(50):15277–15284

Jalan B (1999) Problems and policies in small economies. Croom Helm, London

Katzenstein PJ (1984) Corporatism and change: Austria, Switzerland and the Politics of Industry. Cornell University Press, Cornell

Katzenstein PJ (1985) Small states in world markets. Industrial policy in Europe. Cornell University Press, Cornell

Keohane RO (1971) The big influence of small allies. Foreign Policy 2

Kuznet S (1960) Economic growth of small nations. In: Robinson EAG (ed) The economic consequences of the size of nations. MacMillan, Toronto

Leeds BA et al (2022) Alliance treaty obligations and provisions. Int Interact 28

Macdonald S (1993) European destiny, Atlantic transformation – Portuguese foreign policy under the Second Republic, 1974–1992. Transaction Publishers, New Brunswick, NJ

Macedo EF (1988) Subsídios para o estudo do esforço militar português na década de cinquenta. Os compromissos com a O.T.A.N., 2 vols. Estado-Maior do Exército, Lisboa

Magalhães JC (1987a) Portugal e os Estados Unidos: Relações no domínio da defesa. In: EREI, n. ° 3

Magalhães JC (1987b/1988) Portugal e a integração europeia. In: EREI, n.° 4

Magalhães JC (1995) Portugal e as Nações Unidas: a questão colonial (1955-1974). Cadernos do Lumiar 6. IEEI, Lisboa

Mahoney RD (1983) J.F.K. ordeal in Africa. Oxford University Press, New York

Marquina BA (1986) España en la politica de seguridad del Ocidente. Servicio de Publicaciones del E.M.E, Madrid

Martins F (1995) Portugal e a Organização das Nações Unidas: Uma história política externa e ultramarina portuguesa no pós-guerra (Agosto de 1941-Setembro de 1968), Tese de Mestrado em História dos Sécs. XIX e XX. UNL, Lisboa

Morrow JD (1991) Alliances and asymmetry: an alternative to the capability aggregation model of alliances. Am J Polit Sci 35(4)

NATO/OTAN (1981) Structures faits et chifres, Brussels, s. e

Nogueira F (1980) O ataque (1945–1958), vol IV. Atlântida, Coimbra

Nogueira F (1981) História de Portugal, II supl. In: Peres D (dir.) História de Portugal. Civilização, Porto

Pereira BF (1990) Continuidade na mudança. As relações entre Portugal e os Estados Unidos. In: Política Internacional, n.° 2, vol 1, Jun

Pinto AC (2001) O fim do Império Português: A cena internacional, a guerra colonial, e a descolonização, 1961–1975. Livros Horizonte, Lisboa

Raby DL (1988) Fascism and resistance in Portugal. Manchester University Press, Manchester

Redondo JCJ (1996) Franco e Salazar: As relações luso-espanholas durante a Guerra Fria. Assírio & Alvim, Lisboa

Redondo JCJ (1999) Portugal, Espanha e a formação da NATO. In: Política Internacional vol 3, n. ° 19

Rocha AR (1989) Portugal e a defesa ocidental: Problemas militares e estratégicos (1945-1978). Proserpina, n° 8, Mérida

Rodrigues LN (2002) Salazar-Kennedy: a crise de uma aliança. Ed. Notícias, Lisboa

Ross G (1983) The great powers and the decline of the European states system. Longman, London

Rothstein RL (1968) Alliances and small powers. Columbia University Press, Columbia

Sá TM (2009) Os Estados Unidos da América e a Democracia Portuguesa (1974–1976). MNE/Instituto Diplomático, Lisboa

Sá TM (2016) História das Relações Portugal-EUA (1776–2015) D. Quixote, Lisboa

Salazar AO (1950a) Miséria e medo características do momento actual - discurso de 25 de Novembro de 1947. In: Discursos e notas políticas, vol VI. Coimbra Ed., Coimbra

Salazar AO (1950b) O Ocidente em face da Rússia, de 28 de Abril de 1948. In: Discursos e notas políticas, vol VI. Coimbra Ed., Coimbra

Silva AED (1995) O litígio entre Portugal e a ONU (1960-1974). In: Análise Social, vol XXX, n. ° 130
Stenhouse M, George (1991) Defense policy and strategic importance: the western perspective. In: Kenneth M (ed) Portuguese defense and foreign policy since democratization. Camões Center, Special Report n.°3
Teixeira NS (1993) Da neutralidade ao alinhamento: Portugal na fundação do Pacto do Atlântico. In: Análise Social, vol XXviii n.° 120 (1.°)
Teixeira NS (1998) Rivalidade, subsidiariedade, complementaridade: Que modelo para a identidade europeia de segurança e defesa. Centro de Informação Europeia Jacques Delors
Teixeira NS (1999a) A NATO nas mãos de Kafka ou a metamorfose de uma aliança. In: Política Internacional, vol 3, n.° 19
Teixeira NS (1999b) Portugal e a NATO: 1949-1999. In: Nação e Defesa, 2.ª série, n.° 89
Teixeira NS (2011) A Política de Defesa entre Atlantismo e Europeísmo: Portugal, a NATO e a União Europeia. Tribuna da História, Lisboa
Teixeira NS, Pinto AC (2012) Europeanization of Portuguese democracy. Columbia University Press, New York
Telo AJ (1993) Os Açores e o controlo do Atlântico (1898/1948), Ed. Asa, Porto
Telo AJ (1996) Portugal e a NATO. O reencontro da tradição atlântica. Cosmos, Lisboa
Telo AJ (2001) Portugal e a NATO: Um pequeno poder numa grande aliança. In: Ferreira JM (coord) Política externa e política de defesa do Portugal democrático – II Curso Livre de História Contemporânea. Colibri/Fundação Mário Soares/IHC-UNL, Lisboa
Themido JH (1995) Dez anos em Washington (1971–1981). As verdades e os mitos nas relações luso-americanas. D. Quixote, Lisboa
Thorhallsson B (2011) Domestic buffer versus external shelter: viability of small states in the new globalised economy. In: European political science, vol 10
Thorhallsson B (2019) Small states and shelter theory: Iceland's external affairs. Routledge, London
Vasconcelos A (1989) Los tres rostros del atlantismo português. In: Prosepina, n.° 8, Mérida, Abr
Vintras RE (1975) História secreta da base dos Açores. Ulisseia, Lisboa
Vital D (1967) The inequality of states: a study of the small power in international relations. Clarendon Press, Oxford
Vitorino A (1998) Opções de política de defesa nacional. MDN, Lisboa

Nuno Severiano Teixeira is Full Professor of International Relations at NOVA University-Lisbon, and the Director of the Portuguese Institute of International Relations. He was Visiting Professor at Georgetown University (2017–2019 and 2000), Visiting Scholar at the Institute for European studies, University of California, Berkeley (2004), and Senior *Visiting Scholar* at the Robert Schuman Centre for Advanced Studies European University Institute—Florence (2010). He has published extensively on History of International Relations and History of European integration, Military History, Security and Defense Studies. His latest book, *The Portuguese at War*, was published in 2020 by Sussex University Press. He has served as Minister of Interior (2000/2002) and Minister of National Defense (2006/2009) of the Portuguese Government.

Chapter 5
The Small State and the Superpower: Iceland's Relations with the United States

Skafti Ingimarsson and Baldur Thorhallsson

5.1 Introduction

This chapter analyses the origins and development of Icelandic-United States (US) relations in the Second World War, explains how Iceland became important to the United States during the Cold War period and assesses Icelandic-US relations in the post-Cold War era. Shelter theory provides a good framework to study the complex relations between Iceland and the US from the Second World War to the present for two main reasons: first, the theory presents a wide-reaching framework to study a small state's relations with a larger and more powerful state, as it captures not only the close military and diplomatic ties between countries but also their close encounters in economic and societal affairs; second, shelter theory explains why and how the Icelandic-US economic relations were of no less significance than their political relations. Moreover, the theory accounts for how the relations between the superpower and the small state modernised the latter in societal terms.

The chapter is divided into three main sections. The first section examines whether Icelandic-US relations have provided Iceland with political shelter. It analyses the origins of Icelandic-US relations during the Second World War, explains why Iceland joined NATO and signed a bilateral defence treaty with the US at the beginning of the Cold War period, and details the efforts of the US government to maintain Iceland as a loyal partner during the so-called Cod Wars between Iceland and Britain. Finally, it explores the disintegration of the Icelandic-US bilateral relationship in the post-Cold War era, resulting in the withdrawal of US forces from Iceland in 2006, and assesses the current state of Icelandic-US political relations.

S. Ingimarsson · B. Thorhallsson (✉)
Faculty of Political Science, Centre for Small State Studies, University of Iceland, Reykjavik, Iceland
e-mail: skafti@hi.is; baldurt@hi.is

A. Cunha, B. Thorhallsson (eds.), *Small States and Big Powers*, The World of Small States 10, https://doi.org/10.1007/978-3-031-42345-1_5

The second section examines the extent to which Icelandic-US relations have provided Iceland with economic shelter. It analyses the economic impact of the US military presence in Iceland during the Second World War, explains Iceland's participation in the Marshall Plan, details US economic assistance to Iceland during the Cold War period and assesses the state of Icelandic-US economic relations in the post-Cold War era.

The third section examines whether Icelandic-US relations have provided Iceland with societal shelter. It analyses the US cultural impact in Iceland during the Second World War, explains attempts to minimise the social impact of the American presence by closing off the US military base in Keflavik during the Cold War period, details the importance of grant programmes for Icelandic students in the US and assesses the state of Icelandic-US social relations in the post-Cold War era.

5.2 Political Shelter

5.2.1 The Origins of Icelandic-US Political Relations, 1939–1945

The origins of Icelandic-US shelter relations can be traced back to the Second World War. When the war began on 1 September 1939, the Icelandic National Unity Government declared that Iceland would remain neutral during the conflict. In the interwar period, Iceland had followed in the footsteps of its Nordic neighbouring states and declared its policy of "eternal neutrality" in the Act of Union with Denmark in 1918. According to the treaty, Iceland was a sovereign state in personal union with the King of Denmark, but the Danes continued to represent Icelandic foreign and defence affairs and the countries could sever its union 25 years after the treaty was signed.[1] However, it quickly became clear that neutrality had little significance during the war. The German occupation of Denmark on 9 April 1940 forced the Icelandic government to conduct its foreign and defence affairs. The British government feared that a German invasion of Iceland was imminent and decided to act. On the morning of 10 May 1940, British warships sailed into the port of Reykjavik and landed troops in the capital. The occupation of Iceland had begun.[2]

The Icelandic government reacted to the British occupation with calm. Opposition was futile as Iceland had no army. Therefore, while the government protested the occupation publicly, it otherwise cooperated with the British. In a radio broadcast to the nation, Prime Minister Hermann Jónasson stated that Iceland's neutral policy would be continued and urged people to consider the British soldiers as guests.[3]

[1] Jónsson (1989b, p. 203).
[2] Whitehead (1999, pp. 15–29).
[3] Baldvinsson (2015, p. 269).

Privately, however, the ministers were deeply worried that Iceland would become a battlefield if the Germans decided to invade.[4]

After considering the options, the government concluded that the only chance to maintain neutrality during the war was to secretly request military protection from the United States.[5] The Icelandic policymakers went on a shelter-seeking mission in Washington. The core aim was to seek political and economic shelter from the upcoming power. The Icelandic government had three main foreign policy objectives during the war: first, to gain military protection from the United States; second, to solve Iceland's pressing economic problems by gaining duty-free access for export goods in the US; third, to prepare the termination of the relationship with Denmark and make the Anglo-Saxon powers approve the establishment of a republic in Iceland.

However, convincing the US government to provide military protection for Iceland was a challenging task. Communications between the countries were opened when the two governments exchanged consuls shortly after the Germans occupied Denmark.[6] The new Icelandic consul was Vilhjálmur Thor, a businessperson with close ties to Prime Minister Jónasson. Thor, who the Americans later described as a "vigorous advocate of the American occupation," pursued his goal in Washington during the summer of 1940. At an official meeting with Secretary of State Cordell Hull on 5 September 1940, the Icelandic consul maintained that Iceland was part of the Western hemisphere, and that the Monroe doctrine should extend to Iceland. Secretary Hull responded by saying that the issue was under consideration, but other matters were more pressing. However, the Icelanders were insistent. In December, Stefán J. Stefánsson, the Icelandic Minister of Foreign Affairs, raised the issue again in a conversation with the American consul in Reykjavik, asking how the US government would react to an appeal for American protection from the Icelandic parliament. Again, the State Department evaded the question.[7]

The US government's avoidance of the Icelandic question in 1940 was not surprising. Officially, the United States was still neutral in the war. Putting US troops on Icelandic soil could be considered an act of war by Nazi Germany. However, the deteriorating military situation of the British in autumn 1940 forced the issue. At the American-British Staff Conference (ABC-1) in Washington in January–March 1941, the US government decided to support the British in the war against the Germans. According to the ABC-1 agreement, the United States was to provide military protection for Iceland.[8] In February, the Icelandic government realised what was going on, but the exact date of the American arrival was not known.[9] In June, President Franklin D. Roosevelt ordered an American troop

[4] Whitehead (2006, pp. 36–37).

[5] Jóhannesson (2016, p. 37).

[6] Thorsteinsson (1992, p. 172).

[7] Bittner (1983, pp. 123–124).

[8] Bittner (1983, p. 125).

[9] Stefánsson (1966, pp. 193–197).

convoy to be sent to Iceland, but only at the invitation of the Icelandic government. The President feared that the sudden arrival of US troops in Iceland, without approval from the Icelandic government, would undermine confidence in American policy of non-intervention in the affairs of states.[10] However, the Icelanders refused to invite the Americans because they were determined to negotiate a favourable agreement with the US government. The small state was not only in need of political shelter provided by a more powerful state, but also economic shelter. When the Icelandic-US negotiations began in late June, the Icelandic government listed 15 conditions for the US arrival. The four most important were: first, the United States would send forces to defend Iceland and promise not to interfere in Icelandic affairs; second, the US would negotiate favourable trade agreements with Iceland; third, the United States would recognise the independence and sovereignty of Iceland; fourth, the US would promise to withdraw their forces from Iceland at the end of the war. In addition, the Icelandic government requested that Britain agreed to revise Icelandic-British trade agreements and recognise Icelandic independence and sovereignty.[11] This meant that the US and British governments would recognise the establishment of a republic in Iceland when the termination clause of the Act of the Union came into force in 1943. However, Danish politicians were upset about Iceland's intention to establish a republic during the German occupation of Denmark.[12] The Icelandic government concluded an agreement when all the conditions had been met. On 1 July, messages were exchanged between Prime Minister Jónasson and President Roosevelt and on 7 July public announcements in Reykjavik and Washington coincided with the arrival of the first American troops in Iceland. Two days later, the Icelandic parliament ratified the agreement.[13]

The Icelandic-US defence agreement in July 1941 was a remarkable achievement for the Icelandic government. In 14 months, the government had achieved its three main foreign policy objectives during the war and gained political and economic shelter from the US. However, the drawback was that Iceland was now within the US sphere of influence. President Roosevelt's decision was also of historical significance as the US had taken a major step towards entering the war.[14] The strategic military importance of Iceland was demonstrated during the conflict as tens of thousands of US troops were stationed in Iceland, many of whom were transferred from there to the battlefields of Europe. In fact, the Joint Chiefs of Staff concluded as early as 1942 that it was important to have US military bases in Iceland after the war.[15] The Americans developed close relations with the Icelandic government during the conflict. The Allies honoured their promise when the United States, and Great Britain formally recognised the founding of the Icelandic Republic on 17 June

[10]Bittner (1983, p. 130).
[11]Jónsson (1969, pp. 729–733).
[12]Thorhallsson (2021, p. 132).
[13]Whitehead (2006, p. 44).
[14]Corgan (1992, p. 145).
[15]Ingimundarson (1996, p. 28).

1944. Many Icelanders, who regarded the event as the culmination of the independence struggle with Denmark, which had lasted almost one hundred years, were deeply affected.[16] As a token of their gratitude, Sveinn Björnsson, the newly elected President of Iceland, went on his first official visit to the United States in August 1944, where he was greeted by President Roosevelt in the White House.[17] A year later, the Second World War ended when the Japanese surrendered on 2 September 1945.

5.2.2 Forging the Icelandic-US Political Alliance, 1945–1951

According to the defence agreement, the American forces were to leave Iceland at the end of the war. The Truman administration, however, wanted to maintain the US military presence in Iceland. On 1 October 1945, the Americans requested a long-term lease of three bases in the area surrounding Reykjavik. The request caused deep divisions within Icelandic society and threatened to destabilise the so-called Innovation Government, which consisted of the centre right Independence Party, the Socialist Party, and the Social Democratic Party. The pro-soviet Socialist Party was against such an agreement with the US.[18] The Prime Minister and leader of the Independence Party, Ólafur Thors, tried to resolve the crisis and proposed a compromise solution which granted landing rights to the Americans. The result was the Keflavik Agreement in October 1946, under which the US agreed to abrogate the defence agreement and withdraw American forces from the country within 6 months. The Icelanders took possession of the Keflavik Airfield, but US civilian contractors ran the airfield, which was an important stepping-stone for aircrafts flying across the Atlantic towards the Allied occupied zone in Europe.[19] Nevertheless, the Socialists were against any political and military cooperation with the Americans and broke away from the government.

The Keflavik Agreement was a setback for US policy in Iceland. State Department officials were, however, determined to achieve their objectives. The American policy over the next years was a mixture of political pressure and economic incentives. In February 1947, a new coalition government was formed in Iceland. This was beneficial to US policy as the socialists were placed in opposition.[20] Influential politicians like Bjarni Benediktsson, the Minister of Foreign Affairs and member of the Independence Party, were advocates of Western cooperation and deeply worried about developments on the European continent. The communist coup in Prague in February 1948 caused anxiety in Western capitals, including

[16] Thorhallsson (2021, p. 132).
[17] Kristjánsson (2001, pp. 6–10).
[18] Ólafsson (2020, pp. 259–260).
[19] Whitehead (1998, pp. 26–27).
[20] Ólafsson (2020, p. 262).

Reykjavik. The Icelandic government finally concluded that neutrality was no longer a viable option in foreign affairs and decided to forge close military and economic relations with the United States. The result was that Iceland joined the Marshall Plan in April 1948 and NATO on 30 March 1949, amidst mass protests in Reykjavik.[21] The formation of a new centre right coalition government a year later, consisting of the Independence Party and the centre agrarian Progressive Party, was also helpful to the Americans. When the Korean War broke out in June 1950, the government decided to abandon the principle of demilitarisation. The Icelandic-US Defence Agreement was signed on 5 May 1951. According to the agreement, the US obtained a military base at Keflavik Airport. Two days later, American forces returned to Iceland after an absence of only 4 years.[22] The US again fully sheltered Iceland.

5.2.3 *The Rebellious Ally, 1951–1991*

Iceland had now been integrated into the western defence community.[23] Icelandic-US relations, however, remained problematic for two reasons. First, the Icelandic-US Defence Agreement was controversial in Iceland, especially amongst socialists and nationalists. In fact, opposition towards the US military presence grew steadily and, in February 1956, a parliamentary resolution was approved on the withdrawal of US forces from Iceland. The situation became serious when the first Icelandic left of centre coalition government took office in August the same year.[24] The government, however, never implemented the resolution because of economic difficulties and the volatile situation in the Cold War. Thus, the US was able to preserve the military status quo in Iceland by providing the government with economic assistance and generous loans. The situation was resolved with the formation of the Reconstruction Government, consisting of the Independence Party and the Social Democratic Party in November 1959 and the stabilisation of Icelandic-US relations.[25]

The second reason was that Icelandic politicians wanted to promote Icelandic national interests by taking advantage of Iceland's strategic military importance in the middle of the North Atlantic. One of the most important objectives of Icelandic foreign policy after the Second World War was the implementation of the exclusive fishing zone around Iceland.[26] The problems began when the Icelandic centre right coalition government extended the fishing limits around Iceland from three to four nautical miles in May 1952. The British, who had fished in Icelandic waters for centuries, reacted by imposing a ban on the landing of fresh fish from Iceland. This

---

[21] Whitehead (1991, pp. 75–110).

[22] Jóhannesson (2004, pp. 117–118).

[23] Corgan (2002, pp. 69–71).

[24] Whitehead (1998, pp. 67–71).

[25] Ingimundarson (1996, pp. 361–362).

[26] Valdimarsson (1993, pp. 50, 76).

led to a prolonged dispute between the two countries which was resolved in 1956 when the British government accepted defeat.[27]

The second round in the Icelandic-British dispute began in 1958, when the Icelandic government announced that it was extending its fishing limits from 4 to 12 nautical miles. This time the British protested and sent the Royal Navy into the disputed waters to protect British trawlers from harassment by Icelandic gunboats. Thus began the First Cod War.[28] Icelandic politicians declared that Iceland's membership in NATO and the American presence in Keflavik had both come under threat. Appalled by the conduct of the Icelandic government, President Dwight D. Eisenhower remarked that the whole episode reminded him of Bismarck's expression, "the tyranny of weakness." Nevertheless, the Icelandic strategy worked and in 1961 the British had to accept another defeat.[29]

By now it was clear that Iceland's negotiating position was strong and many Icelandic politicians were prepared to use the US military base in Keflavik as a bargaining chip in the Cod Wars.[30] The pro-western Reconstruction Government, however, managed to normalise relations between Iceland and Britain and, as a result, the fishing zone dispute lay dormant for 10 years. But it flared up again when the second centre left coalition government took office in July 1971. The government's policy was to expel the US forces from Iceland.[31] In September 1972, the government extended Iceland's fishing limits from 12 to 50 nautical miles. This triggered the Second Cod War and British warships again sailed into the disputed waters. The Icelandic government responded by declaring that any agreement on the future of the US military base in Keflavik was impossible if British warships were within the Icelandic fishing zone. Henry Kissinger, who was President Nixon's national security adviser, flew from Washington to Reykjavik to mediate, only to return stunned by the audacity of the Icelanders. In late 1973, the Second Cod War ended in a compromise which favoured Iceland. Once again, the Icelanders had benefitted from Iceland's strategic military importance during the Cold War.[32]

The formation of a centre right coalition government in Iceland in August 1974 raised hopes in Washington that a lasting stability could finally be found in Icelandic-US relations. However, the determination of the Icelanders became apparent when the government declared an exclusive economic zone of 200 miles in July 1975.[33] Yet again, the British responded by sending in the Royal Navy. Thus began the Third Cod War, which quickly escalated and became a genuine problem within NATO. By 1976, the Icelanders had become so infuriated that they severed diplomatic relations with London. The dispute ended in June 1976 with an agreement

[27] Jóhannesson (2004, pp. 118–119).
[28] Thorhallsson et al. (2018, p. 545).
[29] Jóhannesson (2004, p. 121).
[30] Ingimundarson (2001a, p. 296).
[31] Ingimundarson (2001b, p. 128).
[32] Jóhannesson (2004, p. 124).
[33] Ingimundarson (2011, p. 134).

which stipulated that all British ships were to be withdrawn from the 200-mile fishing zone within 6 months.[34]

The conclusion of the Third Cod War marked a turning point in Icelandic foreign policy during the Cold War. The Icelandic government had reached its main foreign policy objective, which was to implement an exclusive fishing zone around Iceland. True, the Icelandic cause was helped by the fact that the law of the sea was undergoing rapid changes, and later in the year Britain itself adopted a 200-mile exclusive economic zone.[35] But the relevance of the Cod Wars and the US military base in Keflavik is demonstrated by the fact that the presence of US forces in Iceland ceased to be a major issue in Icelandic politics when the Cod Wars ended. In fact, no Icelandic government was formed based on the theme of the withdrawal of US troops from Iceland and of abrogating the Defence Agreement from there on.[36] Instead, Iceland became a more active participant in NATO by participating in defence planning and political debates.[37] In 1986, Reykjavik was chosen as the venue for the Reagan-Gorbachev summit in Reykjavik, which played an important part in ending the Cold War in 1989.

5.2.4 Icelandic-US Political Relations, 1991–2006

The fall of the Soviet Union in 1991 exposed the weakness in the Icelandic-US defence relations and had extensive consequences for Icelandic-US political relations in general. Iceland's military importance in the North Atlantic evaporated and the US need for military facilities in Iceland declined significantly.[38] As the Bush administration began to reorganise its defence policy in 1992, the State Department wanted to withdraw the bulk of the US forces from Iceland. This included all F-15 fighter jets and the AWACS-surveillance planes stationed in Keflavik. The Icelandic government responded by threatening to abrogate the Defence Agreement, emphasising the need for a permanent or credible defence in Iceland. Although the Clinton administration backed down in 1993, over the next few years the State Department withdrew all but a handful of F-15 fighter jets and one AWACS-surveillance plane from Keflavik. What followed was a prolonged debate between Icelandic and US officials about the number of planes to be situated in Iceland.[39]

The Icelanders managed to hold their own in the debate until the September 11 terrorist attacks in New York and Washington in 2001. As the "War on Terror" began in 2002, the US government decided to enforce changes to the Icelandic-US

[34] Rastrick and Ísleifsson (2004, p. 388).

[35] Jóhannesson (2004, p. 127).

[36] Ingimundarson (2011, p. 139).

[37] Jónsson (1989a, pp. 33–35).

[38] Bjarnason (2008, pp. 155–156).

[39] Ingimundarson (2008, pp. 9–12).

bilateral defence relationship. As a result, Iceland was removed from a list of areas seen as vital to US continental defence. In 2003, the Bush administration informed the Icelandic government that the fighter jets would be removed from Iceland.[40] Again, the Icelandic government responded by threatening to abrogate the Defence Agreement, but in a show of good faith, also decided to put Iceland on the US State Department list of the "Coalition of the Willing" in March 2003, to keep the fighter jets in Keflavik.[41] However, this decision was controversial as most Icelanders were against the US led military invasion of Iraq. By doing this, the Icelandic government managed to buy itself time but was unable to prevent the inevitable. The jet-issue was finally resolved when the US decided, unilaterally, to withdraw its forces from Iceland on 30 September 2006, thereby ending its 55 years presence in Iceland. At the same time, however, the United States reaffirmed its commitments to the Icelandic-US Defence Agreement of 1951 on the base of the North Atlantic Treaty through projected defence.[42]

5.2.5 Icelandic-US Political Relations in the Post-American Era, 2006–2022

The American withdrawal from Iceland was a bitter pill to swallow for many Icelanders, especially for Eurosceptic Atlanticists within the Independence Party, who identified closely with the Icelandic-US Defence Agreement. Some of them expressed anger at the American withdrawal, which they saw as betrayal.[43] The Icelandic government, however, decided not to sever any contractual ties with the United States, thereby committing Iceland to the continuation of the defence relationship with the US.[44] Icelandic officials also began to outline a post-American security policy. The aim was to address the "power vacuum" in the North Atlantic. An important part of this policy was to strengthen Iceland's ties with NATO through temporary air policing arrangements with member states, four times a year, for 2 to 3 weeks at a time. This was seen by politicians as a partial compensation for the shutdown of the US base in Iceland. In fact, it meant that Iceland's NATO membership had taken political precedence over the Icelandic-US Defence Agreement, involving more European NATO partners.[45]

At the same time, the Icelandic government also tried to build expertise on matters of security and defence. During the Cold War, Icelandic over-reliance on American expertise had hampered the development of a skilful Icelandic national

[40] Jóhannesson (2004, p. 130).

[41] Ingimundarson (2008, pp. 20–21).

[42] Ingimundarson (2011, pp. 152–154).

[43] Ingimundarson (2011, p. 163).

[44] Thorhallsson, Steinsson (2019, p. 173).

[45] Ingimundarson (2011, pp. 155–156).

security apparatus, as Icelandic politicians saw little need to develop the country's own security expertise.[46] As a result, the Defence Agency was founded in April 2008 for the express purpose of handling Icelandic defence and security issues. The Defence Agency had a substantial operational budget for projects controlled by the Agency.[47] However, in October 2008 the Icelandic banking system collapsed following a debt-financed spending spree. In June 2009, the Icelandic government decided to dissolve the Defence Agency due to budget cuts, while reaffirming Iceland's defence and security commitments.[48]

The Icelandic government also responded to the American withdrawal by paying more attention to Arctic issues. During the first two decades of the twenty-first century, the importance of the Arctic in global politics due to climate change shifted the region from the margins of Icelandic foreign policy to the centre.[49] One of the goals of Iceland's Arctic policy is to draw US attention to Arctic matters and thus re-establish closer ties with Washington. This policy has been partially successful. During the last decade, Iceland has made a stake holding claim in the Arctic region based on national interests. This policy has been based on a longing to take advantage of Iceland's geostrategic location in the North Atlantic, to be actively involved in the Arctic institutions, and to benefit from future natural resource extraction and prospective opening of new transarctic trade routes.[50] At the same time, Iceland has also been able to establish itself as a venue for the annual Arctic Circle Assembly in Reykjavik, where Arctic matters are discussed.[51] However, the Icelandic government has not been able to turn Arctic issues into a Cold War-style strategic prize. This has to do with US policy in the region. While the US government has reasserted its intentions to protect its broad national security interests in the Arctic, it does not foresee any war-threatening tension in the region in the near future, which explains its limited military interest there.[52]

As for US policy in Iceland, the government of the United States continues to view Iceland as an important NATO ally. According to the Defence Agreement, the United States is committed to defending Iceland in the event of a military threat, but it is mainly up to the US government to decide how and when to activate the agreement.[53] Iceland's strategic military importance has increased again since the Ukrainian crisis began in 2014, because the United States and NATO have intensified their military presence in the North Atlantic in response to increased Russian naval activities in the area. At present, the Russian invasion of Ukraine in February 2022 has forced NATO member states to strengthen their defences. This will also be

[46] Thorhallsson et al. (2019, p. 62).
[47] Ingimundarson (2011, p. 160).
[48] Kristjánsson (2016, p. 177).
[49] Thorhallsson (2018, p. 9).
[50] Ingimundarson (2020, p. 251).
[51] Thorhallsson (2018, pp. 9–10).
[52] Ingimundarson (2020, p. 259).
[53] Ingimundarson (2011, pp. 162–163).

the case in Iceland, although there has been no talk of formally reopening the military base in Keflavik. The invasion has also increased the debate on defence and security issues in Iceland, as in other NATO member states. However, if the US wanted to station military forces in Iceland in peacetime, a high-tension situation in the North Atlantic would be required to reopen the base question in Icelandic domestic politics. The current Icelandic government, which is a three-party coalition spanning the left-right political spectrum, is led by the Left-Green Party, which opposes Iceland's membership of NATO. Any hint of a return of US forces to Iceland would certainly reopen the difficult, even painful, Cold War debates in Icelandic politics and society.[54]

Meanwhile, the bilateral Icelandic-US defence agreement and Iceland's NATO membership remains the cornerstone of Iceland's defence policy and will continue to be so for years to come.[55] Since the Defence Agreement with the US is based on the North Atlantic Treaty, NATO's security guarantee applies to Iceland. The Alliance, therefore, continues to fund military infrastructure projects in Keflavik, as it did during the Cold War period, and US forces participate in air policing operations in Iceland. However, there is no discussion of individual NATO member states taking over Iceland's territorial defence. Influential Independence Party members, who are Eurosceptic Atlanticists in the realist tradition, remain committed to the United States in security and defence, despite the American withdrawal in 2006. These individuals, who have influenced Icelandic security policy for decades, argue that the United States is the only real security guarantor, while Europe and the EU are considered militarily weak.[56] As a result, Iceland's defences will continue to rely on other NATO member states, volunteering to assume, on a rotation basis, temporary air surveillance duties with fighter jets for the foreseeable future.

5.3 Economic Shelter

5.3.1 The Origins of Icelandic-US Economic Relations, 1941–1945

Icelandic-US economic shelter relations began during the Second World War when US troops arrived in Iceland. In accordance with the defence agreement, the US government provided Iceland with comprehensive economic support during the war.[57] As a result, Icelandic society was transformed during the conflict with its economy growing by 38%. By comparison, other European economies shrank by

[54] Ingimundarson (2020, pp. 258, 262).

[55] Thorhallsson and Steinsson (2019, p. 173).

[56] Ingimundarson (2011, p. 163).

[57] Kjartansson (2002, p. 222).

25% on average during the war.[58] The growth was mostly due to the British occupation and the US military presence and the demand they brought into the economy. After arriving, the Allied forces launched various military projects, such as the construction of airfields, docks, roads, bridges, army barracks and other important infrastructure, which required a considerable workforce.[59] The result was that unemployment, which had plagued Icelandic society through the 1930s, vanished and wages increased. Those who suffered were Icelandic sailors, who sailed in the submarine infested North Atlantic, carrying fish to Britain, and bringing consumer goods back from the United States.[60]

To put the Icelandic economic boom during the war into perspective, Iceland's national income was only exceeded by the United States. Iceland ran up trade surpluses with its exports and built up considerable currency reserves. Investment increased from 4 million dollars in 1938 to 29 million in 1945. Indeed, some scholars have argued that Iceland achieved economic objectives during the Second World War that would normally have taken half a century.[61] Before the war Iceland was the poorest country in Northern Europe, isolated and struggling with the effects of the Great Depression. When the conflict was over, it had become one of the richest.[62] The American shelter had made Iceland prosperous.

5.3.2 Forging the Icelandic-US Economic Alliance, 1945–1960

The Icelandic economic boom ended in 1946 when Iceland experienced a sharp decline in national income due to the withdrawal of the British and American forces.[63] After the Keflavik Agreement, the US government stopped subsidising and guaranteeing Iceland's exports which hurt its export earnings. In fact, Iceland's currency reserves decreased from 89 million dollars in 1943 to 5 million in 1946. By 1947, it was clear that the economy was heading into a post-war recession.[64]

However, Iceland's military importance increased as the Cold War began. The Truman administration wanted Iceland to participate in the Marshall Plan because US officials were convinced that political and economic stability in Iceland would serve US strategic military interests, as identified by the national security theory.[65] Indeed, high-level Pentagon officials argued that the Icelandic government would be

[58] Thorhallsson et al. (2019, p. 63).
[59] Thorhallsson et al. (2018, p. 547).
[60] Jóhannesson (2004, p. 116).
[61] Ingimundarson (2011, pp. 24–25).
[62] Kjartansson (2002, p. 247).
[63] Kjartansson (2002, pp. 247–252).
[64] Thorhallsson et al. (2018, p. 548).
[65] Leffler (1990, pp. 143–152).

more susceptible to US military base plans if it participated in the Marshall programme.[66]

US policy towards Iceland during this period had three major objectives: first, to ensure political and economic stability in Iceland; second, to increase the chances that the Icelandic government would accept US base requests; third, to stop Iceland's trade with the Soviet Union despite Iceland's substantial trade with the Eastern Bloc. Thus, the reason for proposing Iceland's participation in the Marshall Plan was to stabilise its economy and maintain the high living standards of the population, as part of the US efforts to maintain its political and military influence in Iceland.[67]

The Icelandic government decided to participate in the Marshall Plan in 1948 to avoid an economic crisis.[68] Over the next few years, Icelandic officials used the strategic military importance of Iceland in the Cold War to obtain maximum aid from the Marshall programme. The strategy worked and Iceland received the highest per capita Marshall aid of all the participating countries. In fact, following the official conclusion of the Marshall Plan in 1952, Iceland even got a 1-year extension due to its military importance.[69] Iceland received twice as much aid per capita as the second highest recipient, with the Marshall Plan accounting for almost 6% of Iceland's GDP when the programme peaked in 1951. As a result, the aid minimised the effects of the 1948–1952 economic slump, financed 17% of Iceland's imports between 1949 and 1953, and enabled substantial capital investments in the fishing industry, energy sector, and agriculture.[70]

At the same time, the US again began to help the Icelandic government to market Icelandic fish abroad. In 1947–1948, the US government subsidised the sale of tens of thousands of tons of saltfish to Greece, Italy, and Occupied Germany and in 1952–1956 the Americans relieved Iceland of some of its unsold fish stocks during the Icelandic-British fishery dispute.[71] By the early 1950s, the US economic support had again become instrumental in sustaining the Icelandic economy and the high living standard of the Icelandic people.[72]

Meanwhile, Iceland continued to trade with the Soviet Union and its satellite states. However, this trade was unpredictable, that is, 1 year the Soviet Union was Iceland's largest trading partner but by the next year the trade had fallen to zero. Many Icelandic policymakers and American officials worried about Iceland's dependence on trade with the Eastern Bloc. This was one of the reasons why Icelandic politicians asked for additional Marshall Aid in 1956–1960. It was also one of the motivating factors behind the willingness of the US to provide Iceland with

[66]Ingimundarson (1996, pp. 150–151).

[67]Ingimundarson (2011, p. 26).

[68]Whitehead (1998, p. 30).

[69]Ingimundarson (2011, p. 27).

[70]Thorhallsson et al. (2019, pp. 63–64).

[71]Thorhallsson et al. (2018, p. 550).

[72]Ingimundarson (2011, p. 27).

extensive shelter. The US assistance prevented Iceland from becoming even more dependent on trade with the Eastern Bloc and growing dependent on the Soviet Union.[73]

The US economic support, however, also had its downside. As the Cold War continued and Iceland's economic reliance on the US became clear, Icelandic politicians refrained from implementing necessary reforms to the economy, thus, in effect, artificially sustaining an unsustainable economic model.[74] This was also reflected in Icelandic relations with international economic institutions. While Iceland participated in the establishment of the Bretton Woods institutions at the end of the Second World War, it had less to do with the Bretton Woods system than was expected. The reason was that the privileged US treatment allowed the Icelandic government to bypass the services of the International Monetary Fund (IMF) and the World Bank and deal directly with the Americans instead. The result was that although Iceland was a part of the Bretton Woods system, the Icelandic government did not in fact comply with the rules on trade liberalisation, at least in the early post-war years. The US would normally use its diplomatic force to back up Iceland's request for exceptions from rules on trade literalisation, such as within the OECD.[75]

5.3.3 Icelandic-US Economic Relations, 1960–2006

By 1960, Iceland had to a certain extent been integrated into the western economic system. That same year, the US government declared that Iceland would no longer receive the same economic assistance in the future. As a result, Icelandic politicians finally implemented the necessary economic reforms to make the Icelandic economy sustainable.[76] However, Iceland could still rely on US economic support. For example, Iceland received favourable loans from the US in the 1960s, which were part of the PL-480 development-assistance programme for underdeveloped countries. The fact that Iceland received the loans, and was the only western country to do so, demonstrates that the Icelandic government still received special treatment in Washington.[77] The last time the US government helped Iceland directly during economic difficulties was in 1969 when the Nigerian market closed due to the Biafran War. In response, the US bought most of Iceland's stockfish, which was subsequently distributed by the Red Cross in Nigeria.[78] However, the US government continued to give Iceland indirect economic assistance. For example, it gave Icelandic shipping companies special rights to manage sea transport to and from

[73] Ingimundarson (1996, pp. 141–149).

[74] Thorhallsson et al. (2019, pp. 65–66).

[75] Thorhallsson et al. (2018, pp. 548–549).

[76] Ingimundarson (2001b, p. 25).

[77] Thorhallsson et al. (2019, p. 68).

[78] Thorhallsson et al. (2018, p. 552).

Iceland on behalf of the US military forces in Keflavik. The same applied to the Icelandic airline Loftleidir which had special rights to land in the United States and offer services at lower prices than carriers that were part of the International Air Transport Association.[79]

Although direct US economic interventions and associated diplomatic assistance had stopped, Icelanders continued to reap the economic benefits of Icelandic-US economic relations. One way which Iceland profited was from the presence of the US military base in Keflavik and the various construction projects that came with it.[80] In 1947, an American construction company undertook all projects related to the base, but it was replaced in 1951 by a semi-private firm set up by the Icelandic government. The new Icelandic firm, which provided jobs for thousands of Icelanders from all over the country, was entitled to all projects it could undertake for the US military forces in Iceland.[81] These projects turned out to be highly profitable and provided Iceland with much needed foreign currency over the next decades. In fact, Iceland's net income from the US military base in Keflavik usually amounted to about 5–10% of its export income through the whole Cold War period, or around 2–3% of GDP from 1970 onwards. When the Cold War ended, the US government continued to fund infrastructure projects at the military base and run the Keflavik Airport. In addition, the US forces managed air-surveillance and operated helicopters, which was crucial to rescue operations at sea around Iceland, until the base was closed in 2006. The small Icelandic economy still enjoyed important economic shelter provided by the US.[82]

5.3.4 *Icelandic-US Economic Relations in the Post-American Era, 2006–2022*

When the US military forces were withdrawn from Iceland, Icelandic-US economic relations had become a shell of what they had been during the height of the Cold War. Icelandic politicians were, however, still convinced that the United States would come to Iceland's rescue in times of economic trouble.[83] It only became evident how wrong they were when Iceland was the first casualty of the international financial crisis in October 2008, when its banking system collapsed. In the run-up to the crash, the Icelandic Central Bank approached the US central bank, as well as central banks in Europe, and requested currency swap agreements. The talks were inconclusive but in September the NY Federal Reserve rejected the idea due to the

[79] Ingimundarson (2022, p. 79).
[80] Whitehead (1998, p. 56).
[81] Ingimundarson (1996, p. 221).
[82] Thorhallsson et al. (2018, pp. 550, 552).
[83] Ingimundarson (2011, pp. 170–171).

relative size of the Icelandic banking system and in the absence of an IMF agreement.[84]

The unprecedented Icelandic economic collapse which followed and the Icelandic government's response to it led to the most bizarre episode in Icelandic-US relations. In a fit of desperation, Icelandic politicians, who were disappointed that the United States had not come to the country's rescue, turned to Moscow as a potential saviour, asking Russia for a 5.4-billion-dollar loan.[85] The Russian government was open to negotiations. An announcement from the Central Bank of Iceland confirming this made headlines around the world. The announcement, however, raised suspicion in western capitals that this was part of an Icelandic Cold War style strategy designed to pressure the West to grant Iceland economic assistance. Indeed, Moscow and Iceland's traditional western Allies called their bluff and when the Icelandic government was forced to turn to the IMF for a bailout at the end of October the game was up.[86] Nevertheless, the US took a neutral position within the IMF when Britain and the Netherlands blocked a rescue package to Iceland due to the so-called Icesave dispute, see chapter X for more details. Accordingly, the US was not even willing to provide Iceland with diplomatic shelter in the wake of its economic collapse.

Disappointed by this turn of events, the Icelandic President, Ólafur R. Grímsson, however, criticised Iceland's traditional western allies for not coming to Iceland's aid, claiming that it was clear the country needed new friends and that Russia should be invited to use the former US military base in Keflavik. The idea had no solid foundation and was soon forgotten.[87] The President also took the initiative to seek diplomatic and economic assistance provided by China in the immediate aftermath of the economic collapse, as discussed in detail in chapter X on the Sino-Icelandic relations.

The fact that the United States did not come to Iceland's rescue during the financial crisis demonstrated that Iceland had lost its strategic military importance at the end of the Cold War and that the Icelandic government could no longer rely on the American superpower to come to its rescue during an economic crisis.[88] However, once the immediate crisis was over Icelandic-US relations stabilised and the "Russian episode" was forgotten. At the same time, Icelandic politicians were forced to admit that the reason behind the Icelandic economic collapse was the erroneous neoliberal economic policy implemented by the centre right coalition government in the years before the crisis and the criminal behaviour of the Icelandic bank managers on the eve of the collapse.[89] As for Icelanders in general, the lesson of the financial

[84] Thorhallsson et al. (2019, pp. 68–69).

[85] Ingimundarson (2011, p. 170).

[86] Ingimundarson (2020, p. 255).

[87] Ingimundarson (2011, pp. 171–172).

[88] Thorhallsson, Steinsson (2019, p. 173).

[89] Hreinsson et al. (2010, pp. 31–47).

crash was that Iceland, as a sovereign state, has to take responsibility for its own actions.

Meanwhile, the United States continues to be the leader of the free world because of its military might and economic power. As such, it remains a key player in maintaining the rules of the international system, as it has done since the end of the Second World War.[90] Therefore, Iceland will continue to rely on the US leadership role in world affairs, as small states usually prosper from free trade and respect for international law. In fact, Iceland's trade with the United States continues to flourish, although it is insignificant compared to its European trade. In recent years, less than 10% of total Icelandic export of goods have gone to the US and less than 10% of total import of goods have come from the US. In addition, Iceland saves a considerable amount each year because the United States continues to pay for its defences.[91] At present, Iceland is seeking a bilateral trade agreement with the US. However, talks on this issue have so far been inconclusive. Therefore, Iceland is likely to continue its quest to strengthen economic relations with the United States once again.

5.4 Societal Shelter

5.4.1 Icelandic-US Social Relations, 1941–2022

The strong political and economic relationship between Iceland and the United States had a profound influence on social and cultural affairs in Iceland. The arrival of the Allied forces during the Second World War created jobs and led to a dramatic rise in the standard of living in Iceland.[92] The labour shortage created by the occupation also altered traditional gender roles in Iceland as women entered the labour market. During the height of the occupation in 1943, about 50,000 troops were stationed among its 130,000 inhabitants.[93] Although relations with the locals were generally satisfactory, many Icelandic men felt threatened by the presence of the Allied troops. Indeed, the interactions between Allied soldiers and Icelandic women became the most controversial aspect of the occupation and led to moral panic that was referred to as the "situation."[94]

At the start of the Cold War, a shortage of housing at the US military base in Keflavik meant that a considerable number of military personnel had to be accommodated in nearby towns, which became a source of bitterness on the Icelandic side. Also, Icelandic men remained suspicious about the interaction between Icelandic

90 Ingimundarson (1996, p. 9).

91 Thorhallsson, Steinsson (2019, p. 174).

92 Kjartansson (2002, p. 220).

93 Jóhannesson (2004, p. 116).

94 Thorhallsson et al. (2019, p. 82).

women and US soldiers throughout the Cold War period as stories of debauchery circulated in the Icelandic media.[95] As a result, the Icelandic government imposed restrictions on US troops interacting with Icelandic society. Part of this segregation policy was a blanket ban of the stationing of coloured troops in Iceland.[96] When this policy became public knowledge in the US in the 1960s, and the Kennedy administration protested, the Icelandic government refused to admit that it was responsible. In fact, the government did not fully abolish the policy until the mid-1970s.[97]

The American presence in Iceland was, however, beneficial to Icelandic society in many ways. As a demonstration of the virtues of American culture, the American government sent hundreds of American musicians, writers, and other artists to Iceland.[98] The US military base in Keflavik also had a profound influence on Icelandic pop culture and was an important source of American popular music and television. This, however, caused objections from the Icelandic side as Iceland did not have its own television station, and thousands of Icelanders received broadcasts from the military base.[99] Finally, fearing the "Americanisation" of Icelandic culture, the Icelandic government decided to establish Iceland's national television channel in 1966.[100]

However, the most lasting social and cultural effect of the American presence in Iceland is Icelandic-US cooperation in education. When the American forces arrived in Iceland during the Second World War, Icelandic students gained access to American educational institutions and Fulbright grants. As the Cold War began, these relations became closer until they peaked during the 1990s. Overall, thousands of Icelandic students have studied in the United States and close to a thousand Fulbright grants have been awarded to Icelanders. However, the US never became the central destination for Icelanders seeking higher education, and the proportion of Icelandic students studying in the United States today is small compared to the number of students studying in European countries.[101]

5.5 Conclusion

Icelandic-US relations arose from specific historical circumstances during the Second World War when the national interests of the small state and the superpower converged. Iceland, as a neutral country with no army, saw the United States as the only option to shelter its political and economic interests during the war. Indeed,

[95] Ingimundarson (2011, pp. 45–54).
[96] Jóhannesson (2004, p. 123).
[97] Thorhallsson et al. (2019, p. 83).
[98] Magnúsdóttir (2000, pp. 30–33).
[99] Jóhannesson (2004, p. 123).
[100] Thorhallsson et al. (2019, p. 85).
[101] Thorhallsson et al. (2018, pp. 552–553).

Iceland took the initiative to seek shelter in Washington. However, when the United States decided to move its Atlantic defences to the east and provide military protection for Iceland to support Britain in the war against Nazi Germany, the Icelandic government rejected Roosevelt's request to invite American forces to the country but agreed that the stationing of US military forces in Iceland served the national interests of the Icelandic people. US troops arrived in Iceland in July 1941. The Allies defended the country from German invasion, secured Iceland's economy with favourable trade agreements, kept shipping routes open and recognised the founding of the Icelandic Republic in 1944 as promised. Finally, when the war ended the US agreed to withdraw its forces from Iceland in accordance with the Keflavik agreement in 1946. Iceland had secured all its original objectives by seeking shelter from the US.

Iceland was now within the US sphere of influence and the US government wanted a long-term lease of military bases in Iceland. As the Icelandic economy headed into a post-war recession, the American policy over the next few years was a mixture of political pressure and economic incentives. When the Cold War began, Iceland decided to abandon its neutrality policy and forge a close military and economic alliance with the American superpower. As a result, Iceland participated in the Marshall Plan in 1948, joined NATO in 1949, and signed the bilateral Icelandic-US Defence Agreement in 1951, when US troops returned to Iceland. Icelandic politicians and policymakers regarded political and economic shelter arrangements with the US as the most suitable way to defend the country and strengthen its fragile economy.

Both sides took full advantage of the Icelandic-US alliance during the Cold War. The United States used it influence and wealth to provide political, economic, and social shelter to Iceland, and used the strategic importance of the US military base in Keflavik to beneficial effect in the struggle against the Soviet Union. At the same time, the Icelanders harvested economic benefits from the presence of American troops in Iceland, both in the form of direct US economic assistance and favourable western loans, and the strategic importance of the military base was used as a tool in the struggle to extend the exclusive fishing zone around Iceland. As a result, Iceland was able to defeat Britain in the Cod Wars from the 1950s until the 1970s, thereby achieving the single most important objective of Icelandic foreign policy since the Second World War. Meanwhile, the US military presence in Iceland speeded up the modernisation of the country and had an important effect on Icelandic culture and on educational standards. Indeed, Iceland enjoyed partial societal shelter provided by its close encounter with the superpower. This was particularly the case from 1941 to the mid- 1990s.

The United States was the main provider of economic shelter to Iceland from 1941 to the late 1960s and Iceland continued to enjoy considerable political shelter (in military terms) until 2006. However, it lost its strategic military importance in the North Atlantic with the collapse of the Soviet Union in 1991. As a result of this the US withdrew its forces from Iceland in September 2006, while reaffirming its commitments to the Icelandic-US Defence Agreement. This brought an end to the Icelandic-US alliance and Iceland became the only NATO member state with no armed forces on its soil. The loss of Iceland's political and economic shelter from the US was demonstrated during the 2008 financial crisis, when the US government refused to grant Iceland economic assistance. Hence, Iceland was left without political (diplomatic backing) and economic shelter at the time of its economic collapse. The Icelandic political elite felt betrayed by Washington. But despite these difficulties, the relations between Iceland and the US have remained stable. The Icelandic-US Defence Agreement remains the cornerstone of Iceland's foreign and defence policy and the countries enjoy good economic and social relations, although they are only a shadow of what they were at the height of the Cold War.

References

Baldvinsson PB (2015) Stríðsárin 1938–1945. JPV, Reykjavík

Bittner DF (1983) The Lion and the White Falcon. Britain and Iceland in the World War II Era. Archon Books, Connecticut

Bjarnason GÞ (2008) Óvænt áfall eða fyrirséð tímamót? Brottför Bandaríkjahers frá Íslandi: Aðdragandi og viðbrögð. University of Iceland Press, Reykjavík

Corgan MT (1992) Aðdragandinn vestanhafs að hervernd Bandaríkjanna á Íslandi 1941 (trans. Unnur Ragnarsdóttir). Saga 30:123–156

Corgan MT (2002) Iceland and its alliances - security for a small state. Scandinavian Stud 8. The Edwin Mellen Press, New York

Hreinsson P, Benediktsdóttir S, Gunnarsson T (eds) (2010) Aðdragandi og orsakir falls íslensku bankanna 2008 og tengdir atburðir, vol 1. Rannsóknarnefnd Alþingis, Reykjavík

Ingimundarson V (1996) Í eldlínu kalda stríðsins. Samskipti Íslands og Bandaríkjanna, 1945–1960. Vaka-Helgafell, Reykjavík

Ingimundarson V (2001a) The Role of NATO and US Military Base in Icelandic Domestic Politics, 1949–1999. In: Schmidt G (ed) History of NATO. The First Fifty Years. Palgrave, New York, pp 285–305

Ingimundarson V (2001b) Uppgjör við umheiminn. Samskipti Íslands, Bandaríkjanna og NATO 1960–1974. Íslensk þjóðernishyggja, vestrænt samstarf og landhelgisdeilan. Vaka-Helgafell, Reykjavík

Ingimundarson V (2008) Frá óvissu til upplausnar - Öryggissamfélag Íslands og Bandaríkjanna, 1991–2006. In: Ingimundarson V (ed) Uppbrot hugmyndakerfis. Endurmótun íslenskrar utanríkisstefnu 1991–2007. Hið íslenska bókmenntafélag, Reykjavík, p 1–66

Ingimundarson V (2011) The Rebellious Ally. Iceland, the United States, and the Politics of Empire 1945–2006. Republic of Letters, Dordrecht

Ingimundarson V (2020) Iceland as an Arctic State. In: Coates KS, Carlin H (eds) The Palgrave handbook of Arctic policy and politics. Palgrave Macmillan, Cham

Ingimundarson V (2022) Unarmed sovereignty versus foreign base rights: Enforcing the US-Icelandic Defence Agreement 1951–2021. Int Hist Rev 44(1):73–91

Jóhannesson G Th (2004) To the edge of nowhere? US-Icelandic defence relations during and after the Cold War. Naval War Coll Rev 57(3):115–137

Jóhannesson G Th (2016) Fyrstu forsetarnir. Embætti þjóðhöfðingja Íslands á 20. öld. Sögufélag, Reykjavík

Jónsson A Kl (1969) Stjórnarráð Íslands 1904–1964, vol 2. Sögufélag, Reykjavík

Jónsson A (1989a) Ísland, Atlantshafsbandalagið og Keflavíkurstöðin. Öryggismálanefnd, Reykjavík

Jónsson H (1989b) Íslensk hlutleysisstefna. Fræðilega hlutleysið 1918–1941. Andvari 114(1): 203–224

Kjartansson HS (2002) Ísland á 20. öld. Sögufélag, Reykjavík
Kristjánsson S (2001) Forsetinn og utanríkisstefnan. Bandaríkjaför Sveins Björnssonar árið 1944. Ný saga 13:4–16
Kristjánsson JÞ (2016) Iceland. A small state learning the intelligence ropes. In: De Graaff B, Nyce M (eds) The handbook of European intelligence cultures. Rowman and Littlefield, New York, pp 171–181
Leffler MP (1990) National security. J Am Hist 77(1):143–152
Magnúsdóttir R (2000) Menningarstríð í uppsiglingu. Stofnun og upphafsár vináttufélaga Bandaríkjanna og Sovétríkjanna á Íslandi. Ný saga 12:29–40
Rastrick Ó, Ísleifsson SR (2004) Stjórnarráð Íslands 1964–2004, vol 2. Sögufélag, Reykjavík
Stefánsson SJ (1966) Minningar Stefáns Jóhanns Stefánssonar, vol 1. Setberg, Reykjavík
Thorhallsson B (2021) Iceland's shelter-seeking behavior. From Settlement to Republic. Cornell University Press, Itacha
Thorhallsson B, Steinsson S (2019) Icelands shelter options in the New Millennium. In: Thorhallsson B (ed) Small state and shelter theory. Iceland's external affairs. Routledge, London, pp 171–204
Thorhallsson B, Steinsson S, Kristinsson Þ (2018) A theory of shelter. Iceland's American period (1941–2006). Scandinavian J Hist 43(4):539–563
Thorhallsson B, Steinsson S, Kristinsson Þ, Devine DJ (2019) Shelter during the American Period. Icelandic relations with the US and International Organisations. In: Thorhallsson B (ed) Small state and shelter theory. Iceland's external affairs. Routledge, London, pp 61–92
Thorsteinsson PJ (1992) Utanríkisþjónusta Íslands og utanríkismál. Sögulegt yfirlit, vol. 1. Hið Íslenska Bókmenntafélag, Reykjavík
Valdimarsson VU (1993) Ísland í eldlínu alþjóðamála. Stefnumótun og samvinna innan Sameinuðu þjóðanna 1946–1980. Alþjóðamálastofnun Háskóla Íslands, Reykjavík
Whitehead Þ (1991) Leiðin frá hlutleysi 1945–1949. Saga 29:63–121
Whitehead Þ (1998) The Ally Who Came in from the Cold. A Survey of Icelandic Foreign Policy 1946–1956. University of Iceland Press, Reykjavík
Whitehead Þ (1999) Bretarnir koma. Ísland í síðari heimsstyrjöld. Vaka-Helgafell, Reykjavík
Whitehead Þ (2006) Hlutleysi Íslands á hverfanda hveli 1918–1945. Saga 44(1):21–64

Skafti Ingimarsson is a Postdoctoral Researcher at the Institute of History at the University of Iceland. His research is focused on Icelandic political, social, and environmental History. He holds a PhD (2018) in History from the University of Iceland and MA (2007) in History from the University of St Andrews in Scotland.

Baldur Thorhallsson is a Professor of Political Science, and founder and Research Director for the Centre for Small State Studies, at the University of Iceland. His research focus has primarily been on small European states, small state theory and Iceland's foreign policy. His recent articles are included in *The Hague Journal of Diplomacy*, *Scandinavian Journal of History* and *Global Affairs*. His latest edited books are titled *Iceland's Shelter-Seeking Behavior: From Settlement to Republic* (Cornell University Press 2021), *Small States and the New Security Environment* (co-editor) (Springer 2021) and *Small States and Shelter Theory: Iceland's External Affairs* (Routledge 2019). He holds a PhD (1999) and MA (1994) in Political Science from the University of Essex in the United Kingdom.

Chapter 6
Iceland's Relations with the Nordic States

Pia Hansson and Auður Birna Stefánsdóttir

6.1 Introduction

The five Nordic countries, Sweden, Denmark, Finland, Norway and Iceland, are known for their consensus-oriented and unified political processes and have long been hailed for their strong welfare systems. Despite the important differences between the countries, there are enduring similarities in the social, political and economic structures that have contributed to these countries being considered as a regional unit. The countries have a long tradition of cooperation and, in fact, the Nordic Council founded in 1952 is the oldest regional partnership in the world. The Nordic countries have a strong regional cooperation framework and also tend to be perceived as a unified region in the international arena.[1] Even though Nordic cooperation has undergone different stages of togetherness and solidarity, it is safe to say that these countries, often referred to as "the Nordics", are a solid and enduring regional construction that they can rely on in times of trouble and uncertainty.[2]

All of the Nordic countries can be defined as small states despite their varying sizes. Traditionally, small states all rely to some degree on forging alliances and advancing their agendas through negotiations and participation in rule-based multilateral institutions. In a world where challenges are increasingly global and rarely solved with military power, power has gained a new meaning, as power itself is more often diffused among stakeholders of specific issues on the global agenda. The tradition of small states working together regionally and internationally is thus an

[1] Hansson and Stefansdottir (2021).

[2] Strang (2016).

P. Hansson (✉) · A. B. Stefánsdóttir
Institute of International Affairs, University of Iceland, Reykjavik, Iceland
e-mail: pia@hi.is; audurstefans@hi.is

A. Cunha, B. Thorhallsson (eds.), *Small States and Big Powers*, The World of Small States 10, https://doi.org/10.1007/978-3-031-42345-1_6

influential tool in today's world when states need to tackle global challenges.[3] It would therefore be logical that, as the smallest in the Nordic family, Iceland would recognise Nordic cooperation as a valuable tool in its foreign policy toolkit. Nevertheless, Nordic cooperation in security and defence was not a priority in Iceland's foreign policy until the US withdrawal from Iceland in 2006, when the country was faced with seeking political and economic shelter from alternative sources.[4]

The aim of this chapter is to explore what role Nordic cooperation plays in Iceland's foreign policy and to analyse whether Nordic cooperation is more important to Iceland as the smallest member of the regional cooperation. We will explore the extent to which Iceland has received and continues to receive political, economic and societal shelter from the Nordic states. Does Nordic solidarity always prevail or are the Nordic countries in some ways constrained when it comes to providing shelter because of the different choices they have made in securing their national economic and security interests? To answer the above questions, analysis of official documents, research papers and media coverage will be used in conjunction with seven anonymous semi-structured interviews with key experts and government officials.

6.2 Iceland and Nordic Cooperation: Political Shelter

Iceland, like other small states, faces inherent size-related difficulties when it comes to reducing risk in the face of a possible crisis. It therefore needs external shelter in order to survive and prosper and is to some extent dependent on the political shelter provided by larger states as well as regional and international organisations.[5] While Nordic cooperation in different forms ranging from academic networks to labour movements has a long history, from the mid-twentieth century it also developed into official cooperation between the Nordic governments. Nordic political cooperation is formed by the inter-parliamentary Nordic Council established in 1952 and the intergovernmental Nordic Council of Ministers, established in 1971. Iceland has certainly benefitted from this regional cooperation over the years, a cooperation that has since led to the establishment of a common Nordic labour market as well as a passport and social security union, preceding similar developments in the EU by many decades.[6]

When it comes to collaboration in the field of foreign and security policy, Nordic cooperation has been characterised by informality and has mostly taken place outside of the institutional Nordic structures. Incidentally, foreign, security and defence policy matters were not high on the Nordic Agenda until the end of the

[3]Tarp and Hansen (2013).
[4]Thorhallsson (2018a).
[5]Thorhallsson (2019).
[6]Hilson (2019).

Cold War and focused mainly on coordinating Nordic contributions to UN peace operations. Even after the Cold War cooperation between the Nordic countries, foreign and security policy has mainly been developed outside of the formal framework of Nordic cooperation. The drawback of this informality is the somewhat non-committal nature of Nordic foreign and security policy cooperation that is reflected in the practical output of the cooperation. Due to this lack of formal structure, foreign and security policy seldom translates into binding commitments or joint positions. Instead, Nordic foreign and security policy cooperation, especially at the higher levels, has focused primarily on sharing information, exchanging views and the joint analysis of current events and developments.

The lack of cooperation in the field of foreign affairs and security after the Cold War can also be explained by the Nordic countries' participation in other regional cooperation that focuses on international engagement, mainly Sweden's and Finland's participation in the EU and Iceland's, Denmark's and Norway's participation in NATO.[7] In this period, Iceland focused mainly on its relationship with the United States built on the bilateral defence agreement. Furthermore, according to Thorhallsson, the Nordic countries were considered too weak to be able to provide Iceland with the political shelter it needed in times of crisis.[8]

This perception shifted when Iceland lost its comprehensive American political shelter with the departure of the US military from Iceland in 2006.[9] This loss meant that Iceland needed to widen its scope when it came to securing its security and defence. Changes in the international security environment and the weakening of multilateral institutions also led to an increased interest from the other Nordic countries in further cooperation in the field of Nordic security and defence cooperation. There is a growing need for the Nordic construct as a "go between", not least because Finland and Sweden are not members of NATO.[10] However, this might change since they now have NATO membership applications pending. In 2009, the Nordic foreign ministers commissioned Thorvald Stoltenberg, former Minister for Foreign Affairs in Norway, to write a report with recommendations on how to strengthen Nordic cooperation in foreign and security policy. That same year, the Nordic Defence Cooperation (NORDEFCO) was established as a structure for Nordic cooperation in defence.[11]

Iceland participated fully in this venture and, in fact, 2 years prior to this had also made bilateral declarations on defence cooperation with both Norway and Denmark.[12] To reinforce the commitment, Iceland and Norway also signed a new joint

---

[7] Iso-Markku et al. (2018).

[8] Thorhallsson (2018a).

[9] Thorhallsson (2016).

[10] Interview, February 6, 2018.

[11] Stoltenberg (2009).

[12] Samkomulag um samstarf á sviði öryggismála, varnarmála og viðbúnaðar milli Noregs og Íslands. (2007). and Yfirlýsing lýðveldisins Íslands og konungsríkisins Danmerkur um samstarf í víðari skilningi i um öryggis- og varnarmál og almannavarnir.

declaration reaffirming the two countries' collaboration on security and defence issues in 2017[13] and just this year, in autumn 2021, Iceland and Sweden signed a joint declaration on defence cooperation. On this occasion, the Swedish Foreign Minister, Peter Hultqvist said "The Joint Declaration underlines the intent of both parties to strengthen our defence cooperation on matters of mutual interest to better respond to the evolving security environment" while Iceland's Foreign Minister, Guðlaugur Þór Þórðarson, emphasised that the declaration was to add to the countries exciting cooperation within NORDEFCO and other multilateral institutions.[14] In addition, Iceland instigated the participation of Sweden and Finland in NATO air policing over Iceland, which came to fruition under the leadership of Norway in the spring of 2014. Denmark has also participated extensively in air policing over Iceland, making all the Nordic countries particularly important for Iceland's security and defence.[15]

Signalling Iceland's increased independence in its security and defence, Alþingi passed a bill on the establishment of a National Security Council in 2016. This, together with the formation of a National Security Policy, was an historical event according to Lilja Alfreðsdóttir, the Foreign Minister at the time.[16] In the new National Security Policy, particular emphasis is given to the importance of strengthening Nordic cooperation on security and defence. [17] This was also manifested in the prioritisation given to Nordic cooperation in the foreign affairs section of the coalition agreement of the Icelandic government that came to power in November 2017. The first sentence of the section states: "Nordic cooperation will continue to be one of the cornerstones of Iceland's foreign policy."[18] Nordic cooperation has therefore become increasingly important in the field of security and defence cooperation in Iceland.

Alongside the substantial deepening of Nordic cooperation in defence in 2009, the Nordic ministers responsible for civil security and emergency management agreed to the so called 'Haga' declaration, which focuses on Nordic cooperation in areas of societal security and crisis preparedness. Ten years later, in 2019, the Nordic Council approved a new strategy on cooperation in societal security, calling for closer cooperation. The strategy is due to the common challenges faced by Nordic societies, e.g. cyber attacks, terror, extreme weather events and natural disasters, pandemics, problems with energy supplies, among others. The Nordic Council emphasises that these threats could all have cross-border repercussions, which call for effective cooperation between the Nordic countries in emergency planning and

[13] Stjórnarráðið (2017).

[14] Ministry for Foreign Affairs (2021, September 15).

[15] Kinnunen (2012).

[16] Arnarsdóttir (2016, June 2).

[17] Þingsályktun um Þjóðaröryggisstefnu fyrir Ísland. Þingskjal 1166–327 mál.

[18] Agreement between the Progressive Party, the Independence Party and the Left Green Movement on collaboration in a coalition government and reinforcing the capacity of the Althingi. (2017, November 30).

rapid responses that are not hampered by borders or doubts about roles and responsibilities.[19]

One of the areas for cooperation focuses especially on the non-traditional threats of cyber attacks and this cooperation with the Nordic countries is explicitly cited as an essential element of Iceland's cyber security policy.[20] Iceland has since set up a Computer Security Incident Response Team (CERT-IS) like the other Nordic countries which has resulted in extensive cooperation with similar units in the other Nordic countries, sharing information about cyber threats, defence methods and equipment.[21]

It should also be noted that Iceland benefits from being a part of the Nordic brand, namely the global perception of the Nordic countries as being devoted to democracy, equality and human rights. Furthermore, Iceland benefits from diplomatic backing that forms an important part of the cooperation between the Nordic countries. An Icelandic government official describes this as follows:

> Being part of the Nordic countries definitely strengthens Iceland; if we were trying to advocate for things on the international arena and were not part of the Nordic countries, we would be working alone. If we take that hypothetical example, I imagine we would be much weaker.[22]

Over the years, Nordic diplomatic backing has been extremely important for Iceland, which runs one of the smallest foreign services in Europe. The Nordic countries are small states with similar cultures and values that are motivated to work together to increase their influence in the larger international arena, and this is especially important to Iceland as the smallest amongst its neighbours. The Nordic countries operate as a coordinated political block in many international contexts, for example in the United Nations (UN), the Organisation for Economic Cooperation and Development (OECD), the International Monetary Fund (IMF) and the World Bank where the Nordic countries have in the past taken turns to occupy powerful seats in the bodies.[23] Nordic cooperation has been a venue for the Nordic countries to coordinate their actions in the UN to maximise their influence, and Iceland has reached many of its decisions on how to vote in the UN on the basis of the conclusions reached at Nordic Council meetings.[24]

Iceland has therefore depended on the other Nordic countries for assistance in international institutions, for example at the UN. However, a government official noted that Sweden and Finland became less interested in cooperation after they joined the EU and transferred their focus to that regional cooperation.[25] The Nordic states have also provided Iceland with extensive administrative assistance within

[19] Nordic Council (2019, 30. oktober).

[20] Ministry of the Interior (2015).

[21] Ministry of Transport and Local Government (2018).

[22] Interview, January 30, 2018.

[23] Schouenborg (2012).

[24] Thorhallsson (2018b).

[25] Interview, February 12, 2018.

EFTA and the EEA frameworks. For instance, in the mid-1960s when Icelandic officials were monitoring free-trade developments in Europe closely, much of their information came through collaboration with the other Nordic countries. The Nordic EFTA member states also saved Iceland considerable administrative cost by providing it with extensive administrative assistance in the first years of EFTA membership in the early 1970s.[26] In the 1990s, Iceland followed the Nordic EFTA member states in joining the EEA and Schengen. The Nordic EU members were also instrumental in helping Iceland secure membership of the Schengen scheme on better terms than they received in the negotiations leading to the signature of the EEA Agreement. Finally, Norway provided Iceland with important economic shelter that gave the country access to the European market. In fact, as Thorhallsson points out, it could be said that Norway paid the bulk of Iceland's entrance fee to the European market. At present, Norway makes significant net contributions to the EU through its membership in the EEA. Iceland is actually a net beneficiary, receiving more from the EU than it pays into it, while Switzerland pays slightly more to the EU than they receive in return.[27] To date, Norway and Switzerland has provided Iceland with considerable diplomatic backing and valuable expertise in all areas covered by the EFTA Convention and the management of the EEA Agreement.[28]

Iceland's diplomatic capabilities have been strengthened by Nordic cooperation as the Nordic states coordinate considerably on foreign policy matters, and the Nordic identity gives them disproportionate international influence and a higher profile in the international arena.[29] Iceland therefore seems to enjoy considerable backing from the Nordic countries and the regional cooperation is valued by government officials. One government official described it as follows:

> It is based on common values, a common culture and history, which enables us to work together on a solid foundation with a great deal of trust between both people and systems and, in fact, it is based on a long experience of deep cooperation.[30]

This deep-rooted trust and solidarity seems to be shared by the other Nordic countries. In 2011, the Foreign Ministers of the five Nordic countries signed the 'Nordic declaration of solidarity', which was incidentally one of the 13 recommendations in Stoltenberg's 2009 report. The declaration emphasised the common interests and values of the countries in promoting democracy, international law, gender equality and sustainable development, and also stressed that these shared values made it natural for the countries to cooperate in solidarity when facing foreign and security policy challenges.[31]

---

[26] Thorhallsson et al. (2018).

[27] Thorhallsson (2018a).

[28] Thorhallsson et al. (2018).

[29] Thorhallsson and Steinsson (2020).

[30] Interview October 15, 2020.

[31] Regjeringen (2011).

Given this declaration of solidarity and the frequent reference made to the importance of Nordic cooperation, it is strange that this Nordic solidarity and cooperation did not seem to materialize when the world was faced with the enormous challenge of COVID-19 at the beginning of 2020. Silja Dögg Gunnarsdóttir, then President of the Nordic Council, called for closer cooperation among the Nordic countries to fight the pandemic. She emphasised the exceptionally close relations and their unique level of trust and added "the friendship and trust we have built up must now show its worth".[32] But it is clear that as the crisis hit the Nordic region, all the Nordic countries responded differently and on a national level, even when it came to drastic political decisions like closing borders. The Nordic solidarity and cooperation that the political elite so often mentioned was lacking, as one government official describes:

> ...there was full-scale panic, as in other countries, so rash actions were taken without informing anyone in advance, and it certainly caused frustration and discomfort when the border was closed without notice between countries that are as intertwined as the Nordic countries and which live, study, work and have family on the other side of the border.[33]

In general, despite cooperation between the Nordic countries on different levels, mainly on how to react to the effects of the pandemic, the countries acted unilaterally first and collaborated later. Solidarity, understood as something that goes beyond cooperation, does not seem to hold when the region is faced with an unexpected global crisis. The Nordic region, just like the global community, tends to go national in times of crisis. Many Nordic leaders have called for deeper cooperation on the response to the crisis but, as one Icelandic government official pointed out, this can be hampered by the competitive spirit of the Nordic countries with everybody defending their responses to the pandemic, making it difficult to move forward and reach a unified position.[34]

In the 2020 Bjarnason report, a follow-up to the 2009 Stoltenberg report on defence, Bjarnason emphasises that the COVID-19 experience shows that the Nordic countries need to have a Nordic contingency plan for pandemics; moreover, the pandemic has underscored the need for both increased Nordic cooperation on countering hybrid threats and ensuring that autocratic states do not control the global narrative. The report proposes that the Nordic countries reconsider their cooperation on total defence so that it complements the work of the EU and NATO in order to better prepare for future pandemics. This cooperation would be based on relevant national authorities coming up with a common system of analysis, an early warning system, integrated contingency planning and finally unified Nordic action. Such a framework might later serve as a model for a Nordic governmental and societal approach in times of major crises.[35]

---

[32] Nordic Council (2020).

[33] Interview, October 7, 2020.

[34] Hansson and Stefansdottir (2021).

[35] Bjarnason (2020).

It seems that Nordic solidarity has its limits in times of crisis as demonstrated by the Nordic countries' unilateral actions at the start of COVID-19. However, even though the Nordic countries do not give Iceland full political shelter, Nordic cooperation has provided and keeps providing it with crucial political and diplomatic backing in the international arena. Iceland has received important diplomatic shelter from its Nordic neighbours, vital for the limited Icelandic foreign service, as well as partial security shelter, especially after the country lost its comprehensive American military shelter.

6.3 Iceland and Nordic Cooperation: Economic Shelter

As small open economies, all the Nordic countries have been well integrated in both the regional and international economy. The Nordic region is the 11th largest economy in the world and has an open labour market which has enabled people from Nordic countries to enjoy the freedom to work anywhere in the region. The economic development of these countries since the Second World War has been similar even though they have different market orientations. Trade between the Nordic countries has been important over the years despite exports to Britain, Germany and Russia generally exceeding intra-Nordic trade.[36] In the past, there have been several failed attempts to increase Nordic economic cooperation and integration, most notably with the idea of a Nordic single market and a proposal for a Nordic Economic Union (NORDEK) with the aim of generating economic growth and social well-being.[37] The failure to establish such a union was in part caused by the diverse economic interests of the Nordic countries and, in the case of Iceland, the fact that marine products were not covered in the proposed version of the union.[38] Each of the five Nordic countries have had differing economic relationships with Europe, with Finland currently being the only one to have adopted the euro, and Iceland and Norway the only ones not to have become members of the EU.

As the Nordic markets are small and diverse and rely on European markets, the Nordic countries are unable to provide Iceland, or each other, with sufficient economic shelter.[39] However, Iceland has been given considerable economic shelter from the Nordic countries through the common Nordic labour market, diplomatic backing and burden sharing arrangements as well as on occasion through participation in European integration.[40] Nordic cooperation has, for example, eased Iceland's economic transition and adaptation to the European integration process. Iceland considered following the United Kingdom, Norway, Denmark and Ireland and

[36] Strang (2016).

[37] Sonne (2007).

[38] Jónsson (2009).

[39] Thorhallsson et al. (2018).

[40] Thorhallsson (2019).

applying for membership of the EU in the early 1960s but came to the conclusion that its economy was too underdeveloped.[41] The Nordic states have provided Iceland with extensive administrative assistance within EFTA and the EEA frameworks as explained above. Iceland also obtains considerable diplomatic backing from both Norway and Switzerland in all areas covered by the EFTA Convention and the management of the EEA Agreement.[42] As one interviewee described it when asked about Iceland's economic cooperation with the Nordic countries:

> Iceland definitely benefits more from Nordic cooperation than it has put into it. Being part of a "club" that has considerably more resources and is better connected to the international community and the EU has been an asset for Iceland economically, there is no doubt about that. Nordic support on information gathering and expertise on new developments is invaluable for Iceland and saves a lot of time and effort on our part.[43]

Besides cooperation in EFTA and the EEA, Iceland has also worked closely with both the Nordic countries and the Baltic states since the early 1990s in the World Bank Group and the IMF, granting it a role within these institutions. Iceland has appointed representatives to serve on the governing bodies of the World Bank Group through the membership of the Nordic and the Baltic states. It has also chaired the delegations of these states to the IMF.

It can therefore be said that the Nordic countries provide Iceland with partial economic shelter through their considerable diplomatic backing, assistance and burden-sharing in EFTA and the EEA as well as in other international organisations. Nevertheless, Nordic solidarity has its limits and even though the Nordic countries may at times be more willing than others to assist their small neighbour, their responses to Iceland's request for assistance during the 2008 economic crash was not entirely positive.[44] Iceland was hit hard in the global credit crunch in 2007–2008 resulting in the collapse of its three international banks, Landsbanki, Kaupthing and Glitnir, in October 2008, in what was one of the world's greatest national financial crises.[45] The collapse of Landbanki, Icesave's parent bank, meant that the Icelandic regulators did not have enough money to pay back foreign customers, leaving them without access to the money in their Icesave accounts. The existing protection against banking collapse proved insufficient. As a member of the EEA, Iceland had established a Depositor and Investor Guarantee Fund, but this was only legally required to hold much smaller assets than would be required in a serious crisis. So although they had emergency money, its was not enough for all accounts. When the rescue funds proved insufficient, the laws were ambiguous as to who was responsible for repaying Icesave's international customers, with Iceland claiming that it had fulfilled its responsibilities even though they could not repay foreign customers, and the Netherlands and the UK claiming that Iceland was responsible for paying back

[41] Thorhallsson (2018a, b).

[42] Thorhallsson et al. (2018).

[43] Interview, October 12, 2021.

[44] Thorhallsson (2018b).

[45] Bergmann (2017).

the minimum deposit guarantee on foreign accounts.[46] The dispute resulted in the British Prime Minister, Gordon Brown, using sections of a law known as the "Anti-terrorism, Crime and Security Act 2001" to freeze Landsbanki's assets in an effort to keep the bank from pulling its funds out of the country. This was the final blow for Iceland's largest and last remaining bank, Kaupthing.[47]

The relationship between Iceland and the Nordic countries at the height of and in the aftermath of the 2008 economic crash in Iceland shows contradiction in Nordic solidarity. As one interviewee put it: "The IMF rescue package was dependent on other countries extending part of the loans, so if the Nordic countries had not come through for us then we would not have been able to receive the IMF rescue package, as no other countries provided any significant help." Therefore, it can be said that the only economic help in the financial crisis came from Nordic countries. At the same time, these countries took part in blocking the IMF rescue package to try to get Iceland to capitulate to the demands of Britain and the Netherlands on the Icesave issue.[48] Former Prime Minister Jóhanna Sigurðardóttir was disappointed with the lack of understanding from the Nordic countries and had expected more support and Ólafur Ragnar Grímsson, who was President at the time, also expressed his disappointment with the Nordic countries' position in the Icesave dispute,[49] It can therefore be said that they regarded their relations with the UK, the Netherlands, and the EU, as more valuable than "Nordic solidarity" with their small Nordic partner.[50]

A common Nordic labour market has also proved to be highly beneficial for Iceland, not least in the aftermath of the economic crash. One interviewee described it as follows:

> The common Nordic labour market that enables Icelandic people to work anywhere in the Nordic region is very important for the Icelandic economy and Iceland in economic downturns. It was especially helpful after the economic crisis in 2008 as many Icelanders moved to the Nordic countries to work and this eased the pressure on the Icelandic labour market and the central budget.[51]

Therefore, even though the political elite in Iceland was disappointed with the lack of Nordic solidarity in the Icesave dispute, ultimately the Nordic countries came through for their smallest neighbour. Iceland has in fact received considerable economic shelter through Nordic cooperation, the common labour market and not least through having access to diplomatic backing and expertise that has saved Iceland much time and effort in international institutions like EFTA and the EEA, as well as the IMF and the World Bank.

---

[46] Bier (2020).

[47] Bergmann (2017).

[48] Thorhallsson (2016).

[49] Sigurðardóttir (2013, January 31).

[50] Thorhallsson (2018a).

[51] Interview, October 12, 2021.

6.4 Iceland and Nordic Cooperation: Societal Shelter

Iceland as a small state depends on the free flow of ideas across its borders to make up for a limited knowledge base. Iceland's societal relations with other countries in terms of technological, educational and cultural ideas, norms and practices is therefore vital to the country's prosperity.[52] Nordic cooperation in the form of close relations and exchange of ideas has been especially important to Iceland's societal shelter. While relations with Nordic countries was minimal during the Second World War due to the German occupation of Denmark and Norway, Iceland's strong social relations with the countries resumed once the war ended. Even though Iceland has always had a close relationship with the US and been influenced culturally by the States, Iceland has mainly looked to its Nordic neighbours when it comes to modules on how to organise its public policy, especially social policies.[53]

The Nordic countries share a basic cultural unity and are in fact often seen internationally as a single entity. This close tie means that the Nordic countries have traditionally looked to each other for guidance on policies and ideas. They have learned from each others' experiences and often use examples from one or more of the other Nordic countries to justify the introduction or rejection of new ideas or the implementation of specific policies. The end of World War II saw the start of closer formal cooperation between the Nordic countries at senior political and administrative levels and this furthered the coordination of public policies and even today contributes to Nordic countries adopting similar policies on a number of topics.[54] This close tie with the Nordic countries resulted in Iceland developing its welfare system based on the Nordic Welfare Model, hailed internationally as one that combines economic competitiveness with social equality and inclusion. Iceland has also extensively mimicked other policies that were developed by its neighbours, such as on women's rights and LGBT rights legislation.[55] Through Nordic cooperation, Iceland is also part of the common Nordic labour market as well as the Nordic Passport Union, the Nordic Convention on Social Assistance and Social Services and the Nordic Convention on Social Security. This cooperation has enabled Icelandic people to live, work and educate themselves in the Nordic Region, thus contributing to the country's knowledge base and to the management of a small volatile economy.[56]

Nordic cooperation also enjoys widespread public support with the population according to an extensive survey carried out by The Nordic Council of Ministers and the Nordic Council in 2017. It reveals that more than 90% of the population consider Nordic cooperation important or very important, with two-thirds of respondents

[52] Thorhallsson og Steinsson (2018).

[53] Thorhallsson et al. (2018).

[54] Kuhnle (1978).

[55] Thorhallsson and Steinsson (2020).

[56] Norden (n.d.) Nordic agreements and legislation.

supporting more Nordic cooperation. Not surprisingly, the Nordic cooperation perceived to be most important in everyday life is (1) the opportunity to be able to move and work freely in the Nordic region, (2) to be able to travel between the Nordic countries without border controls, (3) the opportunity to study and (4) use social security measures wherever you live in the region. The shared values and the similar social structure of the Nordic countries are considered the most important foundations for Nordic cooperation according to respondents. The typical Nordic values most mentioned are freedom of speech, equality, human rights and democracy.[57] Based on the study, the Nordic population seems to see themselves as belonging to a group of like-minded small welfare states and they are proud of many of the region's characteristics. The Nordics, including Icelanders, value the opportunity the cooperation provides for them to live, work and educate themselves in the other Nordic countries, as it widens their education and work choices.

Nordic cultural and educational cooperation is linked to the common ideals of the Nordic welfare state, in which open accessible higher education is considered important. Nordic student mobility has a long history and in fact predates formalised cooperation within the Nordic Council of Ministers, which started in the 1950s. A number of Nordic agreements and instruments have been developed to enable Nordic students to study in other Nordic countries, including the Nordplus programme for exchange students and the Nordic agreement on admission to higher education in 1996. Historically, mobility within the Nordic region has varied and the mobility patterns have been uneven within the countries, where in particular Iceland and Norway have a particularly large number of students studying in the other Nordic countries. In fact, Iceland has far higher proportions of students abroad than any other Nordic country, with almost half of Icelandic mobile students going to other Nordic countries.[58] This is not surprising given that education opportunities in Iceland are more limited due to its size. Although the agreement between the Nordic countries stipulates that the sending country pay for the education provided by the receiving country, Iceland holds an exemption to this. In 2014, this exemption was worth more than 3.2 million euros. In the 2012–13 academic year, 1049 Icelandic students studied in other Nordic countries but only 106 students from the Nordic countries studied in Iceland.[59] Iceland therefore receives considerable educational support from the other Nordic countries and seems to be more dependent on this cooperation than the other Nordic countries.

Nordic research cooperation is also important to the exchange of ideas in Iceland. The Icelandic research community relies on Nordic research funding mainly through its cooperation in NordForsk, established in 2005 by the Nordic Council of Ministers. Although Iceland does not receive large amounts in research funding from NordForsk, it receives substantially more than it contributes, as demonstrated by the contribution of 40 million NOK in 2018 versus the 68 million NOK of funding

[57] Andreasson and Stende (2017).

[58] Elken et al. (2015).

[59] https://www.althingi.is/altext/145/s/1512.html

received.[60] When asked about Iceland's contribution to Nordic research funds, one interviewee commented that although the other Nordic countries sometimes claim Iceland does not pull its weight in the fund, they are generally very tolerant of it fully participating without contributing as much as the other countries.[61] Although European Funds are bigger (the overall budget of Horizon Europe is 95.9 billion euros), the Nordic funds can be a good foundation for researchers that are taking their first steps in international research projects, since the communications between the Nordics are often more informal and laid back, according to an interviewee. Furthermore, the collaboration between Nordic partners when applying for funding to the EU's key funding programmes is invaluable.[62]

The above mentioned examples clearly demonstrate that Nordic cooperation is an integral part of the societal structure in Nordic countries. However, while the Nordic Prime Ministers adopted a new strategy in 2019 called *Our vision 2030*, with the aim of becoming the world's most sustainable and integrated region, their funding for cooperation has been declining sharply for the past two decades. In proportion to Nordic GDP and government expenditure in general, funding for cooperation is only half that of about 30 years ago. Whilst the countries themselves have increased funding for cultural affairs, the funding provided for joint Nordic cultural cooperation has diminished.[63] This is a matter of concern for Iceland, which has received substantial societal shelter from the Nordic countries and may have benefitted disproportionately from the cooperation.

6.5 Conclusion

Despite some limitations as shelter providers, the Nordic countries have supported Iceland politically, economically and socially over the years. Nordic cooperation has led to similar value systems, norms and lifestyles in the Nordic countries and even though the cooperation has experienced different stages of togetherness and solidarity, the Nordic states still form a solid and enduring regional construction. Although Iceland is more reliant on the US in foreign and security matters through the bilateral defence agreement and NATO membership, the diplomatic shelter provided by the Nordic countries has been vital internationally to the limited Icelandic foreign service in the international arena. As the smallest of the Nordic states, Iceland benefits more from Nordic cooperation in international institutions as it depends to a degree on the assistance of its neighbours to fulfill its responsibilities in international cooperation. The Nordic brand has gained momentum and respect

[60] Herou, Anna. Ten Years of Nordic Research Funding. 2009–2018. Retrieved from: http://norden.diva-portal.org/smash/get/diva2:1365795/FULLTEXT08.pdf. Accessed 4 July 2023.

[61] Interview. December 2, 2021.

[62] Interview. December 2, 2021.

[63] Felixson (2019, August 20).

internationally. Being part of the Nordic club has also given Iceland a stronger voice on the international stage and allowed it to punch above its weight. Furthermore, the partial security shelter provided by the Nordics through the NORDEFCO cooperation and bilateral declarations of defence cooperation was important when the country lost its comprehensive American military shelter. The Nordic countries also participate extensively in Iceland's airpolicing and provide vital expertise and support for cyber security.

It can also be said that Iceland has received considerable economic shelter through Nordic cooperation via the common Nordic labour market and diplomatic backing and burden sharing when it comes too participation in European integration. Iceland has also worked closely with both the Nordic countries and Baltic states in the World Bank Group and the IMF, which granted it a role within these institutions. The size of the other Nordic countries means they are often better connected and have more resources than Iceland. Access to the diplomatic backing and expertise of the other Nordic countries in EFTA, the EEA and other international institutions has been an asset to Iceland and certainly saved the Icelandic government a great deal of time, effort and money. Nordic cooperation has also enabled Icelanders to work anywhere in the Nordic region, which is especially useful in a small volatile economy. Even though Iceland has received economic shelter from the Nordic countries, Nordic solidarity has not always been consistent in times of crisis, as was the case in the aftermath of the economic crisis in Iceland in 2008. The Nordic countries may have felt constrained due to their relationship with other larger countries and EU members.

Nordic cooperation is also an integral part of Iceland's societal structure. Through the close cooperation with the other Nordic countries, Iceland has based its welfare system on the Nordic model and adopted other policies and ideas on issues such as women's rights and LGBT rights legislation. Iceland also benefits from a long history of Nordic cooperation in education and research, that is vital for Iceland as the smallest of the Nordic countries and, in turn, makes it more dependent on this cooperation. Inclusion in the Nordic agreements that are the foundation for the common Nordic labour market has enabled Icelanders to live, work and educate themselves in the Nordic region, which has strengthened Iceland's knowledge base and contributed to cultural exchanges that in turn have led to a greater understanding of the Nordic region. In fact, Nordic cooperation seems to enjoy widespread public support in all Nordic countries, especially when it comes to the opportunity to move and work freely throughout the region.

Our findings support the claim that Nordic cooperation does provide Iceland with considerable political, economic and societal shelter. Nonetheless, Iceland needs additional shelter from other providers in the international system. It is therefore in Iceland's interest to maintain strong Nordic cooperation. Considering the Nordic Prime Ministers' ambitious plan for the region to become the most sustainable and integrated region in the world by 2030, it was however discouraging that the Nordic countries acted unilaterally when the pandemic hit by closing their borders. Funding for Nordic cooperation has also declined sharply over the past two decades, suggesting a lack of political will to maintain and strengthen the cooperation.

References

Agreement between the Progressive Party, the Independence Party and the Left Green Movement on collaboration in a coalition government and reinforcing the capacity of the Althingi. (2017, November 30)

Andreasson U, Stende T (2017) Ett värdefullt samarbete: Den nordiska befolkningens syn på Norden. Nordic Council of Ministers, Copenhagen

Arnarsdóttir E (2016, June 2) National Security Council Established. Icelandic Review

Bergmann E (2017) The Icesave dispute: a case study into the crisis of diplomacy during the credit crunch. Nord Med 12

Bier J (2020) It's a small, small, small world: the Icesave dispute and global orders of difference. Politics Space 38(7–8):1291–1307, 1299–1300

Bjarnason B (2020) Nordic Foreign and Security Policy 2020

Elken M, Hovdhaugen E, Jenssen JW (2015) Higher education in the Nordic countries. Evaluation of the Nordic Agreement on Admission to Higher Education. Nordic Council of Ministers

Felixson T (2019, August 20) Norrænt samstarf – öflugt eða orðin tóm? Stundin. https://kjarninn.is/skodun/2019-08-20-norraen-samstarf-oflugt-ad-ordin-tom/. Accessed 4 July 2023

Hansson P, Stefansdottir A (2021) Nordic solidarity and COVID-19. Small States Territories 4(1): 29–44

Herou A. Ten Years of Nordic research funding. 2009-2018. http://norden.diva-portal.org/smash/get/diva2:1365795/FULLTEXT08.pdf. Accessed 4 July 2023

Hilson M (2019) The Nordic region. Nordic.info

Iso-Markku T, Innola E, Tilikainen T (2018) A stronger north? Nordic Cooperation in Foreign and Security Policy a new security environment

Jónsson G (2009) On the sidelines: Iceland and the Nordek negotiations, 1968–1970. In: Hecker-Stampehl J (ed) Between Nordic ideology, economic interests and political reality: new perspectives on Nordek. Finnish Society of Science and Letters, Helsinki, pp 159–167

Kinnunen T (2012) Finland, Sweden to help NATO in Iceland air. Reuters. https://www.reuters.com/article/us-finland-iceland-idUSBRE89T0K720121030. Accessed 4 July 2023

Kuhnle S (1978) The beginnings of the Nordic welfare states: similarities and differences. Acta Sociologica 21:9–35

Ministry for Foreign Affairs (2021, September 15) Iceland and Sweden sing joint statement. https://www.government.is/diplomatic-missions/embassy-article/2021/09/15/Iceland-and-Sweden-sign-Joint-Declaration-on-defence-cooperation/. Accessed 4 July 2023

Ministry of the Interior (2015) Icelandic National Cyber Security Strategy 2015–2026

Ministry of Transport and Local Government (2018) Cybersecurity capacity review. Republic of Iceland. Global Cyber Security Center

Norden (n.d.) Nordic agreements and legislation. https://www.norden.org/en/information/nordic-agreements-and-legislation/

Nordic Council (2019, October 30) Nordic council approves closer cooperation on societal security. https://www.norden.org/en/news/nordic-council-approves-closer-co-operation-societal-security. Accessed 4 July 2023

Nordic Council (2020) Nordic council letter to prime ministers: work together in times of crisis

Regjeringen (2011) Nordic declaration on solidarity. Norwegian Government, Oslo

Samkomulag um samstarf á sviði öryggismála, varnarmála og viðbúnaðar milli Noregs og Íslands (2007)

Schouenborg L (2012) The Scandinavian international society primary institutions and binding forces, 1815–2010. Routledge

Sigurðardóttir G (2013, January 31) The Icesave conflict: Iceland did not break the rules. Nordic Labour J. http://www.nordiclabourjournal.org/nyheter/news-2013/article.2013-01-31.3016781167. Accessed 4 July 2023

Sonne L (2007) NORDEK: a plan for increased Nordic economic co-operation and integration 1968-1970

Stjórnarráðið (2017) Joint Declaration between Iceland and Norway on defence cooperation. https://www.stjornarradid.is/lisalib/getfile.aspx?itemid=b49f91f4-3ede-11e7-941a-005056bc530c. Accessed 4 July 2023
Stjórnarráðið. Yfirlýsing lýðveldisins Íslands og konungsríkisins Danmerkur um samstarf í víðari skilningi i um öryggis- og varnarmál og almannavarnir
Stoltenberg J (2009) Nordic cooperation on foreign and security policy. https://www.regjeringen.no/globalassets/upload/ud/vedlegg/nordicreport.pdf. Accessed 4 July 2023
Strang J (2016) Nordic political and economic cooperation: context. History and Outlook
Tarp MN, Hansen J (2013) Size and influence: how small states influence policy making in multilateral arenas. DIIS Working paper 2013:11
Þingsályktun um Þjóðaröryggisstefnu fyrir Ísland. Þingskjal 1166–327 mál
Thorhallsson B (2016) Do small states need shelter? The economic and political turmoil in Iceland. In: Baldersheim H, Keating M (eds) Small states in the modern world: vulnerabilities and opportunities. Edward Elgar, Cheltenham, pp 42–56
Thorhallsson B (2018a) Nordicness as a shelter: the case of Iceland. Global Affairs 4:1–14
Thorhallsson B (2018b) A small state in world politics: Iceland's search for shelter. In Stjórnmál og stjórnsýsla sérhefti um vald og lýðræði á Íslandi: 61–82
Thorhallsson B (2019) Insight 218: shelter theory and Iceland: options for a small state
Thorhallsson B og Steinsson S (2018) The theory of shelter. Research Policy Briefs. Small States and the New Security Environment
Thorhallsson B, Steinsson S (2020) Nordic cooperation as a form of governance: Iceland's sheltered society. In: Briguglio L, Byron J, Moncada S, Veenendaal W (eds) Handbook of governance in small states. Routledge
Thorhallsson B, Steinsson S, Kristinsson T (2018) Nordic cooperation and shelter implications. In: Thorhallsson (ed) Small states and shelter theory: Iceland's external affairs

Pia Hansson is the Director of the Institute of International Affairs and its three centres, the Centre for Small States Studies, the Centre for Arctic Studies and Höfði Reykjavík Peace Centre. She holds a B.A. degree in Communication from the University of Minnesota and an M.A. degree in International Relations from the University of Iceland. Pia also pursued an M.F.A. programme in Television Production at the City University of New York. For years, Pia worked as a Broadcasting Producer and Director, both in Iceland and abroad, until she became the Media Specialist at the Embassy of the United States in Iceland from 2000–2006. In the winter of 2007–8 Pia served as the Head Spokesperson for the Sri Lanka Monitoring Mission (SLMM), a Nordic ceasefire monitoring mission in Sri Lanka, on behalf of the Icelandic Ministry for Foreign Affairs.

Auður Birna Stefánsdóttir is an expert at the Institute of International Affairs. She holds a B.A. degree in Anthropology and an M.A. in International Relations from the University of Iceland. Before starting work at the Institute of International Affairs Auður worked as a project manager at the Icelandic Human Rights Center. Auður has been part of the team at the Institute of International Affairs since 2016 and has been involved in diverse research projects during that time. She has for example coordinated a research project on refugees integration opportunities and challenges in Iceland, a review on Iceland's National Action Plan on Women Peace and Security, edX course on small states and leadership, and she is the project manager of the Arms Control Negotiation Academy (ACONA) to name a few.

Chapter 7
Portugal's Contemporary Relations with Africa: A Limited Shelter?

António Raimundo

7.1 Introduction

Africa is a traditional dimension of Portugal's external relations with a long and complex history of engagement. Its African presence dates back to the fifteenth century when the small Iberian state initiated its 'Golden Age of Discovery', laying the ground for a vast, long-lasting, but also scattered and fragile empire.[1] For an extended period this presence was not very significant, but with the disintegration of the Luso-Brazilian Empire and the European 'Scramble for Africa' in the nineteenth century, the importance of the continent for Portugal's self-image and international ambitions grew. The borders of its African colonies were then established, comprising the large territories of Angola and Mozambique as well as the exiguous Portuguese Guinea and the small Atlantic islands of Cape Verde and São Tomé and Príncipe. More systematic attempts at human occupation and economic exploitation were also initiated during that phase and were further reinforced in the twentieth century under authoritarian rule.[2] Resisting the 'Winds of Change' in Africa, from the early 1960s to the early 1970s Portugal's New State fought bitter colonial wars in Angola, Guinea and Mozambique that left deep social and political wounds on all sides.

The overthrow of Portugal's dictatorship in 1974 led to a rapid and turbulent process of decolonisation.[3] This break from the past meant Portugal ceased to be a pluricontinental empire and became a small peripheral European state. This new and diminished international status, in turn, entailed a redefinition of the country's role,

[1] See, for example, Costa et al. (2014), Newitt (2009).

[2] Oliveira (2016).

[3] Oliveira (2017).

A. Raimundo (✉)
University of Minho, Braga, Portugal

A. Cunha, B. Thorhallsson (eds.), *Small States and Big Powers*, The World of Small States 10, https://doi.org/10.1007/978-3-031-42345-1_7

but one that would still bear the marks of the past. Africa, in particular, lost much of its previous importance to the country's external outlook, but continued to be one of the geographical areas of major interest for the diplomacy of the new democratic regime.[4] With the passage of time, old scars faded and Portugal gradually managed to rebuild its ties with its ex-colonies, which remained the main focus of the country's presence in Africa.[5] The creation of the Community of Portuguese-Speaking Countries (CPLP) in 1996 was an important milestone for the close relationship Lisbon currently enjoys with all its former colonies. Based on an intricate mix of historical, geopolitical, cultural and economic reasons, these post-colonial relations have not only been perceived domestically as significant in themselves, but also in view of the value they can add to other key vectors of Portugal's foreign policy, such as the European Union, NATO and the United Nations.[6] In fact, Portuguese decision-makers have explored the potential synergies between these different dimensions by playing an intermediary or facilitator role.[7]

This chapter examines the importance of Africa for contemporary Portuguese foreign policy. Despite its practical relevance, there is a paucity of systematic and up-to-date academic research on the topic.[8] The present study tries to narrow this gap by considering whether Portugal's small size has had a say in its policy towards Africa and, in particular, towards its former colonies. This problematique is addressed from a shelter theory perspective, which posits that small states seek political, economic and societal shelter from larger states and international institutions to alleviate the inherent vulnerabilities of being small in an anarchic international system.[9] Accordingly, the chapter assesses whether and to what extent Portugal has been seeking and has received political, economic and societal shelter from Africa, more particularly from Angola, Portugal's largest and resource-rich former African colony. In view of its status as an ex-Portuguese colony and a still developing country, Angola can be seen as a 'hard case' for shelter theory as applied to Portugal, especially in the economic domain. However, the ex-metropole has maintained close and intense political-diplomatic, economic and sociocultural bilateral ties with Angola, which concurrently has had pivotal importance for Lisbon's broader agency on African matters. After becoming independent, in 1975, Angola descended into a long and devastating civil war, but its return to peace in 2002 paved the way to greater domestic stability, economic growth and international ambition.[10]

Drawing on secondary and primary sources, the bulk of the analysis centres on the twenty-first century, but a broader contextualisation is also provided to better illuminate patterns of continuity and change in the long run. A particular focus is

[4] Cravo (2012), Teixeira (2003).

[5] Carvalho (2018), Raimundo (2019a).

[6] Raimundo (2013a, 2019a).

[7] See, for example, Cravo (2012).

[8] See Raimundo (2019b, pp. 16–17).

[9] Thorhallsson (2018), Thorhallsson and Steinsson (2019).

[10] Ball (2017), Soares de Oliveira (2015).

given to the recent global financial meltdown and subsequent Eurozone crisis, when Portugal went through great difficulties. This period of national vulnerability as well as crisis in Portugal's EU shelter is assumed to be a propitious situation to observe potential Portuguese shelter-seeking attitudes and behaviour towards Angola. Since Portugal's bilateral relationship with Angola has tended to be linked to wider normative and policy frameworks, attention is also given to some of these more relevant linkages, particularly in the CPLP, EU and UN contexts. The chapter argues that Angola has only provided a limited shelter to Portugal.

7.2 Political Shelter: Some Valuable Diplomatic Support

This first section examines the degree to which Portugal has relied on cooperation with Africa, particularly with Angola, when it comes to its foreign and security policy. More precisely, it considers whether and to what extent Lisbon has been seeking and has received political shelter from its former African colony in contemporary times. Political shelter basically refers to military or diplomatic backing by another state or international organisation.[11] In the past, Portugal's colonial project in Africa was a key foreign policy priority, prized even for reasons of national sovereignty and survival. But this strong emphasis on the African colonies, highly visible from the late nineteenth century, was complemented by the crucial protection provided by the centuries-old alliance with Britain, Portugal's main political shelter until the mid-twentieth century when it was gradually replaced in that role by the country's 'special relationship' with the USA and participation in NATO.[12] After transition to democracy and decolonisation in the mid-1970s, Portugal's redefined identity as a Euro-Atlantic country meant that European integration became a key national priority, with the European Union turning into an additional major political shelter, namely for diplomatic and soft security matters. As for Portugal's post-colonial relations in Africa (and with the wider Portuguese-speaking world), they have mainly been articulated as part of a third pillar of the country's foreign policy, alongside Europe and transatlantic relations, but with a less central significance.[13] Indeed, while important, Portugal's relations with its former African colonies, and with the wider Africa region for that matter, have represented at best a (secondary) complement to the country's main contemporary political shelters, i.e. the Atlantic Alliance and the EU.

Despite the many constraints and challenges, since decolonisation Portugal has gradually developed close relations and important levels of political cooperation with all its former African colonies, at both the bilateral and multilateral level. This has been particularly the case with Angola, with which Portugal has nurtured an

[11] See Thorhallsson and Steinsson (2019, p. 24).

[12] See, for instance, Telo (1996).

[13] See Cravo (2012), Sá (2015), Teixeira (2003).

intense and deep bilateral relationship.[14] However, in view of the challenging process of post-colonial adjustment as well as Angola's own structural limitations and difficulties, the level of cooperation and political backing that Lisbon could receive from its ex-colony was for a long time highly constrained and has thereafter remained testing. The bilateral relationship was immediately affected by the civil war that broke out in Angola in 1975, just a few weeks after independence. Strong post-colonial tensions and resentment were other important complicating factors, especially during an initial phase still in the Cold War. From the second half of the 1980s, the relationship improved significantly and opened the door for an important Portuguese involvement in the Angolan peace process.[15] Backed by Washington and Moscow, Lisbon played a central mediation role in the negotiations that led to the 1991 Angolan peace agreement. With the rapid restart of war, Portugal stepped back from its mediator role but continued to be involved in the Angolan peace efforts as an observer and contributing to successive United Nations peacekeeping operations.[16] Meanwhile, as an EU member Portugal was also pressing Brussels to provide political and financial support for the stabilisation of its ex-colony and greater attention to southern Africa in general.[17] While these efforts contributed to upgrading Portugal's bilateral relationship with Angola, they appear as mainly one-sided. While one can concede that Angola's stability was also in Portugal's own interest and that Lisbon's endeavours in different international settings buttressed its Africanist diplomatic specialisation and influence, it is harder to find evidence here of Angola as a 'shelter' for Portugal than vice versa.

From the second half of the 1990s and early 2000s, some important elements of change emerged. Against the increased stability brought by Angola's gradual return to peace in 2002 as well as the new opportunities offered by its post-war reconstruction, Portuguese representatives sought to advance the bilateral relationship by stepping up formal contacts with Luanda and promoting new initiatives in different areas.[18] Specifically in the political domain, an important bilateral initiative was the signing in 1996 of an agreement on military technical cooperation, similar to others Portugal had already formalised in the late 1980s with all its other former African colonies. This agreement provided the first formal framework for further bilateral activities in this area, including military training and logistical support, which have contributed significantly to the capacity-building of Angolan armed forces.[19] Also in 1996, the creation of the CPLP, much fostered by Portugal and initially with limited commitment from Angola, represented the institutionalisation of a new multilateral platform to deepen the cooperation among Portuguese-speaking countries in areas

[14]For an overview of relations see, for example, Seabra (2019).

[15]See, for instance, MacQueen (1997, 2003a), Reis (2019), Reis and Oliveira (2018), Venâncio and Chan (1996).

[16]Venâncio and McMillan (1993).

[17]Neves (1996), Raimundo (2020).

[18]Seabra and Gorjão (2011).

[19]Seabra (2011), Seabra and Abdenur (2018).

such as the promotion of the Portuguese language, education, economy and diplomatic cooperation.[20] Since the late 1990s, the CPLP has also given gradual and tentative steps in the security domain, including regular meetings of defence ministers, a common strategic analysis centre and small joint military training exercises.[21] Simultaneously, at the EU level Portugal continued to raise awareness of African issues, drawing on its historical ties in the region and making effective use of the rotating EU Presidency to expand its visibility and influence in the continent and beyond.[22] These examples show a more balanced picture than in the past, with new mechanisms and possibilities of cooperation being created, from which (also) Portugal was starting to derive more direct benefits and some support.

Against growing domestic difficulties at the beginning of the century, drastically aggravated by the post-2008 global and Eurozone crises, Portugal increased its efforts to deepen relations with Angola, which in turn was going through a period of unprecedented political stability and rapid economic growth. Under this new context, Portuguese authorities intensified their official visits to Angola and started pressing more openly for the formalisation of a bilateral 'strategic partnership', including regular high-level consultations. Both countries also began cooperating more within the CPLP, much due to Angola's increased interest in the platform's opportunities for its growing international ambitions.[23] Moreover, Lisbon persisted with its role as 'promoter' of African matters in Brussels, namely supporting an enhanced EU-Angola political dialogue.[24] In return, Portugal managed to obtain some political backing from its ex-colony, but not without important limits. For instance, during a 2011 visit to Angola by Portuguese Prime Minister Pedro Passos Coelho, aimed at raising support for his crisis-hit country, Angolan President Eduardo dos Santos offered his help, noting without providing further details that "Angola is open and available to find a set of solutions that are advantageous for both countries in a spirit of solidarity and mutual help".[25] On that same occasion, Prime Minister Passos Coelho advocated the development of a common strategic agenda for Portugal, Angola and Brazil, enabling them to 'bridge' the two sides of the Atlantic and three continents. [26] While not much came out of this trilateral grand design, the formalisation of the coveted bilateral 'strategic partnership' between

[20]Carvalho (2018, pp. 153–157), Hewitt et al. (2017), Santos (2003).

[21]MacQueen (2003b), Tavares and Bernardino (2011).

[22]Raimundo (2020), Robinson (2015), Vines (2012).

[23]For instance, in 2013 Angola agreed to raise its contribution for the CPLP Secretariat (up to the level of Portugal's own contribution), even if its actual payments have remained inconsistent. See Seabra (2019, p. 84).

[24]These efforts successfully led to the signature of the 2012 'EU-Angola Joint Way Forward' cooperation agreement.

[25]Reuters: "Portugal PM: Angolan capital welcome in privatisations", 17.11.2011. https://www.reuters.com/article/portugal-angola-idUKL5E7MH3I020111117. Accessed 4 July 2023.

[26]Angop: "Governante luso defende agenda estratégica entre Angola, Brasil e Portugal", 17.11.2011. https://www.portaldeangola.com/2011/11/17/governante-luso-defende-agenda-estrategica-entre-angola-brasil-e-portugal/. Accessed 4 July 2023.

Portugal and Angola was subsequently postponed several times by Luanda. [27] A clearer example of political shelter dynamics is provided by the diplomatic support Portugal has received in international organisations, such as UN bodies. For example, the country's bid for its UN Security Council (UNSC) term in 2011–2012 was unanimously supported by its fellow CPLP members and by a large number of votes from the African group. [28] Apart from their favourable vote, CPLP countries took an active part in Portugal's UNSC campaign, namely through public statements, lobbying activities and information sharing, a form of support that helped raise additional votes. [29]

In sum, this overview shows that Angola has only provided partial or limited political shelter to Portugal, one which has been more significant in diplomatic than security terms. As seen above, their bilateral relationship evolved in a tense and unbalanced manner for a long period after decolonisation, with the former colonial master being a clearer source of political shelter for its ex-colony than the other way round. While Portugal provided important diplomatic, military and administrative support for the peace and stabilisation process of Angola, the latter's stark internal difficulties throughout that phase were a blatant constraint for more reciprocal cooperation and support. Later, Angola's increased stability and self-confidence opened room for potentially greater cooperation, both at a bilateral and multilateral level. But although a more win-win picture eventually emerged, important challenges endured. The deep hardship Portugal went through in the early 2010s in the context of the Eurozone crisis provided a key opportunity and test for Angola's support. While Portuguese representatives clearly sought shelter from its ex-colony on that occasion (mainly economic, but to a lesser extent also political), Luanda's level of support was, however, less evident. In fact, whereas a degree of post-colonial sensitivity continued to complicate the bilateral relationship, Angola's portfolio of international partners had meanwhile expanded. Moreover, the important degree of cooperation and mutual support achieved at multilateral level has been far from unlimited or devoid of difficulties. In reality, Angola's growing international ambitions and agency also made some divergent interests between Luanda and Lisbon more evident, namely within the CPLP. [30] These general trends and challenges are likely to continue in the foreseeable future.

---

[27] The 'strategic partnership' process was suspended in 2013 due to Portuguese judicial investigations on corruption and money laundering involving members of the Angolan elite. Later, the bilateral relationship was complicated by other diplomatic 'irritants' that were only overcome around 2018 through a series of reciprocal high-level visits and new agreements.

[28] Portugal had already received similar support for its 1997–1998 temporary Security Council seat. See Seabra (2019, pp. 86–87).

[29] See Cravinho (2010, p. 29).

[30] See, for instance, Seabra and Gorjão (2011, p. 11), Seabra (2019, p. 85).

7.3 Economic Shelter: Significant Cooperation, Rather than Direct Support

This second section deals with the evolution of Portugal's relations with Africa in the economic domain. More specifically, it examines the extent to which Portugal has looked to Angola for economic shelter in recent times. Economic shelter refers to economic assistance or other forms of economic support, such as favourable market access, beneficial loans or a currency union, provided by another state or international organisation. [31] As mentioned above, Africa only gained more importance for Portugal in the late nineteenth century, against a background of acute domestic difficulties and increased geopolitical competition among European empires. Angola was considered the 'crown jewel' of Portugal's colonial project in Africa, namely due to its extended territory and valuable natural resources such as cotton, coffee, diamonds and oil. It was also the colony that received the greatest number of Portuguese settlers, attracted by the rapid economic growth the territory experienced in the context of the Second World War. In the 1950s, Angola accounted for almost half of Portugal's colonial trade, which in turn represented around 25% and 14% of the country's total exports and imports respectively. [32] But while Portugal's colonial project worked as a kind of domestic 'buffer' against external economic shocks and pressures, Britain was Portugal's main economic shelter throughout this period due to its central importance in terms of trade, foreign investment or financial assistance. [33] By the 1960s, significant changes in Portugal's society and economy were starting to move the country's external orientation away from its African Empire. Even though the colonies continued to be important suppliers of raw materials and critical markets for less competitive Portuguese goods, with the country's increased industrialisation and liberalisation, its external economic relations became increasingly centred in Western Europe.

Similar to other domains, Portugal's economic relations with Africa in the post-colonial era have been mainly concentrated in the five Lusophone countries, with Angola occupying a preeminent place. [34] The overall importance of these economic ties has been relatively small, namely in comparison with Europe, which has been a clearer economic shelter for the country. [35] But despite lagging far behind the significance of other markets, Portugal's economic relations with Africa have still been highly valued, namely for diversification reasons bearing in mind that they take place outside the competitive European context. In fact, the five ex-colonies (especially Angola) have represented important markets for many Portuguese companies, which have kept significant shares of specific sectors of these economies, very often

---

[31] See Thorhallsson and Steinsson (2019, p. 25).

[32] Ferreira (2005).

[33] Telo (2008, p. 237).

[34] See Mah (2019).

[35] For instance, in 2016 Africa was the second regional destination for Portuguese exports (around 8% of total), but far behind Europe (around 80% of total). See Mah (2019, p. 126).

taking advantage of historical, cultural or personal ties. [36] As noted by some observers, these companies, together with other Portuguese interest groups, have been very influential and efficient in shaping Portugal's policy towards Angola. [37] In intimate conjunction with the broader role Angola plays for Lisbon's diplomacy, these factors have led Portuguese authorities to consistently support the reinforcement of bilateral economic ties.

Decolonisation led to a sharp decrease in Portugal's economic links in Africa. While the country's past preferential arrangements in the continent came to an end, the ensuing civil wars in its largest ex-colonies as well as the more general instability and fragilities of their economies further deteriorated the significance of these economic ties. [38] Although not substantial, Portugal started to provide assistance to its former African colonies soon after decolonisation. Such Portuguese support is all the more significant as it started when the country was itself a recipient of foreign assistance. [39] Portugal's accession to the EU in 1986 and its subsequent participation in the Euro currency strongly reinforced the country's economic integration in Europe. Another implication was that Portugal's economic relations in Africa became partly framed by EU common mechanisms and norms, namely regarding external trade and aid. [40] Under its new European status, Portugal's aid efforts towards its former African colonies were also stepped up, both at bilateral and multilateral levels. Whereas the economic liberalisation and prospects of greater stability in some of the Lusophone African countries in the early 1990s led to an increase in Portuguese investments, trade levels remained low. [41] By the same token, economic cooperation at the CPLP level has struggled to produce tangible results. Intra-bloc exchanges have been constrained by geographical distance, different development levels among its members and their respective engagement in distinct regional blocs. With few resources available, the organisation's main added value in this area has been one of facilitating the exchange of information and experiences to favour greater cooperation among its members. [42] This general pattern of cooperation was partly modified in the context of the economic difficulties Portugal went through from the turn of the century.

Under the severe effects of the post-2008 global and Euro area crises, Portuguese decision-makers prioritised economic diplomacy matters and the intensification of relations with extra-European partners, namely with Lusophone countries and China.[43] This emphasis was particularly conspicuous under the centre-right Portuguese government of Pedro Passos Coelho that steered the country through the worst

[36] Ferreira (2002).

[37] Soares de Oliveira (2005, pp. 61–62), Vines (2012, p. 374).

[38] Ferreira (2002).

[39] Between 1975 and 1991 Portugal was on the OECD list of developing countries.

[40] See Raimundo (2013b).

[41] For example, in 1995 Lusophone Africa only represented 2.7% of Portugal's total exports.

[42] Hewitt et al. (2017, pp. 300–304).

[43] See, for example, Sousa and Gaspar (2015).

of its financial crisis during the Troika years (2011–2014). [44] This government's programme expressly stated that "Portugal must invest in the consolidation and deepening of the CPLP, intensifying trade, services and investment relations aimed at building a large economic space". [45] The document also stressed the idea of reinforcing bilateral relations with individual Lusophone countries, notably with Angola which at the time happened to have one of the fastest-growing economies in the world due to high international prices for its rising oil production. More explicit evidence of Portugal's shelter-seeking behaviour was visible during Prime Minister Passos Coelho's visit to Angola in November 2011, when he was quoted as saying: "[w]e should take advantage of this moment of financial and economic crisis to strengthen our bilateral relations". [46] One form of economic support expressly sought from Angola on that occasion was the facilitation of Portuguese exports. Indeed, in the context of the adoption of a new customs tariff for Angolan imports, Prime Minister Passos Coelho mentioned: "[w]e wish that this could be done without creating an additional problem at a time when we are going through great difficulties". [47] He also expressed the hope for "some opening with regard to Portuguese exporters", defending that "some time should be given so that they could adjust to this process". [48]

A few indicators further demonstrate the importance Angola came to have for Portugal in the context of the latter's economic crisis. Supported by a series of credit lines, Portuguese exports to Angola grew considerably, more than tripling between 2004 and 2009 (see Fig. 7.1). Subsequently the level of exports suffered from the effects of the global recession, but it remained significantly high until 2014 when the sharp fall of global oil prices started to have a stronger effect on Angola's economy and its capacity to pay for imports. Also significant, between 2004 and 2008 Angola moved from the ninth to the fourth position as the main destination for Portuguese exports, remaining Portugal's main market outside the EU until 2014. [49] That same year, 9440 Portuguese companies exported to Angola, most of them small and for

---

[44] In order to cope with its financial crisis, in May 2011 Portugal signed a 78 billion euros Economic Adjustment Programme with the European Commission, the European Central Bank and the International Monetary Fund (IMF) that lasted until June 2014.

[45] Governo de Portugal (2011), Programa do XIX Governo Constitucional, p. 107. All quotations in this article originating from non-English sources are the author's own translation.

[46] BBC: "Angola's Eduardo dos Santos offers help to Portugal", 18.11.2011. https://www.bbc.com/news/world-africa-15790127. Accessed 4 July 2023.

[47] Lusa: "Passos Coelho espera 'abertura' relativamente a nova pauta aduaneira a adoptar por Luanda". In Público, 17.11.2011. https://www.publico.pt/2011/11/17/politica/noticia/passos-coelho-espera-abertura-relativamente-a-nova-pauta-aduaneira-a-adoptar-por-luanda-1521408. Accessed 4 July 2023.

[48] Ibid.

[49] In 2015, Angola was replaced by the USA as Portugal's main market outside the EU and by 2019 it was again occupying the ninth position as the main destination for Portuguese exports. Source: AICEP Portugal Global, Angola - Ficha de Mercado (2009, 2014, 2015).

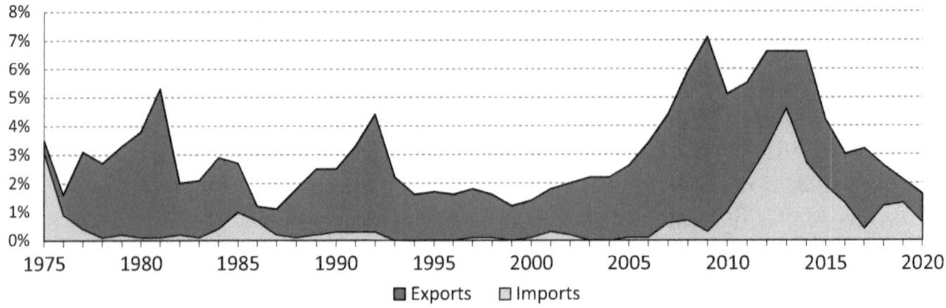

Fig. 7.1 Portugal's trade with Angola, 1975–2020 (% of total). Source: author's calculations based on Banco de Portugal statistics

whom that country was their only export market. [50] Portuguese migration to Angola also increased drastically during this phase, comprising mainly qualified workers trying to escape the crisis in Portugal. In 2009, almost 24,000 Portuguese moved to Angola, compared with less than 200 in 2006. [51] The ex-colony became the main destination for Portuguese emigration outside the EU, with press accounts pointing to around 200,000 Portuguese citizens living there in 2013. That year, Portuguese workers in Angola sent around 300 million euros back to their cash-starved homeland, the highest amount of remittances sent from Africa, but still far from the ones coming from European countries such as France or Switzerland. [52] These figures subsequently decreased with the slowdown of the Angolan economy.

Another revealing indicator was the important rise in Portuguese investments in Angola. According to official data, between 2004 and 2009 the African country moved from fifteenth (1% share) to third position (9% share) as favourite destination for Portuguese foreign investments. [53] More impressive still was the sharp increase in Angolan investments in Portugal, which during the same period went from just 4 million euros to 116 million euros. [54] Despite representing a small share of Portugal's total inward investment, this increased Angolan presence included substantial stakes in strategic sectors such as banking, energy, telecoms and media and it helped many Portuguese companies survive during the economic crisis. [55] However, the association of some of these investments to alleged corruption cases as well as

---

[50] Luís Villalobos, Mais de 5000 empresas dependem a 100% de Angola para exportar, Público, 22.06.2015. https://www.publico.pt/2015/06/22/economia/noticia/mais-de-5000-empresas-dependem-a-100-de-angola-para-exportar-1699691. Accessed 4 July 2023.

[51] Raphael Minder: "Portugal Turns to Former Colony for Growth". In New York Times, 13.07.2010.

[52] Público: "Remessas dos portugueses a trabalhar nos PALOP subiram 13.6% para 316 milhões", 24.03.2014. https://www.publico.pt/2014/03/24/economia/noticia/remessas-dos-portugueses-a-trabalhar-nos-palop-subiram-136-para-316-milhoes-1629528. Accessed 4 July 2023.

[53] AICEP Portugal Global, Angola - Ficha de Mercado (2009, 2014).

[54] Ibid.

[55] See, for instance, Costa et al. (2015).

the widespread discussion about a potential 'reverse colonisation' were arguably less positive ramifications for Portugal's reputation and status. [56] Similar to the other economic indicators above, these reciprocal investments lost steam with the slow-down of the Angolan economy from 2014 onwards, especially Portuguese outward investments in Angola. In fact, as these renewed Angolan difficulties coincided with the recovery of Portugal's economic situation, the old pattern of cooperation between the two countries gained ground once again. For instance, in this more recent context, Luanda authorities have sought to attract Portuguese small and medium companies as well as skilled workers to support the diversification of Angola's heavily oil-dependent economy. [57] By the same token, Lisbon has supported Angola's fight against the Covid-19 pandemic as part of Portugal's wider plan of donating at least 5% of its vaccines to a small group of countries comprising all its former African colonies. [58]

Summing up, the analysis shows that Angola has only provided a limited economic shelter to Portugal in contemporary times. Similar to the previous section's findings, the former colonial master has represented a clearer economic shelter for its ex-colony than vice versa. Since decolonisation, Portugal has consistently supported Angola economically, both through its bilateral instruments and in different multi-lateral bodies. Although such support lost part of its relative importance over time due to Angola's increased options (including important economic partners such as China), it contrasts with the limited assistance that has been reciprocated. For most of the period examined above, Angola's relevance to Portugal in the economic domain was derived mainly from the opportunities of cooperation between the two countries (of a secondary rank), and not so much from Angolan direct support. Only under the exceptional circumstances of Portugal's recent economic crisis was a clear shelter-seeking behaviour visible vis-à-vis the former colony. While the degree of shelter Portugal effectively received is less evident, the economic cooperation between the two sides did intensify during this phase and played a part in the country's economic recovery, providing a 'safety valve' for many Portuguese companies and workers. However, this contribution was not comparable to the substantive direct economic assistance Portugal received from the EU and the IMF during the crisis. Nor was it devoid of costs for Portugal's image and status, as described above. Yet these costs may have been perceived as less significant than the ones derived from the Troika's bailout conditionality. Besides, the indirect support Portugal received from Angola proved short-lived as the subsequent reversal of fortune meant the ex-colonial power was soon back to its more traditional role of

[56] Norimitsu Onishi: "Portugal Dominated Angola for Centuries. Now the Roles Are Reversed". In New York Times, 22.08.2017, https://www.nytimes.com/2017/08/22/world/europe/angola-portugal-money-laundering.html. Accessed 4 July 2023.

[57] Luís Villalobos: "Angola já pagou 176 milhões de euros de dívidas a empresas portuguesas". In Público, 7.03.2019, https://www.publico.pt/2019/03/07/economia/noticia/angola-ja-pagou-176-milhoes-euros-dividas-empresas-portuguesas-1864561. Accessed 4 July 2023.

[58] By December 2021, Portugal had already sent more than 1.8 million vaccine doses to Angola.

backer, rather than recipient of economic support from its ex-colony. This general pattern of cooperation is unlikely to suffer major changes soon.

7.4 Societal Shelter: Upholding Portugal's Status and Identity

This final section considers the evolution of Portugal's relations with Africa in the societal realm. Concretely, it examines whether and to what extent Portugal has been seeking and has received societal shelter from Angola in contemporary times. The concept of societal shelter stresses the importance of cultural transactions, in terms of the transfer of new ideas, norms, lifestyles, ideologies and myths. Such ideational interactions with foreign cultures, ideas and ideologies allow small states to overcome problems that stem from a lack of native knowledge in their small communities and also to avoid isolation and social stagnation. Additionally, small states value relations with other societies in order to obtain recognition of their own status and to ensure their ontological security. [59] Africa has historically been an important source of collective myths and ideologies in Portugal. [60] In the nineteenth century, in particular, under a context of national difficulties and growing imperial competition, Portugal's colonial project in Africa was idealised as an 'El Dorado' and as part of the 'sacred heritage' of the 'Golden Age of Discovery' that needed to be preserved. A sense of vulnerability also fed an imperial nationalism in the country that saw in the African Empire a means to boost its self-image and secure some international prestige.

In the twentieth century, Portugal's authoritarian New State regime actively promoted an imperial mentality among the Portuguese through the educational system, publications, films and public events. These propaganda efforts, made easier by a censorship system, contributed to an increase in Portuguese emigration to the colonies, notably to Angola which, as seen above, was the territory that received the greatest number of white settlers. [61] Moreover, against the growing post-war international pressures for decolonisation, the authoritarian regime tried to legitimise its colonial rule by propagating an instrumentalised version of 'Lusotropicalist' ideas depicting Portugal's colonialism as unprejudiced and open to miscegenation. [62] Some of that exceptionalism and cultural myths would have long-term repercussions in Portuguese society and in the country's international agency, as further explained below. Despite the relevance of those ideas and social interactions related to an African colonial presence, the notion of a societal shelter for Portugal during this

[59] See Thorhallsson and Steinsson (2019, p. 25).

[60] See, for instance, Alexandre (2003), Pinto and Bandeira Jerónimo (2015).

[61] The number of white inhabitants in Angola went from 40,000 in 1940 to 173,000 in 1960. See Alexandre (2003, p. 76).

[62] Castelo (2011).

phase is more easily associated to the strong cultural influence exerted by Western countries, such as England, France, Germany and the United States. In fact, Portugal's colonial ties in Africa, especially under authoritarian rule, can partly be seen as an inward-looking reaction or a form of resistance to such external influences. A reaction that arguably ended up producing more, rather than less, isolation and social stagnation.

After its change of regime and decolonisation in 1974–1975, Portugal's main societal shelters continued to be Western states and organisations, which played an important supportive role in the country's democratisation and modernisation processes. These dimensions of rapid political and social transformation, triggered by the Carnation Revolution, built on broader trends of Westernisation and Europeanisation that were again accelerated by the country's accession to the EU in the mid-1980s. In that context, Europe came to be seen domestically as a kind of material and symbolic compensation for the lost colonial empire and the implied status loss. [63] But while decolonisation represented a departure from Portugal's past in Africa and other external references gained more centrality in the country's outlook, significant post-colonial ties and legacies endured, especially ideational, cultural and social ones. Having moved from imperial power to small state status, Portugal's main democratic elites redefined the country's international identity as Euro-Atlantic, balancing a new European priority with the permanence of traditional Atlantic ties and enhanced relations with former colonies. [64] As regards Portugal's self-conceptions towards Portuguese-speaking Africa, in particular, there was no complete break with the past. Colonial cultural myths lost importance, but were not fully abandoned. [65] They were rather refashioned as a sort of 'Neo-Lusotropicalism' discourse depicting Portugal as "naturally adept at managing post-colonial relations" and as "a particularly able 'bridge-building' state". [66] Moreover, the emergence of a related Lusophony narrative, emphasising the linguistic and cultural bonds between Portugal and its ex-colonies, entailed the "continuation of a form of colonial imagination without an empire". [67] Driven partly by identity and status concerns, these ideas and social imaginary had a profound impact on Portugal's post-colonial reengagement and broader agency on African affairs, gaining added weight during periods of crisis in other dimensions of the country's international identity.

Portugal's post-colonial societal ties with Africa have been closely related to its ex-colonies and, to a lesser extent, South Africa, where a relatively large Portuguese community has lived. One of the main social implications of decolonisation was the return of more than half a million former Portuguese settlers (mostly from Angola), but also thousands of demobilised soldiers and Africans who had served the colonial regime. This massive flow of people, together with subsequent immigration waves

---

[63] Pinto and Teixeira (2002).

[64] Teixeira (2003, pp. 113–118).

[65] See MacQueen (2003a), Pinto and Bandeira Jerónimo (2015, p. 110), Reis and Oliveira (2018).

[66] Reis and Oliveira (2018, pp. 633, 638).

[67] Pinto and Bandeira Jerónimo (2015, p. 111).

from the ex-colonies, contributed to the social, cultural and ethnic diversity of Portuguese society as well as to the endurance of plural and selective memories of empire. [68] On the African side, the decision by the newly independent former Portuguese colonies to keep the old colonial master's idiom as their official language (chiefly as a tool of national unity and external differentiation in their region) favoured the post-colonial reengagement and ensuing collaboration with Portugal. In terms of sociocultural cooperation, what stands out is the important support Lisbon has provided to Portuguese-speaking African states through its bilateral aid in social sectors such as education as well as its cultural diplomacy aimed at promoting the Portuguese language and culture in those countries. [69] By encompassing the transfer and diffusion of Lusophone ideas and norms, this level of assistance has also comprised a dimension of self-help for Portugal. Such complex dynamics of bidirectional societal sheltering effects have been equally visible at multilateral level. For instance, Portugal's advocacy for greater support to Africa in Brussels has simultaneously represented a way to assert the country's specific international identity and an attempt to reinforce its status by playing a facilitator role in EU-Africa relations. [70] Similarly, Portugal's active promotion of the Lusophone community has helped sustain a wide platform for the communication of values and myths linked to a shared heritage that, in turn, has buttressed the country's singularity and relevance in the world. [71]

As seen before, Portugal's emphasis on its post-colonial ties was intensified in the context of the 2008 global financial meltdown and subsequent Eurozone crisis. Under these harsh circumstances and unprecedented difficulties on the European front, Portuguese discourses and narratives linked to the Lusophone World gained force as a complement and, in some cases, even as a rival to the country's European identity. [72] Old cultural myths and Portugal's 'glorious' maritime past were then often evoked in public statements by top political representatives as "a source of comfort and dignity". [73] Moreover, the intensification of economic relations and renewed flows of people between Portugal and its ex-colonies over this period helped nurture cultural and personal ties. As described in the previous section, this was particularly the case concerning Angola, with Portuguese media playing an important role in consolidating the African country's visibility and position within Portuguese society. [74] This 'Angolanisation' went together with a degree of

[68] In 2010, there were around 150,000 to 200,000 Africans living in Portugal, but their visibility was limited (except in domains such as sports or popular culture) and they suffered from social exclusion, thus exposing the limits of Lusotropicalism. See Eaton (2003), Buettner (2016), Vines (2012, p. 380).

[69] See, for instance, Carvalho (2019).

[70] See Vines (2012), Raimundo (2014, 2020).

[71] Sá (2015, p. 58), Zúquete (2013, p. 213).

[72] See Ashby (2017), Zúquete (2013, p. 222), Reis and Oliveira (2018, pp. 647–648).

[73] Buettner (2016, pp. 489–490).

[74] See Figueiras (2021).

de-Europeanisation of Portugal's external relations - a shift also visible in other EU states during this period of crisis. [75] However, this level of shelter-seeking towards Angola was temporary as it subsequently waned, in a trend similar to the one identified in previous sections. Moreover, a stronger version of this attachment was only present among certain sectors of Portuguese society, since the idea of complementarity between different sources of identification prevailed at the official level. Nonetheless, there have been some signs of difficulty in that reconciliation, visible, for instance, in the tension between European and Angolan norms and governance standards alluded to in the previous section, which in turn points to the costs of this sheltering.

Overall, Angola has only supplied a limited societal shelter to Portugal, one which has been more meaningful in terms of the country's status and ontological security than as a source of scientific knowledge and innovation. For these latter aspects, the country has counted on other more significant sources of support and has itself been a clearer shelter for Angola than vice versa. Moreover, the partial societal support Portugal has received from its ex-colony has been intimately linked to broader ideational frames, particularly the Lusophony, which gained more salience and relevance during the recent period of uncertainty and crisis in Europe. Understood as a complement to other sources of identification, this Lusophone dimension has been a central and stable component of the country's identity.

7.5 Conclusion

This chapter set out to examine the importance of Africa for contemporary Portuguese foreign policy from a shelter theory perspective. More specifically, it examined whether and to what extent Portugal has been seeking and has received political, economic and societal shelter from its largest former African colony Angola. The analysis above showed that Angola has only provided a limited or partial shelter to Portugal in all three sectoral dimensions examined. As a source of political shelter, Luanda's support was more relevant in diplomatic than security terms, translated notably in a significant degree of backing within the CPLP and the UN. In the economic domain, Angola's importance was mainly derived from opportunities of bilateral cooperation and not so much from instances of direct support. Finally, as a societal shelter, Angola appeared as more important in supporting Portugal's international status and sense of identity than as a source of knowledge and innovation.

While it is difficult to assess the relative relevance of these three dynamics, an effort in that direction could arguably rank the societal dimension first, followed by the political and economic dimensions, in that order. Still, for all three dimensions Portugal has been a clearer shelter for its former colony than the other way round. Moreover, in all domains Portugal has counted on more evident and significant

[75] See Raimundo et al. (2021).

shelters, such as NATO (security), the EU (economics) and the CPLP (societal). Although the importance of Angola as a potential shelter has tended to increase over time, the assistance it provided to Portugal during the recent Eurozone crisis was still limited. Furthermore, Angola's support has not been devoid of some costs (namely reputational) for its old colonial master, an aspect that future research could develop further.

Ultimately, Africa is a domain where Portugal has perceived itself as *less small*, mainly due to its long and rich history of external engagement. With decolonisation, the country lost status but some echoes of its past grandeur endured, especially for matters related to Africa and the Lusophone World. Portugal's involvement in numerous relevant multilateral arenas helped sustain the country's ambitions and initiatives towards the African continent. Simultaneously, despite the overly optimistic perspectives often noticeable in some Portuguese quarters regarding Angola's evolution, the country has so far remained too weak to be able to provide Portugal with comprehensive shelter, especially in economic and political terms as well as beyond periodic moments of crisis. This points to the limits of Angola as a shelter as well as the interest in deepening the analysis of different views and expectations towards Angola within Portuguese society.

Notwithstanding all the above, it is still significant that a former colonial power turned to one of its ex-colonies in Africa in search of economic support during a national crisis. While other ex-metropoles, including larger ones such as Britain and France, appear to have sought forms of diplomatic or ideational support from ex-colonies in the Global South, dynamics of economic shelter-seeking seem more unusual in this context. In the same vein, Angola's relevance as a shelter for Portugal becomes more significant when the connections between the former and other sources of shelter such as the CPLP or the EU are considered; another aspect that future studies could further explore. Conceptually, these empirical results point to the existence of different degrees and complex dynamics of shelter, including bidirectional simultaneous sheltering effects, instances of shelter reversal and linkages across different sources of shelter. As a whole, these results provide a new, up-to-date and nuanced interpretation of Portugal's contemporary relations in Africa, one which is also theoretically-informed, contextualised and evidence-based, contributing to Portuguese foreign policy studies and to the broader literature on small states foreign policy.

Acknowledgements The author would like to thank Pedro Seabra who commented on an earlier draft of this chapter. This work was supported by the Fundação para a Ciência e a Tecnologia (FCT) under Grant UIDB/CPO/00758/2020 and Grant SFRH/BPD/99579/2014.

References

Alexandre V (2003) The colonial empire. In: Pinto AC (ed) Contemporary Portugal. Politics, society and culture. SSM-Columbia University Press, New York, pp 63–84

Ashby S (2017) The Lusophone world: the evolution of Portuguese national narratives. Sussex Academic Press, Brighton
Ball J (2017) The history of Angola. Oxford Research Encyclopedia of African History. https://doi.org/10.1093/acrefore/9780190277734.001.0001/acrefore-9780190277734-e-180. Accessed 4 July 2023
Buettner E (2016) Europe after empire: decolonization, society, and culture. Cambridge University Press, Cambridge
Carvalho C (2018) Africa and Portugal. In: Nagar D, Mutasa C (eds) Africa and the world: bilateral and multilateral international diplomacy. Palgrave Macmillan, Cham, pp 143–165
Carvalho C (2019) A cooperação Portugal-PALOP no domínio da educação: um instrumento de soft power para a política externa portuguesa? In: Raimundo A (ed) Política Externa Portuguesa e África: Tendências e Temas Contemporâneos. Centro de Estudos Internacionais do ISCTE-IUL, Lisboa, pp 141–165
Castelo C (2011) O Modo Português de Estar no Mundo: O Luso-Tropicalismo e a Ideologia Colonial Portuguesa (1933–1961), 2nd edn. Edições Afrontamento, Porto
Costa JPO et al (2014) História da Expansão e do Império Português. Esfera dos Livros, Lisboa
Costa J et al (2015) Os Donos Angolanos de Portugal. Bertrand Editora, Lisboa
Cravinho JG (2010) A Campanha Portuguesa para o Conselho de Segurança. Relações Internacionais 28:5–37
Cravo T d A (2012) Consolidating partnerships: history and geopolitics in Portugal's twenty-first century foreign policy. In: Royo S (ed) Portugal in the twenty-first century: politics, society, and economics. Lexington Books, Lanham, MD, pp 215–244
Eaton M (2003) Portugal's lusophone African immigrants: colonial legacy in a contemporary labour market. In: Lloyd-Jones S, Pinto AC (eds) The last empire: thirty years of Portuguese decolonisation. Intellect Books, Bristol, pp 99–111
Ferreira ME (2002) Portugal and the Lusophone African countries: continuities and disruptions. Portuguese Stud Rev 10(1):85–107
Ferreira ME (2005) O Império e as Relações Económicas com África. In: Lains P, d Silva ÁF (eds) História Económica de Portugal 1700–2000. Volume III. O Século XX. Imprensa de Ciências Sociais, Lisboa, pp 343–371
Figueiras R (2021) The empire strikes Back? Media freedom, public interest and neoliberalism in the aftermath of the Eurozone economic crisis. Javnost - The Public
Hewitt WE, Burges S, Gomes I (2017) The Comunidade dos Países de Língua Portuguesa at 20 years: an impact assessment. South Afr J Int Affairs 24(3):291–309
MacQueen N (1997) The decolonization of Portuguese Africa: metropolitan revolution and the dissolution of empire. Longman, London
MacQueen N (2003a) Re-defining the 'African vocation': Portugal's post-colonial identity crisis. J Contemp Eur Stud 11(2):181–199
MacQueen N (2003b) A community of illusions? Portugal, the CPLP and peacemaking in Guiné-Bissau. Int Peacekeeping 10(2):1–26
Mah L (2019) Portugal e o bazar africano: mapeando trocas comerciais, fluxos de investimento e de ajuda ao desenvolvimento. In: Raimundo A (ed) Política Externa Portuguesa e África: Tendências e Temas Contemporâneos. Centro de Estudos Internacionais do ISCTE-IUL, Lisboa, pp 121–139
Neves MS (1996) Portugal: A promoter for sub-Saharan Africa. In: Algieri F, Regelsberger E (eds) Synergy at work: Spain and Portugal in European foreign policy. Europa Union Verlag, Bonn, pp 137–163
Newitt M (2009) Portugal in European and world history. Reaktion Books, London
Oliveira PA (2016) Portuguese Empire: 2. Africa. In: MacKenzie JM et al (eds) The encyclopedia of empire. Wiley-Blackwell, New York
Oliveira PA (2017) Decolonization in Portuguese Africa. In: Spear T (ed) Oxford research encyclopedia of African history. Oxford University Press, Oxford

Pinto AC, Bandeira Jerónimo M (2015) Ideologies of exceptionality and the legacies of empire in Portugal. In: Rothermund D (ed) Memories of post-Imperial nations: the aftermath of decolonization, 1945–2013. Cambridge University Press, Cambridge, pp 97–119

Pinto AC, Teixeira NS (2002) From Africa to Europe: Portugal and European integration. In: Pinto AC, Teixeira NS (eds) Southern Europe and the making of the European Union, 1945–1980s. Columbia University Press, New York, pp 3–40

Raimundo A (2013a) The Europeanisation of foreign policy: an assessment of the EU impact on Portugal's post-colonial relations in sub-Saharan Africa. Eur Integ Online Pap 17(1):1–23

Raimundo A (2013b) Between Europeanisation and domestic influences: Portugal's post-colonial relations with Angola. J Contemp Eur Res 9(2):242–260

Raimundo A (2014) Mapping the agency of a small, former colonial power: Portugal and EU political conditionality in sub-Saharan Africa. Perspect Eur Polit Soc 15(4):589–605

Raimundo A (ed) (2019a) Política Externa Portuguesa e África: Tendências e Temas Contemporâneos. Centro de Estudos Internacionais do ISCTE-IUL, Lisboa

Raimundo A (2019b) Política Externa Portuguesa e África: a necessidade de um olhar renovado. In: Raimundo A (ed) Política Externa Portuguesa e África: Tendências e Temas Contemporâneos. Centro de Estudos Internacionais do ISCTE-IUL, Lisboa, pp 13–28

Raimundo A (2020) A Presidência e as Estratégias dos Pequenos Estados: O Caso Português nas Relações UE-África [The presidency and the strategies of small states: the case of Portugal in EU-Africa relations]. Relações Internacionais (68):77–90

Raimundo A, Stavridis S, Tsardanidis C (2021) The Eurozone crisis' impact: a de-Europeanization of Greek and Portuguese foreign policies? J Eur Integr 43(5):535–550

Reis BC (2019) Decentering the cold war in southern Africa: the Portuguese policy of decolonization and Détente in Angola and Mozambique (1974-1984). J Cold War Stud 21(1):3–51

Reis BC, Oliveira PA (2018) The power and limits of cultural myths in Portugal's search for a post-Imperial role. Int Hist Rev 40(3):631–653

Robinson S (2015) Painting the CFSP in national colours: Portuguese strategies to help shape the EU's external relations. Int J Iber Stud 28(2):235–255

Sá TM, d. (2015) Política Externa Portuguesa. Fundação Francisco Manuel dos Santos, Lisboa

Santos LA (2003) Portugal and the CPLP: heightened expectations, unfounded disillusions. In: Lloyd-Jones S, Pinto AC (eds) The last empire: thirty years of Portuguese decolonisation. Intellect Books, Bristol and Portland, pp 67–81

Seabra P (2011) A safe bet: Portuguese technical-military cooperation with Lusophone Africa. IPRIS Viewpoints 39

Seabra P (2019) Um produto de tempos passados? Portugal e África no domínio político-diplomático. In: Raimundo A (ed) Política Externa Portuguesa e África: Tendências e Temas Contemporâneos. Centro de Estudos Internacionais do ISCTE-IUL, Lisboa, pp 73–99

Seabra P, Abdenur AE (2018) Age of choice or diversification? Brazil, Portugal, and capacity-building in the Angolan armed forces. Afr Security 11(3):252–273

Seabra P, Gorjão P (2011) Intertwined paths: Portugal and rising Angola. SAIIA Occasional Paper 89

Soares de Oliveira R (2005) Sobre as relações entre Portugal e Angola ao fim de trinta anos: um ensaio crítico. Relações Internacionais 8:55–72

Soares de Oliveira R (2015) Magnificent and beggar land: Angola since the civil war. Oxford University Press, Oxford

Sousa T, Gaspar C (2015) Portugal, a União Europeia e a crise. [Portugal, the European Union and the crisis] Relações Internacionais (R:I) 48:99–114

Tavares R, Bernardino LB (2011) Speaking the language of security: the Commonwealth, the Francophonie and the CPLP in conflict management in Africa. Conflict Security Dev 11(5): 607–636

Teixeira NS (2003) Between Africa and Europe: Portuguese foreign policy, 1890-2000. In: Pinto AC (ed) Contemporary Portugal. Politics, society and culture. SSM-Columbia University Press, New York, pp 85–118

Telo AJ (1996) Portugal e a NATO: O Reencontro da Tradição Atlântica. Cosmos, Lisboa

Telo AJ (2008) História Contemporânea de Portugal: do 25 de Abril à Actualidade, vol II. Editorial Presença, Lisboa

Thorhallsson B (2018) Studying small states: a review. Small States Territories 1(1):17–34

Thorhallsson B, Steinsson S (2019) A theory of shelter. In: Thorhallsson B (ed) Small states and shelter theory: Iceland's external affairs. Routledge, Abingdon, pp 24–58

Venâncio M, Chan S (1996) Portuguese diplomacy in southern Africa: 1974–1994. South African Institute of International Affairs, Braamfontein

Venâncio M, McMillan C (1993) Portuguese mediation of the Angolan conflict in 1990-1. In: Chan S, Jabri V (eds) Mediation in southern Africa. Macmillan, London, pp 100–116

Vines A (2012) Portugal, the EU, and Africa. In: Adebajo A, Whiteman K (eds) The EU and Africa: from Eurafrique to Afro-Europa. C. Hurst & Co, London, pp 365–384

Zúquete JP (2013) Between land and sea: Portugal's two nationalisms in the twenty-first century. In: Manuel PC et al (eds) Religion and politics in a global society: comparative perspectives from the Portuguese-speaking world. Lexington Books, Lanham, pp 205–226

António Raimundo is Research Fellow at the Research Centre in Political Science of University of Minho and Associate Fellow at the Centre for International Studies of ISCTE-University Institute of Lisbon (Portugal). He holds a PhD in International Relations from the London School of Economics and Political Science. His research has covered topics such as foreign policy, Europeanization, Brexit, Europe-Africa relations and Portuguese foreign policy. He has published in journals such as *Journal of European Integration*, *Journal of Contemporary European Studies, European Politics and Society*. Recently he contributed to *The Routledge Handbook of EU-Africa Relations* (2020) and edited the volume "Política Externa Portuguesa e África: Tendências e Temas Contemporâneos" [Portuguese Foreign Policy and Africa: Contemporary Trends and Themes] (2019).

Chapter 8
Sino-Icelandic Relations

Baldur Thorhallsson and Snaefridur Grimsdottir

8.1 Introduction

Iceland's strategic location is again of importance to world powers. A new race has begun in the Arctic, and Iceland has the potential to serve as a hub on an Arctic shipping route. When Iceland felt deserted and betrayed by its traditional allies (the United States (US), member states of the European Union (EU) and the European Economic Area (EEA), and the Nordic states in the autumn of 2008, it turned to China to seek shelter at the height of the economic collapse. The Sino-Icelandic relations started to gain momentum.

This chapter aims to conduct an extensive analysis of Iceland's policy towards China and the relationship between the countries. It will analyse whether Iceland sought and has enjoyed political, economic and societal shelter from China between 1995–2022. As yet, there has been no comprehensive analysis of Sino-Icelandic relations and there are only a few studies on specific aspects of the relations.[1]

Following the introduction, the chapter is divided into three sections and a conclusion. The first section analyses whether Iceland has benefited from political shelter from China in terms of diplomatic assistance in international organisations, including Arctic cooperation. The possible economic shelter provided by China is

[1] Hauksdottir (2019), Nielsson and Hauksdottir (2020), Lanteigne (2017a, pp. 117–130), Lanteigne (2017b, pp. 60–76), Lanteigne (2010, pp. 362–380), Lanteigne (2014), Thorhallsson (2018, pp. 61–82), Hansen and Hauksdottir (2021, pp. 162–171), Lanteigne (2008, 3–17).

B. Thorhallsson (✉)
Faculty of Political Science, Centre for Small State Studies, University of Iceland, Reykjavik, Iceland
e-mail: baldurt@hi.is

S. Grimsdottir
University of Iceland, Reykjavik, Iceland

A. Cunha, B. Thorhallsson (eds.), *Small States and Big Powers*, The World of Small States 10, https://doi.org/10.1007/978-3-031-42345-1_8

then explored together with current setbacks in Sino-Iceland relations. The third section examines whether China has provided Iceland with societal shelter.

8.2 A Deserted Small State Seeking Political Shelter

As a small state in the North Atlantic, Iceland's political interests with China were scarce until the turn of the twentieth century. The opening of embassies in Reykjavík and then Beijing before the millennium was followed by frequent visits by dignitaries from both countries. Over a period of 10 years, the President of Iceland made two official visits to China, one in 1995 and the second in 2005. Jiang Zemin, the President of China, also paid an official visit to Iceland in 2002.[2]

During the height of Sino-Icelandic political relations, Iceland was the driver of increased relations. However, Iceland's capacity to maintain diplomatic relations is limited to the country's small foreign service. The Chinese government's considerable goodwill towards Iceland is demonstrated by the support it gave to the Icelandic government when it ran for a seat on the United Nations Security Council (UNSC) for 2009–2010. Even though Iceland's bid was ultimately unsuccessful, this support was extremely unusual as the great powers seldom publicly declare their support for states running for the UNSC.[3] On the other hand, Iceland backed China's attempt to obtain permanent observer status on the Arctic Council (which China had started pushing for in 2007). Following Iceland's economic collapse in the international financial crisis in 2008, the Sino-Icelandic relations took a dramatic turn. We will examine the Chinese diplomatic assistance to Iceland in the aftermath of the crash before analysing the states' numerous cooperation agreements and Arctic collaboration.

8.2.1 Political Backing in a Crisis Situation

The Icelandic government was desperate for political and economic shelter in the period leading up to the international financial crisis in 2008, during the height of the crisis and in its immediate aftermath. In the first half of the year, Iceland's long-standing allies were unwilling to provide sufficient backing to strengthen its financial sector. By the time Iceland's entire financial sector had collapsed in October 2008, the country had lost much of its political support. In the immediate aftermath of the economic collapse, Iceland requested assistance from the IMF. However, the United Kingdom (UK) and the Netherlands blocked a negotiated rescue package between Iceland and the IMF in retaliation for Iceland's refusal to compensate British and Dutch citizens who had lost investments in savings schemes operated by the failing

[2] Embassy of the People's Republic of China in the Republic of Iceland (2004).

[3] Friðriksson (2008).

Icelandic banks, known as the 'Icesave dispute'. The British and Dutch position was supported by both fellow EU member states and the Nordic states; these countries linked their loans in the IMF rescue package to the resolution of the Icesave dispute. The United States decided to remain neutral.[4] Iceland considered these actions of its main allies as a betrayal.

In despair, Iceland turned to China to explore the possibility of economic assistance. In a letter to the President of China, Hu Jintao, the President of Iceland, Ólafur Ragnar Grímsson, sought to explore all possible forms of financial assistance from China. Following these communications, the Prime Minister of Iceland and the Chinese Premier Wen Jiabao launched consultations on potential Chinese assistance to Iceland which resulted in both the Chinese President and Premier of China instructing their officials to support Iceland within the IMF.[5] Acutely aware of the stronger political relations between Iceland and China, officials in Brussels frequently asked their Icelandic counterparts what Iceland was doing with China.[6] A high-ranking official in the Icelandic government at the time stated that 'since the era of Chairman Mao, China's policy has always been not to discriminate between large and small states. This policy was made quite apparent with the government of Iceland.[7] The British-Dutch blockage of the IMF continued to push against Iceland until the Icesave dispute was closed. Meanwhile, Sino-Icelandic relations began to flourish.

The countries' discussions about Chinese assistance resulted in a currency swap agreement between the Central Bank of Iceland and the People's Bank of China, signed in 2010. For a small state, this agreement had twofold significance. Not only was it the first time China had signed a currency swap agreement with a Western state, but it was also used to show Brussels what the small island state was capable of achieving.[8] The agreement, which has since been renewed three times, in 2013, 2016 and again in 2020, is due to expire in 2025.[9] This was considered a great success by the Icelandic government since the United States' refusal to sign a currency swap agreement with Iceland in 2008 had not been received well in Reykjavík and generated disappointment amongst Icelandic officials. This situation was aggravated by the fact that the US had signed such an agreement with other states, including the United Kingdom, Japan, Germany and other Nordic States.[10]

---

[4] A former high-ranking representative of the Icelandic government, research participant interview, 26 May, 2020, Reykjavík.

[5] Ólafur Ragnar Grímsson President of Iceland 1996–2016, research participant interview, 22 May, 2020, Reykjavík.

[6] A former high-ranking representative of the Icelandic government, research participant interview, 26 May, 2020, Reykjavík.

[7] A former high-ranking representative of the Icelandic government, research participant interview, 26 May, 2020, Reykjavík.

[8] A former high-ranking representative of the Icelandic government, research participant interview, 26 May, 2020, Reykjavík.

[9] Central Bank of Iceland (2020).

[10] For instance, see Thorhallsson (2019).

Iceland's need for political backing as a small state is further illustrated by the way in which the Sino-Icelandic currency swap agreement was negotiated. The value of this agreement was of a political nature. According to the terms of the agreement, Iceland was able to purchase goods and services from China in Icelandic krónur but was unable to swap physical currency, namely Icelandic krónur, for Chinese yuan. Therefore, although the agreement did not help make payments in foreign currencies, it increased the country's credibility at the time, which was crucial since the economic crash had taken its toll on Iceland's reputation.[11]

Chinese diplomatic backing of Iceland did not sit well with Iceland's allies. US officials conveyed Washington's frustration about the currency swap agreement to Icelandic officials, claiming that China was attempting to gain political influence.[12] But the Icelandic government needed assistance from a major power and hoped that Chinese assistance would serve to gain its allies' attention and increase its trustworthiness internationally following the economic crisis. Nevertheless, as an Icelandic official stated: 'perhaps the main purpose of signing the currency swap agreement at the time was to agitate the United States, NATO and Western-Europe.'[13]

8.2.2 Groundwork for the Sino-Icelandic Relations to Blossom

Indeed, a small show of goodwill from a large state can have a big impact on a small state. Iceland's request for Chinese assistance and the following Chinese diplomatic support resulted in the signing of numerous cooperation agreements between the countries.

The most important of these was the Free Trade Agreement (FTA). Iceland became the first European country and NATO ally to sign an FTA with China, as discussed in detail in the economic shelter section. However, in 2009, the Icelandic government applied for EU membership despite knowing that success would rule out all possibility of an FTA with China, a contract the government had been working towards since 2005. Although this move temporarily halted the FTA negotiations with China, Iceland and China repeatedly indicated their desire for continued political goodwill between the countries. In 2010, Iceland voiced its support of the 'One China Policy',[14] and the two countries expressed their wish to strengthen cooperation.[15] Also in 2010, Chinese Premier Wen Jiabao accepted the

[11] A former high-ranking representative of the Icelandic government, research participant interview, 17 August, 2020, Reykjavík.

[12] A former high-ranking representative of the Icelandic government, research participant interview, 17 August, 2020, Reykjavík.

[13] A former high-ranking representative of the Icelandic government, research participant interview, 17 August, 2020, Reykjavík.

[14] Mission of the People's Republic of China to the European Union.

[15] MBL (2010).

Icelandic President's invitation to make an official visit to Iceland. Moreover, as soon as it was clear that EU membership was not on the cards, Iceland expressed its wish to continue the FTA negotiations.[16]

The case of the Sino-Iceland FTA agreement illustrates the importance to a small state, Iceland, of seeking increased political cooperation with a major power, China. Other European countries were already lining up to try and make an FTA with China, but Iceland wanted to be the first to do so.[17] Thus, the Icelandic Foreign Minister pushed for an official visit to sign the agreement even though the Prime Minister was uneasy about the timing of the visit since it was politically sensitive at the time. There had recently been negative media coverage of an attempt by a Chinese investor, Huang Nubo, to purchase a large area of land in Iceland, discussed below.[18] In fact, the official visit was postponed until the following year, 2012,[19] and the FTA was not signed until 2013.[20] However, during the visit in 2012, the Prime Ministers signed a Memorandum of Understanding (MoU) covering a wide range of topics, including geothermal-, geoscience-, and silicon-cooperation, enhanced cooperation in the Arctic,[21] a cooperation agreement on geothermal energy in developing countries,[22] and an MoU with China Development Bank on finding mutually beneficial investment opportunities for Icelandic and Chinese companies in Iceland and China.[23]

Accordingly, Iceland repeatedly reiterated its wish to strengthen political relations with China in the aftermath of the economic collapse, and this led to Iceland and China creating a foundation in which Sino-Icelandic relations had the potential to expand and blossom.

Later, in 2018, Iceland and China signed an MoU on Electronic Commerce Cooperation and another to establish a geothermal working group between the Ministry of Commerce of China and the Icelandic Foreign Ministry. The first meeting of the working group was held in October 2018.[24]

---

[16] A former high-ranking representative of the government of Iceland, research participant interview, 26 May, 2020, Reykjavík.

[17] A former high-ranking representative of the government of Iceland, research participant interview, 26 May, 2020, Reykjavík.

[18] A former high-ranking representative of the government of Iceland, research participant interview, 26 May, 2020, Reykjavík.

[19] Ministry of Foreign Affairs of the People's Republic of China (2012).

[20] MBL (2013).

[21] RÚV (2012), Jónsson et al. (2013, p. 3).

[22] RÚV (2012).

[23] Invest in Iceland.

[24] Embassy of the People's Republic of China to the Republic of Iceland (2019).

8.2.3 Arctic Cooperation

Iceland was one of the states advocating that China should be granted permanent observer status in the Arctic Council,[25] which China had been pressing for since 2007.[26] As Iceland was in the midst of negotiations for an FTA with China, it considered granting China support to be in its interest.[27] Albeit small, Iceland proved to be a valuable ally to China during these years as the Icelandic Foreign Minister sought to ease tensions between Norway and China,[28] ultimately paving the way for China to be granted permanent observer status in 2013.[29] Nevertheless, even though the relations of Iceland and China in the Arctic Council have been marginal,[30] 'China's limited presence in Iceland may have long-term strategic effects that should not be ignored',[31] as discussed below.

There is considerable debate about whether Iceland is likely to become an attractive location for a shipping hub serving the Arctic. A report on Iceland-Greenland cooperation published by the Icelandic Minister for Foreign Affairs in 2020 identifies Iceland as a valuable location for China to build such a hub.[32] The report explains that the Transpolar Sea route will be the first Arctic Sea route to open. Thus, it underpins the argument for building a shipping route in Finnafjörður, in northern Iceland.[33] However, the report also states that China has already invested in the Northern Sea route through agreements signed with Russia, for example, and that it will be difficult for Iceland to compete with a shipping hub in Norway.[34] Other studies suggest that the Northern Sea route, which is closer to Norway than Iceland, will go ahead and become a reliable shipping route earlier.[35] The Institute of Economic Studies at the University of Iceland also came to the conclusion that while the Northern Sea route remains the most reliable shipping route, it would not be economical to invest in a shipping hub in Finnafjörður. It might however become feasible once the Transpolar Sea route opens.[36] The Institute maintains that as the Transpolar Sea route will not become available for use until nearly 2050, it would be

[25] Arctic Council.

[26] Lanteigne (2014).

[27] High-ranking representatives of the Icelandic and Chinese governments, research participant interviews, May and June, 2020, Reykjavík.

[28] Thorhallsson and Grimsdottir (2021).

[29] Arctic Council.

[30] Information received from the Ministry for Foreign Affairs of Iceland, research participant interviews, 18 June, 2020, Reykjavík.

[31] Dams et al. (2020, p. 25).

[32] Government of Iceland (2020c, pp. 18–19).

[33] Government of Iceland (2020c, p. 19).

[34] Government of Iceland (2020c, p. 19).

[35] Dams et al. (2020, p. 10), Stevenson et al. (2019, p. 85), Laliberté et al. (2016, pp. 256–263).

[36] Institute of Economic Studies (2019, p. 66).

better to invest in a shipping hub in Svalbard, Norway or Russia until that time.[37] Nevertheless, the Foreign Minister's report claims that China might wish to invest in multiple shipping hubs, including in Iceland, due to the Sino-Russian discord in the Arctic.[38] This is interesting in light of a recent joint statement by China and Russia on 4 February 2022.[39] The statement provides a detailed explanation of the close cooperation between the countries and states that no areas of cooperation are off-limits. The statement also extends to the Arctic, where Xi and Putin have pledged to increase practical cooperation via the Eurasian Economic Union and China. Furthermore, direct reference is made to the idea of developing Arctic Sea Routes. China's white paper on the government's Arctic Policy of 2018[40] officially declares Beijing's intention to develop a Polar Silk Road under the aegis of the Belt and Road Initiative, in which Russia is already a participating member. However, the Belt and Road Initiative faced some setbacks following Russia's invasion into Ukraine[41]; on the other hand, China's Arctic presence, including the development of the Polar Silk Road, might benefit from Russia's decline in economic power as Russia may have reduced capabilities 'to counter Chinese influence in many of its Arctic projects'.[42] Even so, the extent to which cooperation between Russia and China is truly unlimited remains unclear, including their cooperation in the Arctic, and as such, the report by Iceland's Foreign Minister might still prove to be accurate.

8.3 Economic Shelter: Good Start and Downturn

8.3.1 The FTA and Investments

When Iceland and China launched a dialogue on the possibility of signing an FTA in 2005,[43] China considered Iceland's small size to be advantageous. Iceland was a small state with a relatively simple market structure and legal infrastructure, which served as a good case for a practice-run of drafting free trade agreements with other European countries.[44] When the FTA came into force in 2014,[45] Iceland's Foreign Minister stated that the FTA was the most important agreement Iceland had signed

[37] Institute of Economic Studies (2019, p. 45).

[38] Government of Iceland (2020c, p. 19).

[39] Leiser (2022).

[40] Belt and Road Portal (2018).

[41] Forough (2022).

[42] Eiterjord (2022).

[43] Vísir (2005).

[44] Current and former high-ranking representatives of the Icelandic and Chinese governments, research participant interview, May – September, 2020, Reykjavík.

[45] Government of Iceland (b).

since the accession to the EEA.[46] The FTA was considered to have economic benefits for Iceland's small market as trade between Iceland and China was expected to increase; indeed, by 2018 it had more than tripled.[47]

Tariff-free access within the FTA for Icelandic fish exports to China was a breakthrough, as marine products amounted to approximately 80–90% of Iceland's total exports to China.[48] However, exported goods to China were just 2.6% of all exported goods from Iceland in 2018,[49] and since Chinese imports to Iceland were increasing, the trade deficit also grew by 39% from 2014 to 2018.[50]

Several challenges remain when it comes to trade in goods with China, many of which relate to Iceland's small size. For instance, the fact that the Icelandic market is much smaller than the Chinese market means that Icelandic companies are often unable to satisfy the minimum order volumes of export products set by Chinese companies.[51] Icelandic companies also find it hard to participate in the large Chinese market. This raises the question of whether they would be better off in a smaller market where they can seek smaller business avenues.[52] Finally, the Icelandic Consumer's Association has accused Icelandic business owners of increasing their profit margin rather than extending the benefits to consumers, as the price of products fell by just 4% well below the anticipated decrease of around 8%.[53]

Moreover, the expansion of trade between the countries is limited by the small number of Icelandic companies and their production rate. For instance, Iceland and China signed an additional protocol on health certification on Icelandic lamb in 2018,[54] and three protocols on health standards were signed in 2019.[55] The additional protocol for Icelandic lamb was considered a breakthrough since China is a large importer of lamb.[56] Nevertheless, Fjallalamb, which owns one of the smallest slaughterhouses in Iceland, is the only company that meets the health standards, and the first export of Icelandic lamb to China took place 2 years after signing the protocol.[57] Notwithstanding, Icelandic companies are interested in entering the Chinese market and seem hopeful that this can come to fruition. For example, Brim and Brim Seafood (previously HB Grandi) want to export Icelandic fish to China.[58] Iceland's Carbon Recycling International has also made an agreement with

46 Finnsson (2014).
47 Government of Iceland (b).
48 Government of Iceland (2016), 3.
49 Government of Iceland (b).
50 Government of Iceland (b).
51 Sigurðardóttir (2015).
52 Sigurðardóttir (2015).
53 Geirsdóttir (2016).
54 Government of Iceland (2018).
55 Government of Iceland (2019).
56 Government of Iceland (2020d, pp. 47–48).
57 RÚV (2020).
58 Júlíusson (2019).

China's Jiangsu Sailboat Petrochemicals in 2021 to build a factory for the production of methanol through carbon dioxide recycling. The total cost of the project is estimated at 35 million USD and operations are expected to commence in 2023.[59]

Foreign Direct Investment was not negotiated as part of the FTA and remains extremely limited. In 2019, Icelandic investment in China amounted to 43 million USD whereas Chinese investment in Iceland was just 28 million USD.[60] The Icelandic Central Bank claims that no Chinese citizen owns a direct investment[61] in Iceland; however, reference is made to Elkem, which is owned by China National Blue Star and operates a smelting company in Grundartangi in Iceland.[62] Meanwhile, the Chinese embassy states that Carbon Recycling International, an investment of 14.5 million USD, is a 'breakthrough in China's direct investment in Iceland'.[63]

Even a single investment in Iceland can make a significant impact given the country's smallness. For example, when Huang Nubo, a Chinese investor, wanted to buy 306.39 square kilometres[64] of land (roughly 0.3% of Iceland's territory) in Grímsstaðir á Fjöllum near Finnafjörður (see discussion below) to build a hotel[65] in north-eastern Iceland in 2012, he claimed that the plot would eventually increase in value due to the opening of shipping routes in the Arctic.[66] This triggered considerable debate in Iceland on whether a Chinese investor should be allowed to buy such a large piece of land—an area close to a potential site of a shipping hub serving the Arctic. After a long debate, the Icelandic Ministry of Interior rejected the bid on the grounds that it did not comply with Icelandic law on foreign land ownership.[67]

8.3.2 *The Offer to Join the Belt and Road Initiative: Still on Hold*

The Icelandic government gradually became interested in the Belt and Road Initiative (BRI)[68] after its launch by President Xi Jinping in 2013 and became a founding member of the Asian Infrastructure Investment Bank (AIIB) in 2015. The idea of the

[59] Carbon Recycling International (2021).

[60] High-ranking representative of the Chinese government, research participant interview, 16 June, 2020, Reykjavík.

[61] A direct investment is when a foreign individual owns 10% or more shares in a local company.

[62] Government of Iceland (a).

[63] Embassy of the People's Republic of China in the Republic of Iceland (2019).

[64] Government of Iceland (2011).

[65] Bergsvein (2011).

[66] RÚV (2013).

[67] BBC News (2011).

[68] A high-ranking representative of the Icelandic government, research participant interview, 26 May, 2020, Reykjavík.

Belt and Road Initiative had already been discussed with Icelandic high-ranking officials before the project's launch.[69] Iceland's attitude towards the BRI was considered positive as the AIIB is seen as a supporting institution of the BRI.[70] Iceland's minister of finance and leader of the centre-right Independence Party is currently on the AIIB board of governors (each member state appoints one governor to the board).[71]

In 2018, China officially invited Iceland to participate in the BRI.[72] Iceland has not yet given a formal reply and officials from both countries have explained that Iceland will not do so unless participation brings concrete added benefits. Indeed, no other Nordic country has officially joined and the US is pressuring the Icelandic government to reject the offer.[73] This is clearly demonstrated by remarks made by former Vice President Pence and former Under Secretary Pompeo about US gratitude towards Iceland for refusing participation in the BRI,[74] undoubtedly contributing to Iceland's hesitancy to accept the BRI offer.

Huang Nubo's investments[75] and the harbour development in Finnafjörður[76] are said to be related to the BRI although there is no concrete evidence of this to date. In 2007, the Icelandic government started researching potential shipping hubs in the country.[77] In 2012, it expressed an interest in conducting an analysis (notably, in cooperation with China, Alaska and the EU) of conditions on the Transpolar Sea route.[78] In 2013, the municipal governments in the northeast of Iceland, the Icelandic engineering consultancy firm Efla, and the German company Bremenports entered into discussions on building a deep-water port in Finnafjörður. In 2019, the parties signed an agreement and developments are pending foreign investment.[79] According to a member of Parliament, building a shipping hub in Finnafjörður would enable local municipalities to seek financing and is not related to the BRI.[80]

In 2021, the Icelandic Foreign Minister drafted a bill for parliament[81] that included most of Finnafjörður in a nearby security zone under full government

[69] A high-ranking representative of the Icelandic government, research participant interview, 26 May, 2020, Reykjavík.

[70] Ólafur Ragnar Grímsson, research participant interview, 22 May, 2020, Reykjavík.

[71] Government of Iceland (2019).

[72] Embassy of the People's Republic of China in the Republic of Iceland (2018).

[73] High-ranking representatives of the Icelandic and Chinese governments, research participant interviews, May and June 2020, Reykjavík.

[74] Vísir (2019).

[75] Gunnarsson (2018).

[76] Jónsson (2019).

[77] Heiðarsson (2007).

[78] Skarphéðinsson (2013, p. 53).

[79] Efla (2019).

[80] A member of Icelandic parliament, research participant interview, 12 April, 2021, Reykjavík.

[81] Ministry for Foreign Affairs (2021).

control.[82] The move was justified by the importance of being able to react to future harbour developments in the area, which already had state security infrastructures including a radar station in close proximity.[83] Moreover, the draft bill stipulates that by declaring the area a security zone, Iceland can honour its international commitments, such as carrying out search and rescue operations, and address environmental and security concerns. The expansion of the security zone has been contested,[84] and the bill has not yet been placed before parliament. During debates in Parliament, an MP stated that the government is attempting to seek financing from NATO because the parties involved have realised that developing a shipping hub in Finnafjörður will not bring any business opportunities.[85] The Minister for Foreign Affairs has dismissed these allegations as pure fiction.[86] However, a US Admiral recently paid a visit to Iceland to explore the benefits of a small, permanent US footprint since the US is evaluating potential investment opportunities in eastern Iceland.[87] Changes in international politics have gradually affected US-Iceland relations, with the US showing more interest since the increased Chinese activity in Iceland and in the Arctic region.

8.3.3 A Setback in Sino-Icelandic Relations

Facing pressure from the US, the Icelandic government gradually shifted its policy towards China from actively seeking shelter during the financial crisis to a cautious approach during the Trump Administration era. Most recently, there have been confrontations between Iceland and China, and the Icelandic government has refrained from seeking any further shelter from the Chinese government. The countries' relations are at a standstill.

In 2019, US Secretary of State, Pompeo, stated that: 'Beijing attempts to develop critical infrastructure (. . .) in some cases, to establish a permanent Chinese security presence'.[88] The Nordic Foreign and Security Policy Report in 2020, written by Iceland's former Minister of Justice and officials at the Ministry for Foreign Affairs, raised a similar warning[89] and NATO is evaluating the challenges from China's increased military capabilities.[90]

---

[82] Friðriksson (2021).

[83] Ministry for Foreign Affairs (2021).

[84] Open government consultation with the public (2021).

[85] Jónsson (2021).

[86] Minister for Foreign Affairs (2021).

[87] MBL (2020a).

[88] US Government (2019).

[89] Bjarnason (2020, pp. 12 and 16).

[90] Government of Iceland (2021, p. 85).

Following US pressure on its allies to refrain from using Huawei telecommunication equipment,[91] Iceland's Minister for Transport and Local Government placed a bill before parliament in spring 2020 stating that any telecommunication frameworks considered sensitive for national security should be made within the EEA, or with a state that has a security cooperation agreement with Iceland.[92] The bill has not yet gone through parliament but China has voiced its disapproval to Icelandic officials.[93] Nonetheless, these disagreements did not hinder Sino-Icelandic cooperation during the Covid-19 pandemic when the countries' respective embassies had frequent communications, including via informal channels such as WeChat.[94]

In the last few years, Iceland has gradually escalated its criticisms of China's human rights violations in line with the approach taken by its traditional allies. However, Iceland did not take the initiative to criticise China on the situation in Xinjiang province during its term on the United Nations Human Rights Council (2018–2019). At the time, no state dared to take the initiative to criticise China's human rights abuses on Uyghurs for fear of facing retaliation from China.[95] However, Iceland took part in Western allies' joint efforts and signed every declaration condemning this situation. Also, Iceland has expressed its condemnation of human rights violations by the Chinese state via a joint statement to the UN Commission on Human Rights in 2019.[96] This was also reflected in a statement by the Human Rights Council in 2020, condemning the situation in Hong Kong.[97] Moreover, the Foreign Minister's reports to parliament in 2020[98] and 2021 state that the uncertainty regarding human rights in China places a shadow on the otherwise good relations between the two countries.[99] China has expressed its dissatisfaction with these remarks.[100]

Lastly, Iceland participated in the EU sanctions on four Chinese officials due to the detention of Uighurs and other Muslim minorities in Xinjiang province.[101] China placed countersanctions, including on one Icelandic citizen.[102] Iceland's Foreign Minister made a formal complaint and expressed his outrage in the national

[91] Cheshire (2020).

[92] Althingi (2020).

[93] A high-ranking representative of the Chinese government, research participant interview, 16 June, 2020, Reykjavík.

[94] High-ranking representatives of the Icelandic and Chinese governments, research participant interview, May and June 2020, Reykjavik.

[95] Information received from the Ministry for Foreign Affairs of Iceland, 15 October, 2022, Reykjavík.

[96] United Nations Human Rights Council (2019).

[97] Government of Iceland (2021, p. 29).

[98] Government of Iceland (2020b, p. 31).

[99] Government of Iceland (2021, p. 25).

[100] A high-ranking representative of the Chinese government, research participant interview, 16 June, 2020, Reykjavík.

[101] Ríkharðsdóttir (2021).

[102] Haraldsson (2020a, b), Haraldsson (2020c).

media.[103] The Chinese Embassy warned that this move 'severely undermines China-Iceland relations'.[104]

8.4 Societal Shelter: Marginal Cooperation

The extent of collaboration between Iceland and China in terms of societal relations (namely, educational, and scientific cooperation) is limited by Iceland's small size. Several moves have been made to enhance societal relations through the signing of cooperation agreements and MoUs[105] to facilitate a platform to boost academic and scientific cooperation,[106] and by encouraging cultural collaboration.[107] However, Iceland's size has meant it cannot fully participate in these initiatives and, as a result, societal cooperation between the countries, in terms of shelter theory, has not properly taken off.

Iceland's contribution to scientific exchanges between the countries has been held back because it is unable to match that of China. The countries have attempted to facilitate exchanges on various platforms through, for example, the China-Nordic Arctic Research Centre (CNARC),[108] the Polar Research Institute of China (PRIC), Arctic Council, and the Arctic Circle. Additionally, Iceland and China are cooperating in a research project focusing on natural science, namely at the Kárhóll Observatory/China-Iceland Arctic Science Observatory (CIAO), which was inaugurated in 2018.[109] However, despite initial research, the exchanges in scientific research and expertise at Kárhóll have not advanced.[110] A high-ranking representative in the Chinese government claims that: '(the reason for limited scientific cooperation in the field) is because the size of your population and number of experts (in Iceland), particularly in the area of Arctic research, are quite limited. That is the

[103] Ríkharðsdóttir (2021).

[104] Embassy of the People's Republic of China in the Republic of Iceland (2021).

[105] See for example: Memorandum of Understanding between the Government of Iceland and the Government of the People's Republic of China (2012), Government of Iceland (2013), Government of Iceland (2012).

[106] See for example: Orkustofnun (2005), and the University of Iceland has cooperation agreements with several Chinese universities. Iceland is also a participant in the Nordic Centre at Fudan University, and more.

[107] The Icelandic embassy in Beijing has a Commercial Counsellor, and Promote Iceland, a public-private company aimed at promoting Iceland business opportunities abroad, has also been very active in facilitating business between the countries, and more.

[108] China-Nordic Arctic Research Centre.

[109] Hauksdottir (2019).

[110] Information from the University of Akureyri, research participant interview, 11 May, 2020, Reykjavík.

reality. So, we (China) definitely want to see more participation from the Icelandic side'.[111] Moreover, when a Chinese state-owned company, Chinese National Offshore Oil Corporation (CNOOC), assisted Iceland's Eykon Energy in its oil exploration in the Arctic in 2014, Iceland revoked the oil exploration permits after surveys did not provide satisfactory results. This was the first time that China became involved in oil exploration in the Arctic.

Cultural and educational exchanges have also been set up but are restricted in scope. The flow of residents between the countries is low and not growing. In 2019, there were 312 Chinese nationals vis-a-vis nearly 20,000 Poles residing in Iceland.[112] Thirty-nine Icelanders were residents in China compared with over 11,000 in Denmark.[113] The University of Iceland is the only university in Iceland that teaches Chinese Studies and the number of students graduating is low. For instance, five students graduated in Chinese Studies at the University of Iceland in 2019, bringing the total number of students since the start of the programme to 50.[114] In addition, the number of exchange students between the University of Iceland and Chinese universities is low.[115] Nevertheless, Chinese students accounted for nearly 15% of graduates (90 out of 629) from the United Nations University Geothermal Training Programme (UNU-GTP) from 1979 to 2019.[116] Although the University of Iceland has signed a contract with the Confucius Institute, which has an allocated office within the University, its activity remains limited and is currently restricted primarily to language teaching.[117]

Mutual cultural activities between the countries are also sparse and mostly limited to the translation of literature.[118] The most noticeable cultural events are organised by the Chinese Embassy in Reykjavik with the Northern Lights Confucius Institute. While the number of Chinese tourists visiting Iceland has been increasing, it remains modest relative to tourists from European countries and the United States. In 2019, nearly 100,000 Chinese tourists visited Iceland (a sharp rise from less than 10,000 in 2007) compared with around 700,000 tourists from the US and 300,000 from the UK in the previous year.[119] Hence, educational, scientific, and cultural cooperation is limited to a small number of experts and students and just a few projects.

---

[111] A high-ranking representative from the Chinese government, research participant interview, 16 June, 2020, Reykjavík.

[112] Iceland Statistics Office (2021b), Registers Iceland (2019).

[113] Government of Iceland (2020a).

[114] University of Iceland (2020).

[115] University of Iceland, International Division, research participant interview, 13 June, 2020, Reykjavík.

[116] Zheng (2019).

[117] An individual with knowledge of the inner workings of the Confucius Institute, research participant interview, 14 April, 2021, Reykjavík.

[118] High-ranking representatives of the Icelandic government, research participant interview, conducted in May and June, 2020, Reykjavík.

[119] Iceland Statistics Office (2021a).

The closest Iceland-China collaboration is in geothermal energy. Arctic Green Energy Corporation (AGE), a private company in Iceland but with headquarters in Singapore, has been remarkably successful in distributing Icelandic expertise in geothermal energy in China.[120] AGE's largest cooperation project is the Sinopec Green Energy joint venture (SGE)[121] with Sinopec Energy, a Chinese state-owned company. SGE is currently the largest geothermal heating company in the world.[122] It holds approximately one third of the market shares of geothermal utilities in China and has around 700 employees working in China (although only 20 Icelandic staff members are stationed in China). AGE also contributes financially to academic research projects in Iceland, mainly within the area of geothermal energy; more specifically, it has contributed over 1 billion ISK since 2006.[123] More recently, AGE and Sinopec Star Petroleum have opened a Research and Development Centre in China in cooperation with the National Energy Authority of Iceland[124] with the aim of gathering and disseminating knowledge about geothermal energy. So far, 50 students have graduated from the centre and some of its teachers are Icelandic.[125] Although AGE is large in scale, its scope is limited to financial injections in academia in Iceland and occasional expertise consultations.

8.5 Conclusions

Iceland's policy towards China has been through four phases since 1995: building closer relations from 1995 to 2007; active shelter-seeking from 2008 to the mid-2010s; gradual deviation from shelter-seeking after the mid-2010s; and a standstill and some confrontations since 2017. Although Sino-Icelandic relations took a dramatic turn in the aftermath of the collapse of the Icelandic economy in 2008, China currently provides only limited economic shelter. Geopolitical shifts have brought policy makers in Reykjavík and Washington closer again.

Bilateral relations gradually increased during the first phase, beginning with diplomatic exchanges and concluding with the possibility of signing an FTA.

The second phase came immediately after the economic crash in October 2008, when the Icelandic government sought assistance from China and was provided with political and economic shelter, i.e. diplomatic support within the IMF, signing of a currency swap agreement, and an FTA agreement. Sino-Icelandic political, economic, and societal relations had never been closer.

---

[120] Arctic Green Energy Corporation, research participant interview, 26 April, 2021, Reykjavík.

[121] Arctic Green Energy Corporation, http://arcticgreencorp.com/

[122] Arctic Green Energy Corporation, research participant interview, 26 April, 2021, Reykjavík.

[123] Arctic Green Energy Corporation, research participant interview, 26 April, 2021, Reykjavík.

[124] National Energy Authority of Iceland (2016).

[125] Arctic Green Energy Corporation, research participant interview, 26 April, 2021, Reykjavík.

The third phase started with a gradual deviation from shelter-seeking due to breakdowns in economic, societal and political cooperation; more specifically, the FTA was not as successful as forecasted, research cooperation did not reach new heights, educational and cultural activities remained restricted, and political cooperation did not evolve.

During the fourth phase, relations gradually ground to a standstill and, more recently, there have been some confrontations. In 2018, Iceland's strategy shifted to refraining from taking a decision on joining the BRI, a hiding strategy or neutral stand within a power struggle between China and the US.[126] Iceland's policy gradually aligned itself more closely with its US, UK and Nordic allies[127] and, lately, the countries have clashed on several issues. Iceland has shown its intention to restrict telecommunication equipment in the country and exclude Chinese companies from the market. Iceland has also indicated an interest in expanding the security zone in Finnafjörður—the location of a potential shipping hub serving the Arctic. Moreover, Iceland increasingly takes part in the international condemnation of China's human rights violations and it participated in the 2021 EU sanctions against China. This is a dramatic policy shift from Iceland's active attempt to seek shelter from China in the immediate aftermath of the economic collapse of the country.

Iceland has again captured the attention of policy makers in Washington. In 2019, on the first visit by a US Secretary of State to Iceland in 11 years, State Secretary Pompeo declared that Iceland would no longer be neglected.[128] Currently, the US is increasing its activity at its former military base in Keflavík.[129] The US has also hinted that it is in favour of signing an FTA with Iceland,[130] and is willing to invest in infrastructures in eastern Iceland.[131]

To conclude, what can we learn from the fact that Iceland turned to China in times of need and when it felt deserted by its Western allies? Firstly, if liberal democracies do not assist each other in crises, they are in danger of losing their small allies to their main rivals. Secondly, Iceland's smallness has been a hindrance in building close economic and societal ties with China. Although the small size of the economy was attractive for China's experiment in making an FTA with a Western state, the small market has since stood in the way of closer economic relations. Thirdly, the Sino-Icelandic relations had the potential to flourish but as soon as Iceland's traditional ally, the United States, turned its attention back to the small entity and opposed Iceland's closer engagement with China, the opportunity for renewed relations with Washington was swiftly taken up. Finally, Iceland and China have already instituted the necessary framework to return to previous shelter-seeking relations if Iceland ever feels pressured to find a new ally.

[126] Fox (1959), Smed and Wivel (2017, pp. 79–98), Wivel and Thorhallsson (2018, pp. 266–77).

[127] MBL (2020b).

[128] Sigurðardóttir (2019).

[129] Cisneros (2020), Harðarson (2019).

[130] Viðskiptablaðið (2019).

[131] Hafstað (2019), Airforce Technology (2020), Cisneros (2020).

References

A former high ranking representative within the Icelandic government, research participant interview, 26 May, 2020, Reykjavík

A former high ranking representative within the Icelandic government, research participant interview, 17 August, 2020, Reykjavík

A high ranking representative within the Chinese government, research participant interview, 16 June, 2020, Reykjavík

A high ranking representatives within the Icelandic government, research participant interview, conducted in May and June, 2020, Reykjavík

A member of Icelandic parliament, research participant interview, 12 April, 2021, Reykjavík

A well connected individual with the inner workings of the Confucius Institute, research participant interview, 14 April, 2021, Reykjavík

Airforce Technology (2020). USAF to upgrade Naval Air Station Keflavik airfield infrastructure. https://www.airforce-technology.com/news/usaf-to-upgrade-naval-air-station-keflavik-airfield-infrastructure/. Accessed 4 July 2023

Althingi (2020) Frumvarp til laga um fjarskipti. Althingi, Reykjavík. https://www.althingi.is/altext/150/s/1354.html. Accessed 4 July 2023

Arctic Council. Criteria for Admitting Observers. https://arctic-council.org/en/about/observers/. Accessed 4 July 2023

Arctic Green Energy Corporation, research participant interview, 26 April, 2021, Reykjavík

Arctic Green Energy Corporation. http://arcticgreencorp.com/. Accessed 4 July 2023

BBC News (2011). China tycoon Huang Nubo angered by Iceland land move. https://www.bbc.com/news/world-asia-15916486. Accessed 4 July 2023

Belt and Road Portal (2018) China's Arctic Policy. https://eng.yidaiyilu.gov.cn/zchj/qwfb/46076.htm. Accessed 4 July 2023

Bergsvein JA (2011) Huang Nubo fær ekki að kaupa Grímsstaði á Fjöllum. Viðskiptablaðið. https://www.vb.is/frettir/huang-nubo-faer-ekki-ad-kaupa-grimsstadi-fjollum/67789/?q=Gr%C3%ADmssta%C3%B0ir%20%C3%A1%20fj%C3%B6llum. Accessed 4 July 2023

Bjarnason B (2020) Nordic foreign and security policy, proposals to the Nordic Foreign Ministers. Ministry for Foreign Affairs, Reykjavík

Carbon Recycling International (2021) CRI Signs Agreement with Jiangsu Sailboat for a 100,000 tons per year CO2 to Methanol Plant. Press release. https://www.carbonrecycling.is/news-media/cri-chemical-plant-project-in-china-will-recycle-150000-tons-of-co2-per-year-to-make-materials-for-solar-panels. Accessed 4 July 2023

Central Bank of Iceland (2020) Ársskýrsla. Central Bank of Iceland, Reykjavík, p 26

Cheshire T (2020) Trump and China respond to UK's ban on Huawei. Sky News. https://news.sky.com/story/uks-decision-to-ban-huawei-from-5g-networks-disappointing-12028776. Accessed 4 July 2023

China-Nordic Arctic Research Center. Member Institutions. https://www.cnarc.info/members. Accessed 4 July 2023

Cisneros M (2020) Air Force awards multiple contracts for airfield construction at NAS Keflavik. U.S. Air Force. https://www.af.mil/News/Article-Display/Article/2359356/air-force-awards-multiple-contracts-for-airfield-construction-at-nas-keflavik/ Accessed 4 July 2023

Dams T, Van Schaik L, Stoetman A (2020) Presence before power: China's Arctic Strategy in Iceland and Greenland. Clingendale report. https://www.clingendael.org/sites/default/files/2020-06/presence-before-power.pdf. Accessed 4 July 2023

Efla (2019). Samstarfssamningur undirritaður. https://www.efla.is/frettir/samstarfssamningur-undirritadur. Accessed 4 July 2023

Eiterjord T (2022) What does Russia's invasion of Ukraine mean for China in the Arctic? The Diplomat. https://thediplomat.com/2022/03/what-does-russias-invasion-of-ukraine-mean-for-china-in-the-arctic/. Accessed 4 July 2023

Embassy of the People's Republic of China in the Republic of Iceland (2019) MoU on Strengthening the Economic and Trade Cooperation between China and Iceland Signed. http://is.china-embassy.org/eng/zbgx/t227266.htm. Accessed 4 July 2023
Embassy of the People's Republic of China in the Republic of Iceland (2004) China and Iceland. http://is.china-embassy.org/eng/zgybd/t98175.htm. Accessed 4 July 2023
Embassy of the People's Republic of China in the Republic of Iceland (2018) Remarks by H.E. Ambassador Jin Zhijian at the Reception Upon Assuming the Post and Celebrations of Chinese New Year. http://is.china-embassy.org/eng/zbgx/rwjl/t1536495.htm. Accessed 4 July 2023
Embassy of the People's Republic of China in the Republic of Iceland (2021) Chinese Embassy Spokesperson's Statement on China's Sanctions on One Relevant Icelandic Individual. http://is.china-embassy.org/eng/zbgx/t1869512.htm. Accessed 4 July 2023
Embassy of the People's Republic of China to the Republic of Iceland (2019) Sino-Icelandic Economic and Trade Relationship. http://is.china-embassy.org/eng/zbgx/jmgx/t1653166.htm. Accessed 4 July 2023
Finnsson K (2014) Viðskiptablaðið. Fríverslunarsamningur við Kína tekur gildi í dag. https://www.vb.is/frettir/friverslunarsamningur-vid-kina-tekur-gildi-i-dag/106949/?q=%C3%96ssur%20Skarph%C3%A9%C3%B0insson Accessed 4 July 2023
Forough M (2022) What Will Russia's Invasion of Ukraine Mean for China's Belt and Road? https://thediplomat.com/2022/03/what-will-russias-invasion-of-ukraine-mean-for-chinas-belt-and-road/. Accessed 4 July 2023
Fox AB (1959) The power of small states diplomacy in World War II. University of Chicago Press, Chicago
Friðriksson G (2008) Saga af Forseta. Mál og menning, Reykjavík, p 462
Friðriksson Ó (2021) Öryggissvæðið stækki um 677 hektara. https://www.mbl.is/frettir/innlent/2021/03/10/oryggissvaedid_staekki_um_677_hektara/. Mbl. Accessed 4 July 2023
Geirsdóttir I (2016) Afnám tolla hefur ekki skilað sér. Morgunblaðið. https://www.mbl.is/frettir/innlent/2016/05/11/afnam_tolla_hefur_ekki_skilad_ser/. Accessed 4 July 2023
Government of Iceland (2011) Ákvörðun vegna erindis um jarðakaup. Ministry of Justice. https://www.stjornarradid.is/efst-a-baugi/frettir/stok-frett/2011/11/25/Akvordun-vegna-erindis-um-jardakaup/. Accessed 4 July 2023
Government of Iceland (2012) Samningar undirritaðir að viðstöddum forsætisráðherrum Íslands og Kína í dag í Þjóðmenningarhúsi. Office of the Prime Minister. https://www.stjornarradid.is/efst-a-baugi/frettir/stok-frett/2012/04/20/Samningar-undirritadir-ad-vidstoddum-forsaetisradherrum-Islands-og-Kina-i-dag-i-Thjodmenningarhusi/. Accessed 4 July 2023
Government of Iceland (2013) Free Trade Agreement Between the Government of Iceland and the Government of the People's Republic of China. https://www.government.is/media/utanrikisraduneyti-media/media/fta-kina/Iceland-China.pdf. 4 July 2023
Government of Iceland (2016) Viðskipti Íslands og Kína. Reykjavík: Ministry for Foreign
Government of Iceland (2018) Viðskiptasamningar undirritaðir í Kína. Ministry for Foreign Affairs. https://www.stjornarradid.is/efst-a-baugi/frettir/stok-frett/2018/09/07/Vidskiptasamningar-undirritadir-i-Kina/. Accessed 4 July 2023
Government of Iceland (2019) Fjármálaráðherra kjörinn varaformaður bankaráðs AIIB, *Ministry of Finance*, Accessed 4 July 2023
Government of Iceland (2020a) Borgaraþjónusta – Aðstoð við Íslendinga erlendis. Ministry for Foreign Affairs.https://www.stjornarradid.is/verkefni/utanrikismal/adstod-erlendis/. Accessed 4 July 2023
Government of Iceland (2020b) Report of the Minister for Foreign Affairs to Althingi, regarding external and international affairs, 150 meeting of the parliamentary assembly. Althingi, Reykjavík
Government of Iceland (2020c) Samstarf Grænlands og Íslands á nýjum Norðurslóðum. Suggestions from the Greenland Committee to the Minister for Foreign Affairs. Ministry for Foreign Affairs. https://www.stjornarradid.is/library/02-Rit%2D%2Dskyrslur-og-skrar/Samstarf%20Gr

%c3%a6nlands%20og%20%c3%8dslands%20%c3%a1%20n%c3%bdjum%20Nor%c3%b0ursl%c3%b3%c3%b0um%20-%20Copy%20(1).pdf Accessed 4 July 2023
Government of Iceland (2020d) Skýrsla utanríkisráðherra um utanríkis- og alþjóðamál 2018-2019. 140 parliamentary session 2018-2019. Althingi, Reykjavík
Government of Iceland (2021) Report of the Minister for Foreign Affairs to Althingi, 151 meeting of the parliamentary assembly, report no. 1321. Althingi, Reykjavík
Government of Iceland (a). Fríverslunarsamningur milli Íslands og Kína. Ministry for Foreign Affairs. https://www.stjornarradid.is/verkefni/utanrikismal/utanrikisvidskipti/vidskiptasamningar/friverslun-vid-kina/. Accessed 4 July 2023
Government of Iceland (b). Viðauki I – Myndræn greining viðskipta Íslands og Kína. Ministry for Foreign Affairs. Received 9 April 2020
Gunnarsson SP (2018) Vilja að Ísland taki þátt. Viðskiptablaðið. https://www.vb.is/frettir/vilja-ad-island-taki-thatt/146356/?q=innvi%C3%B0ir. Accessed 4 July 2023
Hafstað V (2019) US military to invest billions of ISK in Keflavík. Iceland Monitor. https://icelandmonitor.mbl.is/news/politics_and_society/2019/06/24/us_military_to_invest_billions_of_isk_in_keflavik/. Accessed 4 July 2023
Hansen PE, Hauksdottir GRT (2021) Iceland and Arctic Security: US Dependency and the Search for an Arctic Identity. In: Depledge D, Lackenbauer PW (eds) On thin ice? Perspectives on Arctic Security. Trent University, North American and Arctic Defence and Security Network, pp 162–171
Haraldsson J (2020a) Kínverska Covid-19 veiran. Morgunblaðið, Reykjavík
Haraldsson J (2020b) Kínverska sendiráðið enn og aftur. Morgunblaðið, Reykjavík
Haraldsson J (2020c) Kínverskar veirur. Morgunblaðið, Reykjavík
Harðarson BÞ (2019) 14 milljarða framkvæmdir við varnarmannvirki. https://www.ruv.is/frett/14-milljarda-framkvaemdir-vid-varnarmannvirki. Accessed 4 July 2023
Hauksdottir GRT (2019) Pressure in the Arctic: China-Iceland Relations in the Era of U.S-China Rivalry. Institute for Security and Development Policy
Heiðarsson JÞ (2007) Umskipunarhöfn á Íslandi fyrir Íshafssiglingar. University of Akureyri, Akureyri
High ranking representatives within the Icelandic and Chinese governments, research participant interviews, May and June, 2020, Reykjavík
Iceland Statistics Office (2021a) Farþegar um Keflavíkurflugvöll eftir ríkisfangi og mánuðum 2002-2021. https://px.hagstofa.is/pxis/pxweb/is/Atvinnuvegir/Atvinnuvegir__ferdathjonusta__farthegar/SAM02001.px/table/tableViewLayout1/?rxid=6b436daf-b18f-43a3-a2b2-ef09cf205e80. Accessed 4 July 2023
Iceland Statistics Office (2021b) Population by country of citizenship, sex and age 1 January 1998-2020. https://px.hagstofa.is/pxen/pxweb/en/Ibuar/Ibuar__mannfjoldi__3_bakgrunnur__Rikisfang/MAN04103.px/table/tableViewLayout1/?rxid=a5a5fdc4-2cda-43e9-9ec8-5dc74ec11ee7. Accessed 4 July 2023
Information received from the Ministry for Foreign Affairs of Iceland, research participant interviews, 18 June, 2020, Reykjavík
Institute of Economic Studies (2019) Siglingar á norðurslóðum – Ísland í brennidepli, Report no. C19:06 sponsored by the University of Iceland. http://hhi.hi.is/sites/hhi.hi.is/files/sjz/nordurslodir_lok_20_12_19_0.pdf . Accessed 4 July 2023
Invest in Iceland. China Development Bank and Invest in Iceland to cooperate
Jónsson SG 2019) Segir Kínverja standa að baki Finnafjarðarhöfn. Stundin. https://stundin.is/grein/9014/. Accessed 4 July 2023
Jónsson AI (2021) Speech at the 151 meeting of parliamentary assembly, regarding Iceland as a NATO ally. Althingi, Reykjavík. https://www.althingi.is/altext/raeda/151/rad20210311T152138.html. Accessed 4 July 2023
Jónsson ÖD, Hannibalsson I, Yang L (2013) A bilateral free trade agreement between China and Iceland. In: Hannibalsson I (ed) Þjóðarspegillinn. Research paper presented at a conference on

social sciences, sponsored by the Social Science Research Institute at the University of Iceland, p 3. https://skemman.is/bitstream/1946/16786/3/OrnDJonsson_VID.pdf. Accessed 4 July 2023
Júlíusson HV (2019) HB Grandi horfir til sóknar í Asíu. https://www.visir.is/g/2019190409698/hb-grandi-horfir-til-soknar-i-asiu- Accessed 4 July 2023
Laliberté F, Howell SEL, Kushner PJ (2016) Regional variability of a projected sea ice-free Arctic during the summer months. Geophys Res Lett 45:256–263
Lanteigne M (2008) The Falcon and the Dragon: Commercial Diplomacy and the Sino-Icelandic Free Trade Negotiations. Working Paper 2. Center for Small State Studies, University of Iceland, pp 3–17
Lanteigne M (2010) Northern exposure: cross-regionalism and the China-Iceland Preferential Trade Negotiations. China Q 202:362–380
Lanteigne M (2014) China's emerging Arctic strategies: economics and institutions. Institute for International Affairs, Centre for Arctic Policy Studies. https://ams.overcastcdn.com/documents/Marc_Lanteigne2.pdf. Accessed 4 July 2023
Lanteigne M (2017a) 'Have you entered the storehouses of the snow?' China as a norm entrepreneur in the Arctic. Polar Record 53(2):117-130
Lanteigne M (2017b) Iceland's small state diplomacy with China. In: Sverdrup-Thygeson B, Lindgren WY, Lanteigne M (eds) China and Nordic Diplomacy. CRC Press, Florida, pp 60–76
Leiser M (2022) Russia and China to deepen cooperation in the Arctic. https://thebarentsobserver.com/en/arctic/2022/02/russia-and-china-deepen-cooperation-arctic The Barent Observer. Accessed 4 July 2023
MBL. Össur í Kína (2010). https://www.mbl.is/frettir/innlent/2010/07/13/ossur_i_kina/ Accessed 4 July 2023
MBL (2013) Fríverslunarsamningur Íslands og Kína undirritaður. https://www.mbl.is/vidskipti/frettir/2013/04/15/ossur_island_faer_forskot_a_kinamarkad/. Accessed 4 July 2023
MBL (2020a) Skoða varanlega viðveru Bandaríkjahers. https://www.mbl.is/frettir/innlent/2020/10/30/skoda_varanlega_vidveru_bandarikjahers/. Accessed 4 July 2023
MBL (2020b) Þjóðaröryggi er alltaf í forgangi. https://www.mbl.is/frettir/innlent/2020/07/14/thjodaroryggi_er_alltaf_i_forgangi/ Accessed 4 July 2023
Memorandum of Understanding on Chinese-Icelandic Research Cooperation on Arctic Issues between the Polar Research Institute of China and the Icelandic Centre for Research (2012). https://karholl.is/images/PDF/MoU%20Rannis%20PRIC.pdf. Accessed 4 July 2023
Minister for Foreign Affairs (2021) Speech at the 151 meeting of parliamentary assembly, regarding Iceland as a NATO ally. Althingi, Reykjavík. https://www.althingi.is/altext/raeda/151/rad20210311T152820.html. Accessed 4 July 2023
Ministry for Foreign Affairs (2021) Bill for parliament on the 150th parliamentary assembly 2020-2021. Ministry for Foreign Affairs, Reykjavík
Ministry for Foreign Affairs of Iceland, Information received 15 October, 2022, Reykjavík
Ministry of Foreign Affairs of the People's Republic of China (2012) Premier Wen Jiabao Holds Talks with His Icelandic Counterpart Sigurdardottir. https://www.fmprc.gov.cn/mfa_eng/topics_665678/wjbispg_665714/t925277.shtml. Accessed 4 July 2023
Mission of the Peoples Republic of China to the European Union (2010) Chinese, Icelandic FMs hold talks on bilateral ties. https://www.fmprc.gov.cn/ce/cebe/eng/dshdjh/t716348.htm. Accessed 4 July 2023
National Energy Authority of Iceland (2016) Cooperation Agreement of Sino-Icelandic Geothermal Research and Development Center. https://orkustofnun.is/media/mou/MoU-Ki%cc%81na.pdf. Accessed 4 July 2023
Nielsson E, Hauksdottir GRT (2020) Kina, investeringer og sikkerhetspolitik: Politikk og perspektiver i Norden – Island. Internasjonal Politikk 78(1):68–78
Ólafur Ragnar Grímsson President of Iceland 1996-2016, research participant interview, 22 May, 2020, Reykjavík

Open government consultation with the public (2021) Drög að frumvarpi til laga um breytingu á varnarmálalögum nr. 34/2008 (öryggissvæði o.fl.). https://samradsgatt.island.is/oll-mal/$Cases/Details/?id=2932#advices. Accessed 4 July 2023

Orkustofnun (2005) Stærsta jarðvarmaveita í heimi verður byggð í Kína í samstarfi við íslensk fyrirtæki. https://orkustofnun.is/orkustofnun/frettir/nr/869. Accessed 4 July 2023

Ragnarsdóttir SK (2019) Aukið samstarf við Kína á sviði menntamála. RÚV. https://www.ruv.is/frett/aukid-samstarf-vid-kina-a-svidi-menntamala. Accessed 4 July 2023

Registers Iceland (2019) Erlendir ríkisborgarar búsettir á Íslandi í maí 2019. https://www.skra.is/um-okkur/frettir/frett/2019/05/13/Erlendir-rikisborgarar-busettir-a-Islandi/. Accessed 4 July 2023

Ríkharðsdóttir K (2021) 'Óviðunandi' segir Guðlaugur Þór. Morgunblaðið. https://www.mbl.is/frettir/innlent/2021/04/15/ovidunandi_segir_gudlaugur_thor/. Accessed 4 July 2023

RÚV (2012) Mótmæla heimsókn Wen. https://www.ruv.is/frett/motmaela-heimsokn-wen. Accessed 4 July 2023

RÚV (2013) Jarðarkaup á Íslandi langtímafjárfesting. https://www.ruv.is/frett/jardarkaup-a-islandi-langtimafjarfesting. Accessed 4 July 2023

RÚV (2020) Lambakjöt frá Fjallalambi á markaði í Kína. https://www.ruv.is/frett/2020/04/02/lambakjot-fra-fjallalambi-a-markad-i-kina. Accessed 4 July 2023

Sigurðardóttir M (2015) Samningur við Kína skilað litlu. Morgunblaðið. https://www.mbl.is/greinasafn/grein/1560491/. Accessed 4 July 2023

Sigurðardóttir K (2019) Lýsti vonbrigðum sínum við Mike Pompeo. RÚV. https://www.ruv.is/frett/lysti-vonbrigdum-sinum-vid-mike-pompeo. Accessed 4 July 2023

Skarphéðinsson Ö (2013) Ár Drekans. Sögur, Reykjavík

Smed UT, Wivel A (2017) Vulneraility without capabilities? Small states strategy and the international counter-piracy agenda. Eur Security 26:79–98

Stevenson TC, Davies J, Huntington HP, Sheard W (2019) An examination of trans-Arctic vessel routing in the Central Arctic 2019 Ocean. Marine Policy 100:83–89

Thorhallsson B (2018) A small state in world politics: Iceland's search for shelter. Icelandic Rev Polit Adm 14(1):61–82

Thorhallsson B (2019) Small states and shelter theory: Iceland's external affairs. Routledge

Thorhallsson B, Grímsdóttir S (2021) Lilliputian encounters with Gulliver: Sino-Icelandic relations from 1995 to 2021. Reykjavik: institute of international affairs and the centre for Small state studies, University of Iceland

United Nations Human Rights Council (2019) A joint statement on Xinjiang at the United Nations. United Nations, Geneva. https://www.hrw.org/sites/default/files/supporting_resources/190708_joint_statement_xinjiang.pdf. Accessed 4 July 2023

University of Akureyri (2020) Information received from the University of Akureyri

University of Iceland (2020) Information compiled by the University of Iceland Registration Office

University of Iceland. International Division. Research participant interview, 13 June, 2020, Reykjavík

US Government (2019) Looking North: Sharpening America's Arctic Focus. Speech by Michael R. Pompeo at the Arctic Council Ministerial, Finland

Viðskiptablaðið (2019) Trump íhugar fríverslun við Ísland. https://www.vb.is/frettir/trump-ihugar-friverslun-vid-island/157219/. Accessed 4 July 2023

Vísir (2005) Samið um fríverslun. https://www.visir.is/g/2005505130326/samid-vid-kina-um-friverslun. Accessed 4 July 2023

Vísir (2019) Hvatti Íslendinga til að hafna Huawei. https://www.visir.is/g/2019190909459/hvatti-islendinga-til-ad-hafna-huawei. Accessed 4 July 2023

Wivel A, Thorhallsson B (2018) Brexit and small states in Europe: hedging, hiding or seeking shelter? In: Diamond P, Nedergaard P, Rosamond B (eds) The Routledge handbook of the politics of Brexit. Routledge, London, pp 266–277

Zheng TT (2019) UNU Geothermal Training Programme in Iceland: Role in Capacity Building for China's Geothermal Energy Development. Presentation delivered at the Icelandic Chinese Trade Council's (IKV) seminar on Iceland - China energy cooperation

Baldur Thorhallsson is a Professor of Political Science, and founder and Research Director for the Centre for Small State Studies, at the University of Iceland. His research focus has primarily been on small European states, small state theory and Iceland's foreign policy. His recent articles are included in *The Hague Journal of Diplomacy*, *Scandinavian Journal of History* and *Global Affairs*. His latest edited books are titled *Iceland's Shelter-Seeking Behavior: From Settlement to Republic* (Cornell University Press 2021), *Small States and the New Security Environment* (co-editor) (Springer 2021) and *Small States and Shelter Theory: Iceland's External Affairs* (Routledge 2019). He holds a PhD (1999) and MA (1994) in Political Science from the University of Essex in the United Kingdom.

Snaefridur Grimsdottir (Snæfríður Grímsdóttir) is an Adjunct in Chinese Studies at the University of Iceland. Her research is mainly focused on security studies and China. She holds a BA (2015) in Chinese Studies from the University of Iceland, an MA in Diplomatic Studies (2016) from the University of Malta and an MA in Conflict, Security and Development (2018) from King's College London.

Chapter 9
The Many Shades of Shelter: Portugal and Iceland's Quest for Political, Economic and Societal Shelter

Alice Cunha and Baldur Thorhallsson

Foreign policy is one of the most complex policies of every state, and Portugal and Iceland are no exception. On the other hand, not all small states are alike and their shelter seeking behaviour may have many shades. The "Small States and Big Powers: Portugal and Iceland's Foreign Relations" chapters analyse the importance of relations with big powers or regional and international organisations from a shelter theory perspective, detailing the degree of political, economic and societal shelter that they have provided to Portugal and to Iceland over time. We also set out to examine whether their different size and capabilities matter in their relations with larger states and in regional/international organisations. Are all small states similar units that need the same level of shelter or does the size difference of small states, such as in our cases of Portugal and Iceland, lead to distinct foreign policy behaviour? Moreover, we consider the countries' location on the geopolitical map and their contrasting history.

Our case studies begin with an analysis by Nuno Severiano Teixeira who argues that Portugal has known two different models of international insertion. Firstly, the classical model which is characterised by an opposing perception between the continent and the sea, a strategic distancing from Europe, a tendency to favour alliances with the maritime powers and the diversification of extra-peninsular alliances—which lasted for five centuries and guided Portuguese foreign policy until 1974. Secondly, the democratic model which consists of maintaining Portugal's strategic interests in Europe and the Atlantic (complementary for the first time), of

A. Cunha (✉)
Universidade NOVA de Lisboa, Lisbon, Portugal
e-mail: alice.cunha@fcsh.unl.pt

B. Thorhallsson
Faculty of Political Science, Centre for Small State Studies, University of Iceland, Reykjavik, Iceland
e-mail: baldurt@hi.is

A. Cunha, B. Thorhallsson (eds.), *Small States and Big Powers*, The World of Small States 10, https://doi.org/10.1007/978-3-031-42345-1_9

building postcolonial relations, constructing a closer relationship with Spain, and enhancing its participation in multilateral organisations.

Despite being in transition from the classical to the democratic model, Portugal has changed priorities from Africa to Europe. However, the Atlantic remains a constant, with NATO membership playing a key role. The chapter examines why Portugal was invited to be a founding member of NATO, why the government at the time decided to take the offer, and the consequences of NATO membership. The invitation to be a founding member of NATO is explained by the geostrategic value of the Azores archipelago and the Lages military base, which was part of the USA post-war military defence system and proved vital during the Cold War. The traditional anti-communism of the authoritarian regime and the Russian threat to world security justified accession, but more out of necessity than of belief as the regime also had no sympathy for post-war multilateral diplomacy. After joining, however, NATO membership became a reference for Portuguese foreign policy, not only during that regime, but also in the democratic regime that followed.

Bearing all of the above in mind, Nuno Severiano Teixeira therefore concludes that shelter theory does not fully explain Portugal's accession to NATO as it was not the Portuguese state that was seeking political and security shelter but the other way around; that is, it was due to the recognition of the country's strategic geographic importance to the organisation. However, the author also concludes that, in fact, NATO membership has provided Portugal with political and military shelter ever since it has been a member. Moreover, NATO membership additionally and simultaneously translated into a new alliance with a big power (the USA) and improved relations between Portugal and the USA, meaning that the transatlantic dimension of the Portuguese foreign policy thus acquired these two dimensions.

This led to several military cooperation agreements between the parties (on the Azores base, the Mutual Defence Assistance Act, USA-Portugal mutual assistance), the creation of the Ministry of National Defence in Portugal in 1950, and the implementation of a series of reforms to comply with the military commitments within the framework of NATO. This promising start, though, was short-lived as the following decade stands out for the international contestation directed at the Portuguese colonies and difficult relations between Portugal and the USA. This was largely due to Portugal's non-fulfilment of its military commitments to NATO, which continued until the country became a democracy in 1974. At the time, the Portuguese government's foreign policy was focused primarily on keeping the colonies, and the resulting war efforts in these colonies led Portugal to suspend many of its military commitments to NATO, which, in turn, also resulted in many NATO members contesting the Portuguese colonial policy, the USA included.

The nature of the political regimes also plays a role in each country's definition of foreign policy, with continuities and changes. In the case of Portugal, the democratic regime endorsed its membership and commitment to NATO as a fundamental principle of Portuguese foreign policy and for the country's international alignment. And in spite of the significant changes during the post-Cold War period in the military and security policies of both the USA and NATO, Portugal remained a reliable and active member.

In addition to political shelter as a result of NATO membership—in the concrete form of security—, the use of the Lajes base has also granted Portugal with monetary compensation and military aid; however, the international organisation's focus on cooperation in the field of security and defence is such that its shelter does not extend to the economic and societal shelter.

In some cases, relations between a small state and a superpower are asymmetrical. That certainly applies to relations between Iceland and the United States. In the chapter by Skafti Ingimarsson and Baldur Thorhallsson, they address the origins and development of Icelandic-US relations during World War II, the Cold War, and the post-Cold War period.

From the political shelter perspective, Iceland considered military and economic protection from the United States during WW II to be the best option to prevent a German invasion. The political relationship that developed between the two states during and after the war led to over half a century (1951–2006) of US military presence in the country, which made the US the main provider of political shelter to Iceland.

The heyday of Icelandic-US relations came during WW II and the Cold War. During this period, Iceland concluded the Icelandic-US Defence Agreement in 1951—not without controversy—and secured extensive US economic aid and diplomatic support to create a Republic in June 1944. In the post war period, the US also provided Iceland with important diplomatic backing in international organizations (such as the IMF, the World Bank and the OECD) and during the Cod Wars with the UK. Both sides took advantage of the Icelandic-US alliance during the Cold War, with Iceland promoting its national interests by using its important strategic position in the North-Atlantic, while the US benefited from installing military facilities. When the Cold War ended, the US unilaterally withdrew its military forces from Iceland in 2006 but assured its commitment to defend Iceland via NATO. Overall, and specifically regarding political shelter, there was a logical continuation in Iceland-US relations as they were first motivated by WW II, then NATO membership in 1949 and finally by a bilateral defence treaty at the beginning of the Cold War which lasted far beyond the fall of the Soviet Union.

The above-mentioned agreements with the US were not only of a political nature; they also secured a trade deal with favourable trade conditions and economic aid, leading to important economic shelter. After considerable economic support during WW II, Iceland participated in the Marshall Plan in 1948 to stabilise the economy and enable investments, ending up as the highest per capita Marshall Plan recipient. The end of the Cold War marked a turning point in Icelandic-US relations. The low-point occurred in 2008 at the time of the international financial crisis when the Icelandic economy collapsed and, unlike during the Cold War, the US refused to provide the country with economic assistance. This came during the period the authors termed the "Post-American Era", namely between 2006 and 2022.

As for societal shelter, the US presence in Iceland was beneficial to Icelandic society in many ways, namely in arts, pop culture, and particularly in education, with access to American universities and Fulbright grants. However, it is the Nordic states and not the US that have been Iceland's main provider of societal shelter. Ultimately,

Ingimarsson and Thorhallsson's chapter indicates that political and economic shelter is only provided as long as it is beneficial for the shelter provider, as shown with the closure of the Keflavik military base and the absence of any direct assistance or diplomatic support during the Icelandic financial crisis. Nevertheless, the bilateral defence treaty is still in place, there has been a considerable increase in US military activity in the so-called security zone in Keflavík and trade with the US has continued, although it is much less than trade with European countries.

For purely geostrategic reasons, from a unilateral perspective both Portugal and Iceland have benefited from political and military shelter provided by the USA, while they have gained from NATO in a multilateral dimension. In the two cases, the extension of that shelter decreased when the military bases in the countries were no longer of determinant strategic importance. That does not mean that the big powers ceased to be shelter providers, but in practice they transferred or delegated their role as core shelter providers to a multilateral organisation, NATO. Accordingly, the concession and maintenance of military facilities is no longer a strictly bilateral agreement, but a matter for NATO.

In the chapter on Iceland and Nordic cooperation, Pia Hansson and Auður Birna Stefánsdóttir explore the link between Nordic cooperation and Iceland's foreign policy. In particular, the extent of the political, economic and societal shelter provided by the Nordic states and the resulting constraints. Nordic cooperation is based on geographic proximity, shared values, cultural similarity and a long history of interaction and cooperation. As small states, the Nordics benefit from working together to further and protect their interests in the international arena. As the smallest of the five, Iceland has benefitted greatly from this close cooperation, the pooling of resources and diplomatic backing from the Nordic states. It can also be said that being part of the "Nordic brand" has given Iceland more political clout in the international arena than it would otherwise have as a small state.

Through this cooperation, Iceland has been part of a common Nordic labour market as well as of a passport and social security union that preceded similar developments in the EU by many decades. Furthermore, when Iceland needed to look for alternative sources for its security following the departure of the American military, partial security shelter was provided by the Nordic states resulting in several bilateral defence agreements.

As highlighted in the chapter, Nordic cooperation and solidarity is of great value for Iceland as a small state. However, in times of crisis, Nordic solidarity does not always materialise. This was for example the case at the onset of the Covid-19 crisis, as each country adopted unilateral measures, some even as drastic as closing borders without consultation. In short, in times of prosperity, Nordic cooperation works well and provides Iceland with considerable shelter through diplomatic backing, but in times of crisis this cooperation has proven to be fragile. It is therefore in Iceland's interest to work towards a stronger Nordic cooperation and simultaneously supplement it by seeking shelter from other shelter providers.

There have been several attempts to increase Nordic economic cooperation and integration over the years, for example in establishing a Nordic single market and a Nordic Economic Union. However, these efforts failed as the Nordic states are reliant on bigger markets. Therefore, Iceland does not receive sufficient economic shelter from the Nordic states alone. Nevertheless, the common Nordic labour market can be perceived as providing partial economic shelter as it enables Nordic citizens to live, work and study in the region.

The Nordic countries also provide Iceland with economic shelter through their considerable diplomatic backing, assistance and burden sharing, mostly regarding EFTA and the EEA. Nonetheless, Nordic economic shelter seems to have its limits when bigger interests are at stake as was evident in the economic crisis in 2008. The Nordic states were conflicted in their support for Iceland because of their relations with the bigger powers involved, namely the UK, the Netherlands, and the EU. Ultimately, however, the Nordic states came through for Iceland by backing the IMF rescue package.

When it comes to societal shelter, Iceland has benefitted disproportionately from Nordic cooperation in education and research. Iceland receives considerable educational support from the Nordic states, with a large number of students from Iceland studying in the other Nordic countries. This is not surprising given that education opportunities in Iceland are more limited due to its size. In fact, Iceland holds an exemption when it comes to paying for the education provided, which can also be defined as economic shelter. In addition, the Icelandic research community relies on Nordic research funding and benefits from close cooperation with Nordic research colleagues. Iceland, therefore, receives considerable educational support from the other Nordic countries and seems to be more dependent on this cooperation than the other Nordic states.

Nordic cooperation has undergone different stages of togetherness where crises have sometimes revealed weaknesses in Nordic solidarity. Overall, Iceland receives substantial political shelter through diplomatic backing, partial economic shelter through a common labour market and burden sharing in the EEA and EFTA, and valuable societal shelter through Nordic cooperation in education, research and culture.

António Raimundo addresses the importance of Africa—specifically Angola—for contemporary Portuguese foreign policy and he argues that Angola has only provided limited shelter to Portugal in all three dimensions.

Post-colonial relations not only in Africa but also with Brazil are one of the pillars of Portugal's foreign policy: the pillar of the Portuguese-speaking world. Although the country had to redefine its priorities in foreign policy after the end of the Estado Novo authoritarian regime in 1974, Portugal managed to develop and strengthen relations with its former colonies in the aftermath of decolonisation and over time. This included both bilateral and multilateral relations, the most prominent of which was the creation of the Community of Portuguese Speaking Countries (CPLP) in 1996, designed to promote the Portuguese language, cooperation in the economic, social and cultural fields, and diplomatic collaboration between its Member States.

Nevertheless, bilateral relations between Portugal and Angola have gone through different phases depending on the political context, and it was only at the time of the 2008 global and Eurozone crises that Portugal actively sought to deepen its relations with Angola as a potential economic shelter provider. Despite the different context, this is a similar case to that of Iceland's actions vis-a-vis China, as explained ahead.

For a long time after decolonisation, it was Portugal that provided Angola with some kind of political shelter. However, Angola's growing international ambitions and agency highlighted some divergent interests between the two countries, not only in the context of CPLP, but also in world affairs; the most recent example of this is Angola's abstention from the condemnation of Russia's invasion of Ukraine at the United Nations.

Yet Portugal has also benefited from some diplomatic backing from Angola, namely in international organisations such as the United Nations, and the country's bid for its UN Security Council term in 2011–2012. Nevertheless, it is only a limited amount of shelter and only in terms of diplomacy.

As for economic shelter, the EU has been Portugal's chief economic partner since 1986, and it is Portugal that has for the most part been providing Angola with economic shelter. The major shift regarding Angola came in the context of the sovereign debt crisis and ensuing Portuguese financial crisis (2010–2014), when the government sought extra European partners, not only in Africa, but also China. At the time, Angola was one of the fastest-growing economies in the world and, as a result, it became the main destination for Portuguese exports outside EU countries. This was accompanied by a significant increase in migration of qualified workers to Angola, the most popular destination outside the EU, as well as a very marked growth in Angolan investments in Portugal including in strategic sectors such as banking, energy and telecoms. But it also entailed a discussion about the origin of the money and corruption. However, this level of economic shelter-seeking towards Angola was temporary and has since diminished.

At the societal level, bilateral relations between the two countries take the form of educational cooperation and cultural diplomacy aimed at promoting the Portuguese language and culture, but again not from Angola to Portugal but the other way around.

Overall, due to Portugal's imperial past, Africa (and, in this case, Angola) is often perceived as a destination for shelter and not the provider, apart from during exceptionally difficult economic periods when Portugal strives to diversify its partners.

An important lesson is that the 2008 international financial crisis played a role in redefining the seeking of economic shelter for both Portugal and Iceland. Although Portugal continued to benefit from the economic shelter provided by the EU (which it considered insufficient) it turned mostly to Africa. On the other hand, Iceland was abandoned by all its old allies (the US, the Nordic States and other European states) and therefore sought economic shelter from China.

Relations between the shelterer and the sheltered also change over time. When the US refused to provide Iceland with assistance in the 2008 financial crisis, the country sought shelter in the second biggest economic power, China. This was a breaking point for the countries' relations and indicates two things: firstly, cooperation agreements (such as the one between Iceland and the Nordic states on the one hand, and between Iceland and the US on the other) are not as reliable as close regional integration based on legal grounds and commonly agreed rules shared by all parties (such as in the European Union); secondly, small states have options, especially if they have something to offer. And Iceland can offer its strategic location, currently in the context of the Arctic, and has the potential to become a hub on an Arctic shipping route. If small states' traditional allies do not offer shelter in times of need, they are in real danger of losing their small allies to their rival powers.

Baldur Thorhallsson and Snaefridur Grimsdottir focus on the Sino-Icelandic relations between 1995 and 2022 in the context of Iceland's foreign policy towards China. Until the beginning of the twenty-first century, Iceland had little political interest in China. But following Iceland's economic collapse in 2008, their bilateral relations changed significantly with Iceland actively seeking shelter from China. Initially, Iceland turned to China to explore the possibility of economic assistance, but what started out as a statement of trust in the Icelandic economy (with a currency swap agreement between China and Iceland), led to cooperation in several sectors and the signing of numerous agreements, the most important of which was the free trade agreement in 2013.

At the political level (diplomacy), China also supported Iceland in the IMF for their rescue package, and their application for the UN Security Council for the years 2009–2010, and Iceland reciprocated with its support for China being granted permanent observer status within the Arctic Council. There was a trade-off: the signature of the free trade agreement, diplomatic backing within the IMF and a statement of trust (in the interest of Iceland), against the conceding of the permanent observer status within the Arctic Council and willingness to consider Chinese involvement in a hub in the northeast of Iceland (in the interest of China).

Although Iceland also joined the Asian Infrastructure Investment Bank, the offer to join the Belt and Road Initiative is on hold, namely because the US is pressuring Iceland to reject it. This is another twist in the plot as the increased Chinese activity in Iceland and, in particular, its interests in the Arctic region, have made the US renew their interest in Iceland. This indicates that Iceland has a preference for its traditional ally, the US, and that it only prioritised relations with China in times of need in the aftermath of its economic crash. Regardless of the good economic relations with China (and despite their asymmetry), Iceland has criticised China for human rights violations, and this has undermined Iceland-China relations.

In the societal realm, the two countries have also reached agreement to enhance educational, scientific and cultural cooperation, but this cannot really be referred to as societal shelter. Thorhallsson and Grimsdottir conclude that, in shelter terms, the Sino-Icelandic relations are currently restricted to marginal economic shelter.

The European Union is a unique regional organisation and the most advanced example of political, economic and even societal integration. That also has an impact on its relationship with its Member States, in two directions: the powers obtained from the Member States, and the benefits provided by them individually and as a whole. As the EU deepens its policies and broadens both its powers and areas of action, the degree of shelter it provides to smaller Member States may increase. In fact, the influence and impact of regional and multilateral organisations, such as the

EU, in providing shelter to small states should not be underestimated even during crises (financial, pandemic or energy), as they operate on the basis of a fixed set of rules and, in the specific case of the EU, also on common values and solidarity.

In her chapter, Alice Cunha assesses the extent to which EU membership has provided Portugal with shelter. A Member State since 1986, Portugal has received political shelter from the EU at various moments: in securing democracy in the early years after accession, and even prior to this while the country was negotiating to join the EU; in ensuring post-decolonisation insertion in the international system; international visibility when holding the rotating presidency of the Council of the EU; diplomatic backing in other multilateral organisations and on specific matters, such as East Timor's independence. Regarding security, NATO is still the prime provider, but aligned with the EU.

As for economic shelter, external economic funding has been essential for the Portuguese economy throughout its history, and the EU became its main economic shelter provider after accession. First, Portugal holds a long track-record as a net beneficiary of EU funding, with investment and structural funds contributing to the country's economic and social development in all policy domains. Second, taking part in the internal market also brings indirect economic and financial benefits from the EU. Third, as a member of the currency union, Portugal received economic shelter during the sovereign debt crisis in the form of a bailout. Unlike the previous two examples of economic shelter, the conditionality underlying the bailout came at a very high cost for the country. This shows that shelter is not a simple and unchanging arrangement between two states or organisations, but one that evolves in line with the shelter provider's demands or interests. From the perspective of the small state, it may also lead to looking for other shelter providers, even if only momentarily.

Finally, as far as societal shelter is concerned, the European Union was to some extent regarded as a novel national project after the loss of the colonial empire. Thereafter, EU membership entailed the Europeanisation of Portuguese society. The national turnout for the European Parliament elections may be low, but the percentage of Portuguese that feel they are EU citizens is quite high, as is the number of nationals that live, work or study in another EU country.

Overall, the EU is the international organisation that best fits into the three categories of shelter for Portugal, even if we include big powers such as France or Germany whose bilateral relations with the country are mainly dealt with in the EU framework, or the USA, which acts mostly as a security provider via NATO. On the other hand, this is a risk for Portugal as it is heavily dependent on EU membership.

Iceland has a track-record of European cooperation that dates back to the late 1960s. But, most importantly, it has been able to maintain a beneficial position by securing access to all aspects of cooperation that it considers favourable, while abstaining from those they do not believe to be in the national interest. In his chapter, Baldur Thorhallsson explains why Iceland joined EFTA, the EEA and Schengen but not the European Union.

EU membership is a highly divisive topic in Iceland. Over the years, the Icelandic governments have carefully examined the advantages and disadvantages of EU membership, but opposition to the Common Fisheries Policy and the Common Agricultural Policy as well as the transfer of power from Reykjavik to Brussels have been an obstacle to membership. However, in 2009, Iceland applied for EU membership a few months after its economic crash, and at a time when Iceland's other allies refused to bail it out. But the accession process, which lasted until 2013, was extremely controversial and a new government put it on hold largely due to the so-called Ice-save dispute. The accession process is still frozen and Iceland's participation in the European project remains partial. Nonetheless, the country is closely integrated with the EU through membership in EFTA, the EEA and the Schengen Area.

Iceland joined EFTA in 1970 as part of a strategy to improve its access to European markets (including the EU internal market via a free trade agreement) and to facilitate exports of fish and other marine products. EFTA membership led to substantial economic growth for the country. In 1994, Iceland became a founding member of the EEA; this granted it access to the EU internal market and required it to adopt EU legislation and implement the four freedoms of movement (except for the areas of agriculture and fisheries). This provided substantial economic shelter not only in relation to market access, but also due to greater capital injection into the economy and increased participation in several other policy sectors of the EU. In the framework of the EEA, the downside is that Iceland has limited access to the EU's decision-making process despite having to comply with EU legislation. All in all, the EFTA and EU/EEA member states are by far Iceland's most important trading partners, and Iceland has ultimately benefited from their economic shelter. However, they did not provided Iceland with shelter during the economic crisis.

On a different note, the EEA has provided Iceland with unexpected, important and wide-ranging societal shelter through access to EU institutions of higher education and the free movement of people, which has enabled Icelanders to live abroad with the same rights as other EU nationals. Some policies, such as environmental and competition law, have been transformed by EEA legislation, which has also had a significant impact on the public administration and its duty to implement it. Moreover, Iceland is an associated member of several European agencies that deal with crisis management.

From a political shelter point of view, however, Thorhallsson claims that EU shelter is limited to the Schengen membership and the implicit soft security agreements in the areas of border control, judicial cooperation and cyber security.

In short, the chapters show that Portugal and Iceland do not receive full and unlimited political, economic and societal shelter from any big power, regional or international organisation. Some shelters are limited by their scope (e.g., NATO), others by their domestic agenda (e.g., the USA), or affected by major problems (e.g., the Nordic States during the Covid pandemic) and incapacity (e.g., Angola). Small states have to seek shelter from several actors in order to secure comprehensive political, economic and societal shelter.

In the case of Portugal, it is clear that the EU has been the main provider of political, economic and societal shelter since its membership in 1986. On the other hand, for Iceland, the European project is currently the main provider of economic shelter, the Nordic states and the EU/EEA the most comprehensive providers of societal shelter and the US the most important provider of military shelter.

Iceland used its location as a bargaining chip with the USA during WWII and the Cold War and more recently with China in relation to the Arctic. Iceland enjoyed extensive political and economic shelter from the US during the Cold War but later had to shift its shelter-seeking behaviour towards Europe. Hence, the EEA (the EU) has become an importance provider of shelter for Iceland in the last three decades. In contrast, Portugal only made limited use of its location as a bargaining chip with the USA (Lajes' USA military base). In fact, geography matters, and physical space is a valuable commodity both on the offer and demand sides.

In the midst of the 2008 international financial crisis, Iceland was abandoned by its traditional shelter-providing partners (USA, Nordic States and other European states), but Portugal did not lose the EU's economic support. Also, despite being in different situations during the crisis, Iceland and Portugal both sought economic shelter from other actors, namely China in the case of Iceland and Angola in the case of Portugal. Nevertheless, after the crisis, these economic shelter-seeking endeavours lost their original attraction and have since been moderated. Iceland and Portugal have both returned to their shelter seeking relations with traditional long-term allies.

Our findings also indicate that both Portugal and Iceland need to balance their international relations with shelter provided by different actors. Their size and political and economic capabilities matter in their bilateral and multilateral relations. It is therefore in both countries' interest to maintain strong cooperation not only with big powers, but also regional and international organisations, depending on their field of action, in order to flourish politically, economically and socially.

To summarise, our cases of Portugal and Iceland within the shelter theoretical framework shed a new light on shelter theory:

1. the nature of shelter relations can change over time, including the transfer of shelter provided by an actor bilaterally to shelter provided by the same actor within a multilateral sphere (e.g., the US as a security provider to Iceland);
2. the lack of traditional options—mostly in times of crisis—leads small states to search for alternative shelter providers, but almost exclusively in the economic domain (e.g., the cases of China and Angola during the 2008–2014 financial crisis);
3. in the above situation, shelter is sometimes only provided for a short period of time and is not always a stable and enduring relationship (for example, the cases of China and Angola);
4. there are different kinds of shelter depending on the time and the need, and they may come at a cost (such as Iceland implementing the EU/EEA rules without having much say on them);

5. the nature and quality of shelter may also vary over time and work better in times of prosperity (e.g., the cooperation with the Nordic states, the EEA, the EU) or, alternatively, in times of crises (e.g. Angola and China); whereas shelter during times of prosperity tends to be stable, shelter in crisis situations is mostly transitory and may not deepen after the crisis ends;
6. shelter can evolve and lead to a spillover effect from the political domain to the economic and even societal realms (e.g. the wide reaching support of the US to Iceland throughout the Cold War);
7. smallness does not always lead to shelter-seeking behaviour, as demonstrated in the case of Portugal joining NATO;
8. the same is true of the influence of the nature of the political regime, which can lead to or move away from seeking shelter provided by regional organisations (case of the Portuguese authoritarian regime);
9. a small state can become heavily dependent on one big power or a regional organisation, which in itself constitutes a considerable risk and may lead to it not seeking more reliable shelter providers (for instance, the economic assistance from the US to Iceland may have delayed Iceland's participation in the European project);
10. size is indeed an important variable, but it is not the only one as geography, geopolitical shifts, the political regime, history and culture are also vital determinants when seeking and granting shelter;
11. finally, our findings indicate that the different size and capabilities of Portugal and Iceland were not relevant to their need for economic, political and societal shelter during the period under review.

Dr. Alice Cunha is Assistant Professor with Habilitation in International Relations at the NOVA University of Lisbon—School of Social Sciences and Humanities (NOVA FCSH), and Researcher at the Portuguese Institute of International Relations (IPRI), where she has worked on European Integration, an area in which she has published extensively. Her main research interests are related to enlargement studies, Europeanization, European funds and Portuguese foreign policy. She is a member of the European Union Liaison Committee of Historians.

Baldur Thorhallsson is a Professor of Political Science, and founder and Research Director for the Centre for Small State Studies, at the University of Iceland. His research focus has primarily been on small European states, small state theory and Iceland's foreign policy. His recent articles are included in *The Hague Journal of Diplomacy*, *Scandinavian Journal of History* and *Global Affairs*. His latest edited books are titled *Iceland's Shelter-Seeking Behavior: From Settlement to Republic* (Cornell University Press 2021), *Small States and the New Security Environment* (co-editor) (Springer 2021) and *Small States and Shelter Theory: Iceland's External Affairs* (Routledge 2019). He holds a PhD (1999) and MA (1994) in Political Science from the University of Essex in the United Kingdom.